In her debut cookbook, registered dietitian, food lover, and YouTube star Abbey Sharp shares fun, satisfying, and unbelievably healthy recipes that will ignite your love affair with food.

In 100 recipes, Abbey shows us how she eats: healthy and nourishing meals that are packed with flavour like PB and J Protein Pancakes, Autumn Butternut Squash Mac and Cheese with Sage Panko, Stuffed Hawaiian Burgers, Chicken, Sweet Potato, and Curry Cauliflower, Chocolate Stout Veggie Chili, Chewy Crackle Almond Apple Cookies, and Ultimate Sticky Toffee Puddings. The recipes in *The Mindful Glow Cookbook* are often plant-centric, and many are vegan, gluten-free, nut-free, and dairy-free. Others contain some protein-rich, lean grass-fed beef, poultry, eggs, or dairy, so there are plenty of delicious recipes for every one and every occasion.

Featuring gorgeous photography throughout, *The Mindful Glow Cookbook* is the perfect cookbook for anyone looking to fully nourish their body, satisfy food cravings, and savour every meal, snack, and decadent dessert in blissful enjoyment.

The

Mindful Glow
Cookbook

The

Mindful Glow
Cookbook

Radiant Recipes for Being
the Healthiest, Happiest You

Abbey Sharp, RD

PENGUIN

an imprint of Penguin Canada, a division of Penguin Random House Canada Limited
Canada • USA • UK • Ireland • Australia • New Zealand • India • South Africa • China

First published 2018
Copyright © 2018 by Abbey Sharp

www.penguinrandomhouse.ca

LIBRARY AND ARCHIVES CANADA CATALOGUING IN PUBLICATION

Sharp, Abbey, author
    The mindful glow cookbook : radiant recipes for being the healthiest, happiest you / Abbey Sharp.

Issued in print and electronic formats.
ISBN 978-0-7352-3401-7 (hardcover).—ISBN 978-0-7352-3402-4 (electronic)

    1. Cooking. 2. Cookbooks. I. Title.

TX714.S447 2018   641.5   C2017-907395-8
                                        C2017-907396-6

Cover and book design by Jennifer Lum
Cover images and interior photography by Kyla Zanardi
Food styling by Dara Sutin
Prop styling by Kyla Zanardi and Dara Sutin
Stylist assistance by Houstin Mausner

Printed and bound in China

10 9 8 7 6 5 4 3 2 1

Contents

Salads, Sidekicks, and Soups

3 P.M. Fix

Happy Hour

Something Sweet

Introduction

Life is about relationships, and we all obsess over cultivating the best. The rock-solid marriage. The best friend. The mother-daughter bond. But in the process of trying to be domestic superheroes, we've forgotten how to nourish the one relationship that we will never be able to divorce: our relationship with food. Let's face it—it's pretty messy. Like Jerry Springer bad. We've all tried at least one buzz-worthy diet under the guise that we'll be healthier and happier if we just weighed ten pounds less, but somehow we never escape that diet rollercoaster cycle of restrict-binge-regret-repeat.

Trust me, I know; I chose this as my profession. I'm a registered *diet*-itian, an educated woman who devoted the early years of her professional life to finding *the one* diet that actually works. Sadly, after $20,000 in tuition fees and weeks of my life lost to memorizing the Krebs cycle, I've come to terms with a fact everyone who's ever dieted already knows: diets don't work. And much like Shakira's hips, statistics don't lie: fewer than 5 percent of dieters who have lost weight actually keep it off. Apparently, it takes more than willpower or an endorsement from Oprah to change our relationship with food. That statistic alone is more depressing to me than my student loans, but it hardly surprises me now.

Diets are physical, emotional, and mental traps. They lure us in with a sexy sales pitch and then supress our self-confidence with every kick at the can. Once you're in, it becomes even harder to get out (but you surely already know that). Diet *culture* is that nagging internal voice that tells us that we're not good enough, that our bodies aren't right, and that we lack self-control, but we hold on under the pretense that the struggle is for our own "good." It's amazing how bad "good" can feel, but that's the diet game.

Diets are controlling and malicious activities that isolate us from our bodies and from each other. They deny us communication with important people who enrich our lives—the people who could make every calorie count. Not only are they emotionally and socially disruptive and *not* helpful, but they can also do great physical harm. I'm talking about hormonal imbalances, weight fluctuations, eating disorders, and more. Seriously, if all these character flaws were listed on a dating app, we would totally swipe left.

While locker-room conversation has led us to view diets as an innocuous part of eating to meet our health goals (you know, we're on them, we're off them, whatev), if we look deeper, their true colours emerge. Diets don't teach us how to eat (and live) well. They teach us that our bodies need to be policed, and that if they are policed well enough, our lives will one day be better. Friends, do not wait for that day.

Why Diets Don't Work

Dieting may be encouraged by our skinny-obsessed culture, but research suggests it may actually be counterproductive to achieving those, ahem, #bodygoals. The shape, size, and weight of our body is a lot more complicated than a simplified equation of energy in and energy out. In fact, we all have a natural narrow weight range—the place where our bodies are most comfortable being—called our "set point." Believe it or not, if we were to never count, track, or control anything we put into our mouths, but rather simply ate in response to hunger and satisfaction, our weight would remain remarkably stable. For most of us, our set point isn't on par with those Victoria's Secret models we see walking down the runway. But, when we do diet, whether we know it or not, our bodies act out.

Let me explain. First, dieting slows down our metabolism so that we conserve the little energy we give it. Second, it messes with our hunger and satiety (fullness) hormones, kicking in cravings for foods that we didn't even know we liked. Third, it makes us feel sluggish, and as a result, we end up taking the elevator up one floor and an Uber to grab coffee a block away. Sure, we may lose a little bit of weight at first, but our bodies will fight *savagely* to get it back. Usually, it comes back with a vengeance, bringing along a few extra pounds *just* to make sure we don't try to pull a fast one again.

A diet is like excess baggage always following us around. We're always either preparing to go on a diet, are on a diet, or have just come off a diet—restricting, binging, regretting, and repeating the diet cycle again and again and again. Unfortunately, studies suggest that our set point tends to go up after each kick at the diet-cycle can, and it rarely comes down, leaving us heavier and hangrier than we were before. To make it painfully clear, dieting actually makes us *gain more weight* than where our bodies naturally want to be.

The reality is that even if dieting did result in long-term weight loss, that would be totally missing the point. Studies suggest that weight is not a good indicator of longevity, the absence of disease, or good health in general. In fact, research indicates that being just five pounds "underweight" is more dangerous than being seventy-five pounds "overweight." Let's face it: we may think being skinnier will make us happier, but dieting in the long run won't do much. According to research, the process of losing weight and adhering to a diet makes people more unhappy and anxious. Nope, we can't hate our way to health or a rippling six-pack of abs.

Clean Eating: The "New" D-Word

These days, "dieting" isn't a sexy word, but it has never gone out of style. It's just been rebranded, repackaged, and resold. Welcome to the world of "clean eating."

This buzzy new diet is more sinister than it appears.

Words like "clean eating" and "wellness" seem to be body-positive, holistic, and even feminist. They "empower" us to combat the "obesity epidemic." They advocate for a world free of toxins, Big Pharma scandals, and, of course, GMOs. So what could possibly be wrong with a "lifestyle" geared towards *feeling your best*? Clean eating may seem softer, even kinder, than the old wave of diet rhetoric, but it is actually more calorically restrictive than any of our moms' grapefruit diets. Do not be fooled when clean-eating programs tell you, "Hey, try me out, I'm different. I've changed and you can too." Their self-righteous colours and militant eating regimens will soon emerge to drag you back down.

I should know: I fell victim myself.

My Story

As a prisoner of weight-loss culture, I know all too well the allure of the diet promise and the dangers that the reality poses. I was never the "fat" kid in school. In fact, I was always teased for my undefined waist, narrow hips, and somewhat boyish form. But eventually, diet culture got me, too, under the pretense of success. Damn perfectionism. It's way less glamorous than our progress-obsessed society makes it out to be.

It started in the dance studio when I was a wee toddler in a tiny kilt. Despite the fact that I was notably one of the top Highland dancers in my company, I would cry myself to sleep before competitions, worrying I wouldn't take home the gold. And, listen, I was *real* good at dancing over those sharp swords! But I became so miserable trying to be the best, I quit before puberty hit.

Next, singing became the outlet to channel my relentless drive. I travelled across America, collaborating with different producers, songwriters, and agents. But slowly, my fear of failure ate away at my breath. And it's kind of hard to sing if you can't breathe. Not surprisingly, I quit that, too.

Seeing the world in black and white, as a failure or success, as good or bad, drove me to find a new chamber to pour myself into. That was university. On the outside, I looked poised and put together, graduating with a perfect GPA, the top honours of the entire university, and a full scholarship from a prestigious graduate program. But on the inside, I was racked with anxiety, physically sick if I got anything less than a perfect grade. (Seriously, I cried when I once got an A minus. I'm still kinda pissed about it.) Surprise, surprise, I dropped out of grad school a day before my first presentation (on societal causes of extreme suffering and distress; *how ironically fitting*).

Constantly striving for perfection affected every aspect of my life. Like a tea kettle, I would let the steam simmer, bubble up, and burst open with a hasty cry until I was so dry, I could then just give up and move on. That is, until my perfectionism invaded one of the most intimate and essential areas of my life: eating. When the pressure became too heavy, I could give up dance, I could stop singing, and I could drop out of school, but I couldn't as easily escape eating. "Easily" is the key word.

My quest for diet perfection started out with innocent intentions. To be quite honest, I didn't care about my weight, my love handles, or the size of my ass. Oh, and I most certainly did not think about how I could achieve the perfect thigh gap, which apparently some folks on Instagram are *obsessed* with. Rather, after some uncomfortable digestive issues, I just wanted to *feel* better (the bait of the entire clean-eating movement). After visiting a naturopathic doctor in my impressionable late-teen years, I was diagnosed with some sort of mysterious sugar intolerance. My treatment? A full "detox" to completely eliminate all sugars from my diet.

My diet went from a well-balanced selection of colourful salads, turkey burgers, and chocolate chip cookies to fitness-model clean—a sad mélange of baked chicken breasts, hardboiled egg whites, massive green salads, and mountains of steamed veggies. What started as

an attempt to kick a sugar habit turned into a full-blown, irrational fear of "unclean" foods. In my quest to feel Gwyneth Paltrow fabulous, to achieve that halo of health, I sacrificed friendships, hobbies, laughter, life, and, oh, about fifty pounds from my already svelte frame. If glowing meant looking like a sunken ghost, then yes, I had that down.

Although it is still not defined as an "official" eating disorder, we now know my condition as orthorexia, a disordered eating pattern characterized by an unfounded fear of eating something deemed "unhealthy" that occurs as often in men as it does in women. Orthorexia was a natural place for me to park my perfectionist tendencies. Eating clean was a way for me to control my surroundings and ensure a pristine, perfect life, free of disease and discomfort. The reality was, I was the farthest that I'd ever been from comfort and control.

When I "cleaned" up my diet from the perceived "toxins" in my life, my goal was never to lose weight. As with most victims of orthorexia, weight loss was the pretty little package neatly gift wrapped and delivered to me with a bow. Diet culture frames it this way so we don't give it back or re-gift it to someone else. Soon, I was being praised for my malnourished body and for my "dedication" to clean eating. At the same time, I was growing increasingly bored eating fat-free chicken and steamed broccoli day after day. The pleasure in food was quickly wilting like a bag of baby spinach in a hot pan as I began to eat merely (barely) to survive. And if you thought turkey breast without gravy was bad enough, it was just the beginning. I was steadily shrinking, taking up less space, silencing my voice and confidence—the quiet manifesto of the diet industry itself.

Apparently, there's a wafer-thin line between being too fat and too skinny, and while it's well documented that bigger people endure a world of social stigma, it can be similarly lonely at the other end of the scale. I quickly fell into a vicious anti-social cycle. My fear of food and my self-consciousness over my disappearing body prevented me from wanting to go out with friends, but not being social only perpetuated my disordered eating and depressive thoughts. I needed an intervention, but one that could only come from me. That was the birth of my blog.

When I was still in university, one of my classmates suggested that I start my own blog to share my kitchen adventures. Being an overachiever, I blindly accepted the challenge, only to go home and Google "how to blog." But thanks to the powers of the interwebs (and a few Wordpress for dummies tutorials), on that day *Abbey's Kitchen* was born. Slowly, as my following grew, I began to get invitations to food launches and restaurant openings. Getting noticed was exciting . . . until I realized that I was terrified of leaving my safe, detoxed kitchen and being pitched right into a deep-fried bowl of sin. Restaurants aren't exactly known for their "clean" eats.

That's when it hit me. I had a choice: give up on the blog or let go of that tight-fisted grasp I had with food. Trusting that my body was smarter than the "rules" I had arbitrarily set, and that if I could just listen to what it was quite literally screaming at me, meant that I could find health *and* happiness. I closed my eyes and I chose to jump. I leaped out of my prison and into the comforting arms of a thin-crust pizza that reignited my love affair with food. And the romance hasn't died.

What You'll Find Inside

If my journey sounds familiar to you, you're not alone. I get hundreds of emails every week from women and men who have similarly hit rock bottom in their quest for clean living and are now ready to make peace with their bodies.

Thankfully, we're finally seeing a counter-movement emerge. *The Mindful Glow Cookbook* is the manifesto for the cause. Here, rehab-seeking ex-dieters will find inspiration, guidance, support, and recipes that are fun, satisfying, and of course super healthful, too. In *The Mindful Glow Cookbook*, the very word "diet" is stripped of its verb status in our vocabularies as we ask ourselves with

curiosity and without judgment, *Hello, beautiful, what do I want to eat today?*

My goal here is to share recipes and menus that are flavourful, nourishing, and subtly grounded in the latest science, though I promise you won't need to fully understand what a *p*-value or statistical significance means. Here's the Coles Notes version: healthy food is the food we enjoy eating the most, that feels best to our bodies, minds, and souls. And since our bodies depend on a wide range of nutrients to thrive, healthy food is varied food—not a rotating handful of "clean-eating" staples that you read about on a celebrity's website and will spend an afternoon trying to find (not to mention blowing half your paycheque). The recipes you'll find here are often plant-centric, and many are vegan, gluten-free, nut-free, and dairy-free. Others contain some protein-rich lean grass-fed beef, poultry, eggs, or dairy.

What you *won't* find is an in-depth nutritional analysis of each recipe. My goal with *The Mindful Glow Cookbook* is not only to share some of my favourite nourishing, delicious recipes but also to give you the tools to let your body be your guide. Arbitrary calories and numbers quickly derail those efforts, so I've purposely left them out. Having said that, I recognize that a lot of you or your families have dietary restrictions, health conditions, preferences, intolerances, and a wide range of nutrition goals, so I have created an easy-to-follow nutrition-labelling system (outlined below) to help you select the recipes that are best for you.

Rather than focus on classically demonized nutrients like carbohydrates, fat, and calories, I make a point to choose and celebrate ingredients that are high in fibre, protein, and healthy fats that stave off those unruly blood sugar spikes and keep us feeling satisfied longer. (And, of course, everything is delicious.) This isn't some sneaky ruse to help you "cut calories" or "crush cravings," but rather because feeling satisfied *feels* good. I don't know about you, but when I'm hangry, it's impossible for me to stay present and enjoy a quiet, mindful meal. Instead, I just want to eat *all the things*, nay, *anything*, to silence my hunger rage *stat*. Choosing nourishing, satisfying foods helps us break the obsessive thoughts that shackle us to food, so we can enjoy each and every bite in peace.

Dairy-free The recipe does not include dairy.

Gluten-free The recipe does not include gluten, for those with celiac disease or gluten intolerance.

Healthy fats The recipe contains 2 grams or more of monounsaturated and/or polyunsaturated fats per serving.

High fibre The recipe contains 4 grams or more of fibre per serving.

High protein 20 percent or more of total calories come from protein in the recipe.

No added sugar The recipe does not include any source of free sugars, including (but not limited to) white sugar, brown sugar, maple syrup, agave, corn syrup, honey, coconut sugar, or molasses.

Nut-free These recipes are free of nut products, so they're allergy- and school-safe. If you're sensitive to only one or two specific nuts, read the ingredients of other recipes carefully to ensure they'll work for you. In many cases, nuts in a recipe can easily be swapped out for an allergy-friendly nut-free butter or seeds.

Vegan The recipe contains no animal products or products made by animals, such as honey.

Vegetarian The recipe contains no meat, but may contain dairy or eggs or other animal products such as honey.

On Mindful Eating

At the core of what we call mindful eating is the idea that nutrition is actually less about *what* we eat than about *how* we eat. Rooted in Buddhist teachings, mindful eating (and the related concept, intuitive eating) is about avoiding distractions while eating, taking the time to slow down and enjoy a meal, and listening to your body for those subtle cues that it's time to eat and time to stop.

Taking on mindfulness may seem like a massive, scary, unpredictable endeavour, but it's actually more innate than we think. We're all born with a natural instinct that guides us to eat when we're hungry and stop when we're not. Babies cry when they need to eat, and they push away the breast or the bottle when they're full. Toddlers get cranky when they're hungry, but will put down the cupcake in all its frosted glory when they've had enough. It has nothing to do with the "willpower" that chronic dieters tend to lust over. Rather, we're born knowing how to do what *feels good*—what truly makes us glow from the inside out. The diet and weight-loss industry wants to keep us feeling vulnerable, so they snatch away our intrinsic sensibility. This loss of connection happens slowly as we age. Perhaps as children we were coerced into joining the "clean plate club" by well-meaning caregivers and teachers who shared that sad PSA about starving children across the globe. Or maybe it wasn't until adolescence, when we were forced to wolf down our lunchbox contents in a record-breaking fifteen minutes before we got scooted outside into the schoolyard. Perhaps we made it unscathed to young adulthood but then read some headline in one of those celebrity magazines about the dangers of eating after 8 p.m. Food rules strangle our natural instincts, they override what our bodies tell us they need, and like most things, interfering with nature tends to have consequences. We end up unhappy, unhealthy, and often heavier than what our intelligent bodies intended for us.

Silencing Your Inner Food Shamer

The key? We've got to stop with the food labels. The so-called "wellness" industry has created an obsession with dichotomizing "clean," "pure," or "good" food with "bad," "toxic," and "poison" food. It's bad enough that something as pleasurable as butter would have to end up on the naughty list, but we ride a dangerous tide when we bundle up our identity into what we put in our mouths. Suddenly, that Insta-worthy smoothie bowl made of alkaline monk tears and Alsatian grey salt has the power to elevate our being to a higher self, while noshing on processed cheese nibs makes us a bad person. Um, no. Kicking a dog makes you a bad person. Eating street meat in a poppy seed bun loaded up with *all the toppings* does not.

Remember the number-one reason diets don't work: nobody likes to feel deprived. And we don't need to be physically starving to be emotionally underfed. Studies suggest that foods perceived as "healthy" are less psychologically satisfying, leading us to consciously or unconsciously eat more even when we're full, all the while dreaming of the "forbidden" fare we so badly crave. Dragging ourselves through a massive bowl of raw kale is a set-up for devouring a family-size bag of potato chips. Why not skip the misery of dry greens, just enjoy a mindful portion of chips, and move on? On the flip side, when we label foods as off limits or "bad," we go into rebellious teenager mode. I mean, I don't know about your questionable teenage decisions, but when I was sixteen, my dad told me that I couldn't wear a lacy black camisole to school. I probably should have listened because, well, I was at school, not a nightclub for vampires (hello, '90s style, I don't miss you). But I wore it anyway because I didn't like to be told what to do. Denying ourselves something we really want tends to force us to the extreme. This means, if you're like me—and you've forbidden yourself *any* ice cream—then you're probably sneaking into your kitchen at 3 a.m. to polish off the Ben & Jerry's. Food rules (like all rules) are meant to be broken, but when we forgo them in the first place, they lose their power.

Removing food labels also has a tendency to make the formally dreaded "clean-diet food" that we would begrudgingly burden ourselves with feel indulgent and pleasurable again. We start to notice the satisfying crisp texture of an almond, the natural sweetness of a ripe summer berry, and the rich, buttery texture of a luscious piece of salmon. We start to eat what *feels good* in amounts that *feel good*. It might even make these foods more nutritious! One study showed that women absorbed 50 percent more iron from a meal they liked than they did from one that lacked flavour, even though the nutrient content was exactly the same. It's not magic, it's science, and it's ingrained in our biological *need* for pleasure. In the process, we start to feel better. We begin to glow.

But if the idea of letting go of food rules and stratified food categories makes you imagine yourself spiralling into an endless pie-eating marathon, take some baby bites first. Like any relationship, trusting your body takes time.

For a lot of us, structure is comforting, so start by creating a reliable "safe" protocol with your "forbidden" foods—you know, the ones you worry you won't be able to stop eating once you start. For me, that was always cereal. It wouldn't matter if it was coated in sugar or the geriatric fibre variety, if it was crunchy and in a big box, I would eat it all. Whatever your "forbidden" food is, begin to allow yourself a small bowl or plate each day.

Then, if you're feeling up to the challenge, step away from social media. Power down at mealtimes so you can escape the barrage of Facebook cat memes and YouTube wipeout videos to slow down and savour every bite.

Next, try beefing up your "forbidden" food with something a bit more satiating—as long as that doesn't interfere with the pleasure factor of the food. Maybe enjoy your cookies with a glass of milk. Or your bread with some natural almond butter. Or, for me, my cereal with some Greek yogurt. By allowing yourself those little pleasures, judgment-free, each day, those foods will soon start to lose their "forbidden" allure. Maybe you'll lose interest in them altogether, or maybe they just become another food in the long, boundless repertoire of tasty eats. It's not good, it's not bad, it's just cereal. And I'm no longer good or bad for loving the hell out of it. Foods may not necessarily be nutritionally equal, but we can make them *morally equal*.

Your Body as a Red-Hot Ferrari

Now that we've neutralized the moral identity of kale, cupcakes, and cocktails and any food is fair game, how do we know how *much* to eat? I start by thinking of my body as a car (I'll obviously be the red Ferrari). When you don't plan ahead and you leave the house on gas fumes, you end up making questionable, desperate decisions. We've all ended up stranded on the roadside, hiking two miles uphill to find that seedy gas station at 2 a.m. while imagining getting kidnapped by a serial killer. (Hey, I know you've had this thought, too.)

On the flip side, you also don't want to fill up your tank so much that fuel spurts out of the nozzle and spills all over the pavement. If you're a reasonable human being (a.k.a. not my husband who leaves me with the car on an empty tank every single time), you fill up before you get to serial-killer-movie-night status. We can do this with our hunger, too. I like to aim to be between a quarter and three-quarters full on my hunger scale, because that feels comfortable to me. Yes, there are times when I'll eat more because, hey, ice cream sammies are my bae. And there are times I let myself get too hungry because I forget to pack a snack for my mind-numbingly long meeting, only to double-fist the muffins and doughnuts when they bring out the snacks. It doesn't *feel* good bouncing between the two fringe borders of our body's innate hunger gauge, but when we occasionally do it anyway, the key is to trust that our body will make up the difference and move on.

Eat when you're hungry, stop when you're not.

But what about those days you slip up, ignore your body, and get caught up in "emotional eating"? Does it mean you "failed" this, too? Intuitive eating may be largely about identifying and listening to your *physical* hunger cues, but it's also about self-love and compassion, and sometimes that means eating because you're sad, bored, or happy. The concepts of comfort foods and indulgences have been hijacked by diet culture, when at their core they should simply mean foods that bring you pleasure. Comfort foods may bring us joy because they remind us of a memory, a feeling, a relationship, a story—they give us a sense of connection. Acknowledge why food is comforting to you, identify which foods make you *feel* good, and honour those whims guilt-free.

What the Research Says

Not only is mindful eating more pleasurable than cutting calories or counting points, but it's a hell of a lot more effective at promoting good health. Compared with dieters, intuitive eaters are better able to improve cholesterol levels, blood pressure, disordered eating behaviours, diet quality, and psychological well-being. Although weight loss shouldn't be the goal, research suggests that mindful eating can help you settle back into your body's naturally healthy weight. Pleasure always trumps pain in the race towards good health.

The Mindful Glow Cookbook reminds us that our worth is much greater than our bodies. It's greater than how much kale we ate, how long our cleanse lasted, or how many likes we got on Instagram for our #fitspo WOD. I invite you to unapologetically make *yourself* the priority and to feel good about that choice. You don't need to count it, control it, and force it, or hate your way to a clean bill of health. Famous psychologist Carl Rogers once said, "People are just as wonderful as sunsets if you let them be. When I look at a sunset, I don't find myself saying, 'Soften the orange a bit on the right-hand corner.' I don't try to control a sunset. I watch with awe as it unfolds." You, your appetite, and your intelligent body, too, can be an awe-inspiring force that unfolds before your very eyes. So out of love for yourself, eat in ways that *feel good* and help you glow from the inside out.

Deliciously yours,
Abbey xo

My Kitchen Tool Obsession

Sneaking in the side door with a shiny new appliance or serving dish is more exciting than bringing home a new pair of designer shoes. Shoes give you blisters, and kitchen tools give you yummy food! While you certainly don't need everything on this list—I suggest substitutions where relevant—the right tools do make cooking easier and more enjoyable. These are some of my go-to kitchen tools for building an epic meal.

Okay, so it may seem like a decade's worth of Christmas lists for Santa, but don't stress if you don't have some, or even any, of the tools on this list. You can totally rock my recipes without most of these toys. But if you're looking to treat yourself to the gift that keeps giving (and doesn't require dry cleaning), then consider this your ultimate wish list.

Baking Sheet

You know you're going to need a few baking sheets to get perfectly baked cookies like my Mayan Salted Avocado Hot Chocolate Brookies (page 235) and crispy golden-brown meats and breadings like my Buffalo Chicken Egg Rolls (page 227) and Crispy Avocado Fries (page 221). I recommend going with a rimmed baking sheet (to catch any juices or spills) with a durable nonstick surface.

Cast-Iron Skillet

When I want to cook something screaming hot and quickly, like my Zucchini Noodle Carbonara (page 67), or when I finish cooking something in the oven, like my Spicy Chickpea Shakshuka (page 47), that's when I bust out the good old cast-iron skillet. When you first get your skillet, you want to "season" it to help protect it while prolonging its nonstick lifespan. Please, don't skip this step. Think of it like spraying your suede Louboutins before a blizzard. First, wash your pan with warm soapy water and dry it thoroughly. Then moisten a piece of towel with vegetable oil and rub it all over the pan. Don't forget the corners and sides—they need some lovin' too! Finally, just pop it into a 450°F (230°C) oven for about 30 minutes to let the heat set the oil into the pan. I recommend repeating this about three times to get a really good initial layer of seasoning before you start cooking. To clean it without ruining all your hard work, wash the pan in hot water without any soap or steel wool. If there are any sticky bits of food on there, just scrub with a paste made of equal parts kosher salt and water and boil a bit of water in the pan. Finally, thoroughly dry the pan with a kitchen towel and finish with a very light coat of vegetable oil. Yeah, I know it seems like a pain, but if you nurture your cast-iron skillet, it will bring you amazingly tasty meals for many years to come.

Food Processor

I believe that a good food processor is the workhorse of the kitchen. I use mine to make big batches of shredded cabbage for my Cider-Braised Sausages and Cabbage with Fresh Apple Salsa (page 97) and shredded cheese for my Autumn Butternut Squash Mac and Cheese with Sage Panko (page 73), but it also combines ingredients smoothly for my Pumpkin Pecan Pie Energy Bites (page 153) and so much more.

High-Speed Blender

In the peanut butter battle of crunchy versus smooth, smooth wins every time. I love some crunchy chips or fried chicken, but for me, smooth foods need to be super smooth. Don't mess with that. That's only possible with a good high-speed blender. When choosing a blender, look for one with a 2 peak horsepower motor, a stable base, an easy-to-clean container, and a pour spout for mess-free use. It's great for my frosty, creamy Tropical Coconut Smoothie Bowl (page 28), light and airy crêpe batter for my Buckwheat Blintzes with Wild Blueberry Sauce (page 35), and spicy condiments such as the Tomatillo Salsa that goes with my Sweet Potato and Black Bean Scramble Breakfast Taco (page 57).

Ice-Pop Mould

Everything tastes better on a stick, and in those sweaty days of summer, there's nothing more refreshing than a cool, icy pop. When choosing an ice-pop mould, look for large rectangular pops without any ridges that tend to snag any goodies you pack inside. Also, I get that treats are always exciting, but be patient when pulling out. I always run my moulds under hot water for at least 15 seconds to ensure they come out smoothly, without any casualties. Use your ice-pop moulds to make my Frozen Banana Berry Pie Pops with Berry Crunch Dip (page 170) and my Tiramisu Paletas for dessert (page 243).

Kitchen Torch

Handling a kitchen torch is a bit of a power trip. There's something tremendously satisfying about lighting things on fire, especially when it makes them taste good. The key to a perfectly caramelized but not burnt sugar topping is to position the torch about 2 inches from the food and continuously move the flame in a smooth, steady motion, almost like you were brushing hair. While the custard on my Macerated Balsamic Pepper Strawberries with Rosé Sabayon (page 267) can be served without the caramelized crust, and my Brûléed Grapefruit with Mascarpone Thyme Cream (page 273) can be popped under the broiler, a kitchen torch gets

the job done perfectly—and can provide hours of adult entertainment.

Mandoline

It may look like a medieval torture device, but the mandoline is one of my favourite inexpensive kitchen tools for getting long, perfect julienne-sliced vegetables. Because really, who has the time or patience to do that by hand? When using a mandoline, always make sure to use the slicing guard or glove it comes with—we want salad, not a trip to the ER. I use my mandoline to shred sprouts for my Brussels Sprout, Apple, and Apricot Slaw with Beer Vinaigrette (page 129), cauliflower for my Shaved Cauliflower, Apple, and Burrata Salad with Apple Cider Vinaigrette (page 115), and fennel for my Crispy Chickpea, Fennel, and Cherry Salad with Tarragon Citronette (page 112).

Microplane Grater

Citrus zest adds a huge hit of bright flavour without added calories, salt, sugar, or fat. It's essential for bringing bright citrus flavour home in my Meyer Lemon Raspberry Cheesecakes (page 249), Peaches and Cream Quinoa Bites with Brown Sugar Crackle Glaze (page 154), and Raspberry Limeade Overnight Oats (page 55). When choosing a microplane, look for one with razor-edge holes and a very thin grate plate to get a super finely grated zest.

Muffin Pans

My hubbie's pet name for me is Muffin (though he pronounces it *moo-fon*), so naturally I eat a lot of them. I suggest having a set of regular-size and mini muffin pans, and going for the nonstick variety so you don't have to be so religious about getting into all of the little crevices with butter or oil. I obviously use them to make my Peanut Butter Banana Chocolate Chip Muffins (page 165), Peaches and Cream Quinoa Bites with

Brown Sugar Crackle Glaze (page 154), and Ultimate Sticky Toffee Puddings (page 239), but they're also key for making perfect Prosciutto, Pear, and Goat Cheese Egg Cups (page 42), Lemon Poppy Seed Yogurt Cookie Cups (page 158), and Meyer Lemon Raspberry Cheesecakes (page 249). I also like having a set of silicone muffin moulds for delicate no-bake recipes that need to be carefully popped out without greasing, like my Chocolate Banana Peanut Butter Cups (page 257) and Fruity Nut Fro-Yo "Cookies" (page 169).

Nonstick Skillets

If you're going to invest in one good pan, I recommend nonstick. A good nonstick skillet is a healthy home cook's BFF, perfect for making tasty weeknight meals without a ton of added fat or the bicep workout required to clean stuck-on scraps. I use mine religiously for my lean protein dishes such as my Ginger Turmeric Shrimp (page 103) and Sweet Tea Bourbon Chicken Breasts (page 83). While I don't usually recommend putting nonstick skillets in an oven over 500°F (260°C), if you think you might, you'll want to look for a coating without any PTFE, which can break down in super-high heat and release harmful gases. You also want to look for one that is free of PFOA, which is a chemical used in some cookware that may have some carcinogenic properties. To clean your nonstick skillet, create a thick paste of equal parts baking soda and water and gently scrub the pan using a brush or non-metallic sponge. Rinse it off well and then let it dry.

Oil Atomizer

I read a lot of "diet" recipes that call for you to spray food with nonstick spray to cut back on calories. Hell, no! Having said that, I get that we all want a nice even coat of oil, which is where my oil atomizer comes into play. An atomizer allows you to use the best-quality oils without any propellants or additives, while still getting the sheer, even spritz of a commercial nonstick spray. Use it for greasing muffin pans or baking dishes, greasing your grill, and ensuring baked snacks stay crispy. It's the key that ups the addictive qualities of my Cheese-Explosion Cauliflower Tots (page 211), Crispy Avocado Fries with Mango Chili Coconut Dip (page 221), Almond Coconut Zucchini Chips with Ginger Plum Dipping Sauce (page 205), Buffalo Chicken Egg Rolls with Blue Cheese Dip (page 227), and Five-Spice Sesame Panko Tofu Poppers with Sweet-and-Sour Orange Dip (page 207). If you don't have an atomizer, simply use a kitchen brush and lightly brush your food or cookware with oil.

Silicone Baking Mat

My husband says I'm a great cook but a terrible cleaner, so crazy-slippery silicone baking mats legitimately save my marriage every night. They're great for getting evenly browned cookies and pastries without added fat, like with my Chewy Crackle Almond Apple Cookies (page 162). To clean a greasy mat, sprinkle it with a little baking soda, rub it with half a lemon to create a paste, and scrub it very gently before rinsing it off with warm water.

Vegetable Spiralizer

Okay, so vegetable "noodles" aren't real noodles, and they are not a stealthy way to cut calories or carbs out of your life. What they are, however, are a damn tasty and pretty way to get new colours, flavours, textures, fibre, and antioxidants into your mouth. I spent months spiralizing zucchini into noodles to try to figure out the best way to keep vegetable "pasta" from getting soggy, and I'm happy to report I nailed it. It all comes down to a little food science lesson in osmosis—the process by which molecules move from a less-concentrated solution to a more concentrated one in an effort to maintain equilibrium. Check it out in my Zucchini Noodle Carbonara (page 67) and Veggie Noodle Pad Thai (page 71).

Kitchen Staples to *Kill It* in the Kitchen

Cooking may be my passion and ultimately what pays my bills, but like everyone else, I'm too busy and tired to do everything from scratch all the time. I totally have days when I'll happily pay the 200 percent markup for pre-sliced pineapple and fancy salad-bar greens. Having said that, keeping a well-stocked pantry and batch-prepping some of my go-to specialty ingredients can save me a pretty penny. And that, my friends, is how you justify more shoes—totally guilt-free. Below are some of my essential kitchen staples.

You don't need to go crazy at Costco buying all of these goodies in one go, since you probably already have a lot of them, and anything else can be collected as needed. To avoid any scary credit card bills, I suggest you just make a master wish list and pop one new novel staple into your cart each week.

Acids

Some people describe themselves as having a sweet tooth. Others love bitter greens, coffee, and hoppy beer. Me? I'm an acid junkie. I have an entire wall in my pantry devoted to these fermented tinctures. (Ice wine vinegar? OMG, yes please!) Fret not. In this book, I keep it to the basics. Balsamic vinegar is my all-time favourite thanks to its fruity flavour and luscious syrupy consistency. It's a must for seducing the sweetness out of Macerated Balsamic Pepper Strawberries with Rosé Sabayon (page 267) and Balsamic Roasted Brussels Sprouts, Grapes, and Figs (page 133). Apple cider vinegar is another favourite for its natural tart and subtle apple flavour. I love it for complementing cozy autumn ingredients like in my Cider-Braised Sausages and

Cabbage with Fresh Apple Salsa (page 97) and my Shaved Cauliflower, Apple, and Burrata Salad with Apple Cider Vinaigrette (page 115). If you want one more, I say go with rice vinegar for its mild, clean, and delicate flavour, perfect for Asian-inspired recipes like my Miso Cucumber, Avocado, and Toasted Sesame Salad (page 124) and Five-Spice Sesame Panko Tofu Poppers with Sweet-and-Sour Orange Dip (page 207). Feel free to switch up the vinegars if you have some fancy ones on hand. They're a great way to add bold flavour without any sodium, added sugar, or fat.

Canned Goods

Fresh isn't necessarily best. I believe that if using a canned product helps you get dinner on the table, it's probably one of the healthiest foods you can buy. Stock up! Furthermore, these days, canned produce is packed at the peak of perfection to lock in nutrients rather than letting them waste away in transit from California or Mexico. When choosing canned foods, I always look for no-salt-added versions so that I can control how much seasoning I add to my dish. No-salt-added canned tomatoes, for example, are a must. Some of you surely have a better situation down in the southern States, but here in Canada, our tomatoes taste like acidulated water nine months of the year. Canned tomatoes are key to adding farm-fresh flavour to dishes like my Caponata and Ricotta Sweet Potato Bites (page 219) and my Chocolate Stout Veggie Chili (page 148). Canned beans and legumes are another staple. Yes, you can totally cook your own beans to save a bit of money, but when I'm debating between canned beans for my Spicy Chickpea Shakshuka (page 47) and ordering take-out, I'm so glad my pantry is stocked.

Dehydrated and Freeze-Dried Fruit

When there's no fruit in the fridge, I go straight to the pantry. Traditional dehydrated fruit (think raisins, dried cranberries and cherries) are great for adding natural sweetness and a satisfying chew—a must for recipes like my Carrot "Cake" Protein Parfait (page 174) and Riesling-Roasted Pears (page 268). In contrast, freeze-dried fruit is a lower-sugar alternative that packs a wicked crispy crunch and bold fruity flavour, so it adds a sweet crackle coating to my Frozen Banana Berry Pie Pops with Berry Crunch Dip (page 170). You'll also notice I use a lot of Medjool dates in my recipes, because when processed in a powerful blender they rival any sugar or syrup. Try them in my Ultimate Sticky Toffee Puddings (page 239) and my Samoas Doughnuts (page 237) to satisfy your sweet tooth naturally.

Fancy Salts

I know salt has a bad reputation and yes, most North Americans consume far too much of it, but I'll never tell you *not* to season your meals. Salt is essential for coaxing big, bold flavour out of food—without it, even I, a dietitian, wouldn't touch kale or chicken breasts. The reality is, the majority of sodium in our diet comes from highly processed convenience foods, not from home-cooked fare, so adding a mindful pinch to your recipes is really no big deal. I would be lying if I said I didn't have about two dozen different types of salt in my pantry, but unless you get your thrills from mundane spices and seasonings like me, you can stick to just a few. Table salt is what a lot of us find in our salt shakers, but I actually only use it for baking and very precise recipes because it dissolves quickly and packs neatly into a measuring spoon. Use it for enhancing the sweetness of desserts like my Key Lime Mousse Parfait (page 258) and Flourless Chocolate

Almond Cake (page 251). Sea salt is a coarser unrefined salt with its mineral content intact and a clean ocean-air flavour. If you're finding most brands a bit too pricey for regular use, kosher salt is a cheaper alternative that still offers that satisfying coarse grind. I recommend seasoning most of your recipes with coarser salts because the texture helps you get a much better "feel" for how much you're picking up and you generally end up using less. Whether you go sea or kosher, both are great general-purpose salts for dishes like my Caprese Frittata (page 45), Sweet Potato and Black Bean Scramble Breakfast Tacos (page 57), and Pomegranate-Glazed Apples Stuffed with Turkey Pistachio Meatloaf (page 89). The other salt I'm totally obsessed with but save only for finishing off plates is fleur de sel. This special sea salt from France has a delicate crackly texture that makes my mouth water just writing about it. Yes, it's pricey stuff—about a hundred times more expensive than table salt—but it takes the pleasure factor up by *at least* that much. I use it for giving a glistening crackling crust to everything from my Ginger Turmeric Shrimp (page 103) to my Spicy Honey Lime Blistered Shishitos with Sesame Panko Crunch (page 134) and my Chocolate Banana Peanut Butter Cups (page 257).

Hot Sauce

Hot sauce isn't just a condiment, it's a lifestyle. Considering there are hot sauce eating competitions and stores exclusively devoted to the stuff, I think it's safe to say hot sauce is red hot. While you are totally free to switch things up with your favourite brand, I do recommend a few staples for different preparations. Sriracha, a thick paste-like sauce made of chili peppers, vinegar, garlic, sugar, and salt, is my go-to for Asian-inspired dishes like my Veggie Noodle Pad Thai (page 71) and my Spicy Honey Lime Blistered Shishitos (page 134). Cayenne hot sauce (such as Frank's Original) is another staple made simply from cayenne pepper, vinegar, garlic, and salt. It gives my Buffalo Chicken Egg Rolls (page 227) their iconic pub-food flavour and is just generally awesome for adding a kick to a bleh meal. If you want to venture into more distinctive hot sauce flavour, I use a lot of harissa as well. Harissa is a mixture of peppers, garlic, coriander, caraway, and lemon that is commonly used in Moroccan and North African cuisines. I love its bittersweet bite and rich aromatics in my Pistachio-Crusted Lamb Lollies with Harissa Yogurt Dip (page 230) and Spicy Chickpea Shakshuka with Silky Eggplant and Runny Eggs (page 47).

Miso

Miso is a fermented soy product that adds undeniable umami goodness and a distinct salty layer to sauces, soups, and dressings. It's the backbone of my Miso Cucumber, Avocado, and Toasted Sesame Salad (page 124) and my savoury Edamame Mango Brown Rice Energy Balls (page 157) that you just can't do without. You can find a wide range of miso pastes in Asian markets, but my recipes call for the light miso variety, which is naturally lower in salt, creamy, mild, and sweet and is usually easy to find at major grocers.

Mustards

Mustard is my condiment of choice. It's pungent, spicy, bright, and acidic, and can turn your mother-in-law's dry leftover Thanksgiving turkey into a damn good lunch. Not only does mustard add big, bold flavour without added sugar or fat, but it actually helps emulsify fats with liquids in vinaigrettes. Sometimes I use a simple Dijon mustard for creamy-smooth dressings, like in my Crispy Chickpea, Fennel, and Cherry Salad with Tarragon Citronette (page 112), but when I'm looking for a bit more texture, I bust out my whole-grain Dijon mustard, as I do in my Charred Broccoli, Quinoa, and Hazelnut Crunch Salad (page 126). Texture also determines which mustard I use in non-dressing preparations. I like the whole-grain for adding a supple poppy texture to my Cider-Braised

Sausages and Cabbage (page 97), while the standard Dijon works to adhere crispy breading without eggs— check out my Almond Coconut Zucchini Chips (page 205) for that hack! Finally, when I really want the mustard flavour to shine without compromising the smooth consistency, I go for a rich spicy brown mustard. It's the happy medium between a coarse whole-grain and a standard Dijon, and is perfect for slathering on my Apple Cider Can Chicken with Maple Mustard Glaze (page 85).

Non-Dairy Milks

I have no qualms about dairy and rely on it for its natural sweetness in recipes like my Parmesan Garlic French Toast (page 38), but in some recipes, a light non-dairy milk may work best. I often keep almond milk, cashew milk, and soy milk on hand for easy breakfasts like my Raspberry Limeade Overnight Oats (page 55) and dairy-free desserts like my Samoas Doughnuts (page 237). I also always keep full-fat coconut milk around for a dairy-free whipped cream. Insider tip: keep it in the fridge so the cream separates from the coconut water for recipes like Piña Colada Napoleons (page 245).

Nut Butters

Real talk. Sometimes my favourite meals are the "desperate" ones I make out of peanut butter and bread when I've run out of eggs, meat, and vegetables. Nut butters keep busy people alive. I love almond butter in my Chocolate-Dipped Banana Crunch Roll-Up Pops (page 166), peanut butter in my iconic Chocolate Banana Peanut Butter Cups (page 257), and cashew butter in my Wild Rice and Bok Choy Salad with Creamy Cashew Dressing (page 123). Can you use them interchangeably? Go for it, live on the edge! You can even use a nut-free alternatives if you're concerned about allergies. Whatever you choose, I always opt for a natural nut butter with no added sugar so that I can control the sweetness of my snack or meal.

Nuts and Seeds

Okay, if you have an allergy, then by all means skip this section (and head to any of the recipes with the "nut-free" label), but I need these tiny nutrition powerhouses in my life. Nuts are crunchy little flavour bombs, perfect for adding texture and staying power to just about any meal or snack. I love them anywhere—on salads, like my Grilled Peaches with Jalapeño, Walnuts, and Blue Cheese (page 138), desserts like my Sweet Summer Watermelon Cake (page 255), mains like my Pomegranate-Glazed Apples Stuffed with Turkey Pistachio Meatloaf (page 89), and snacks like my Chili and Chocolate Nut Mix (page 196). Yes, my pantry looks like a bulk barn, but I like to keep almonds, cashews, peanuts, walnuts, pistachios, pine nuts, pecans, chia seeds, whole flaxseeds, sunflower seeds, and pumpkin seeds on hand. To prevent their delicate oils from going rancid, keep a small portion of each in an airtight container in the pantry for up to 3 months, or for up to 6 months in the fridge. Also, try to resist chopping or grinding nuts and seeds until you're ready to use them. With flaxseed, for example, I always buy it whole and grind it in small batches as I need it for recipes like my Almond-Crusted French Toast (page 40) and Autumn Butternut Squash Mac and Cheese with Sage Panko (page 73). Get crackin'!

Oats and Flours (and gluten-free options)

There are lots of different grains and flours out there, all of which have distinctive baking properties, flavours, and textures. You'll see that I don't discriminate. Rolled oats (gluten-free ones are available) are a hearty breakfast staple for making my Morning Perk Espresso Granola (page 27) and Whipped Proats (page 49), but they also can be milled into a DIY flour (see page 18). Whole wheat flour is my go-to baking grain because it's easy to work with and adds a boost of fibre to both savoury

recipes (like my Cheese-Explosion Cauliflower Tots on page 211) and sweet (like my Mayan Salted Avocado Hot Chocolate Brookies on page 235). For gluten-free options, I love the rich nuttiness of buckwheat flour in my Buckwheat Blintzes (page 35), the fibre-rich goodness of coconut flour in my Peanut Butter Banana Chocolate Chip Muffins (page 165), and the light natural sweetness of brown rice flour in my Samoas Doughnuts (page 237). Even if you're not gluten-free, experiment with some of these nutrient-rich flours!

Oils and Fats

Every few months some oil or fat takes the limelight while another gets a royal beating in the public eye. While headlines love to categorize fats as good or bad, I strongly believe that the reason the research seems all over the place is because almost all fats have redeeming qualities and downsides. Our body needs a wide range of different fatty acids to grow and thrive, so if you consume a wide range of cooking oils and fats, you're naturally going to get a nice balance of those fatty acids. Not only do different fats offer varying nutritional properties, but they also are ideal for different types of food preparations. I generally use a good-quality fruity extra-virgin olive oil as my standard cooking oil and vinaigrette base. It's perfect for adding rich, grassy flavour to my Avocado Protein Smash with Balsamic Roasted Tomatoes (pages 23), my Lemon Cumin Grilled Eggplant (page 76), and my Grilled Peaches with Jalapeño, Walnuts, and Blue Cheese (page 138). And then there's butter. Honestly, Julia Child was right when she said that anything is good with enough butter. I'm sure that's written as *fact* in a scientific journal somewhere. But honestly, butter is best to help you carry flavours without imparting any new ones. I love it in desserts like my Meyer Lemon Raspberry Cheesecakes (page 249), for pan-frying breakfast classics like my PB and J Protein Pancakes (page 33), and for adding rich, sweet flavour to caramelized onions, as in my Prosciutto, Pear, and Goat Cheese Egg Cups (page 42). It's also an absolute *must* for making dreamy nutty brown butter for dishes like my Brown Butter and Orange Cauli-Couscous Salad (page 117). Brown butter is my bae. And then there's coconut oil. Virgin coconut oil only recently made the jump from the media's bad to good books thanks to its unique medium-chain fatty acid profile. Dietitian confession: I'm less jazzed about the alleged health benefits of coconut oil than I am about its tropical aroma and its versatile high smoke point. Also, because it melts so smoothly and hardens to a solid state, it's the key to getting professional-quality chocolate confectionary, like in my Chocolate Banana Peanut Butter Cups (page 257) and my Tiramisu Paletas (page 243). That is reason enough to keep a tub in your pantry. Coconut oil also stands in as a plant-based alternative to butter in vegan recipes like my Almond-Crusted French Toast (page 40). To keep them fresher longer, store your butter in the fridge and your other oils and fats in a cool, dark pantry.

Starches and Thickeners

I like a thin, runny sauce as much as I like running, period. (That is, just *NO*.) Thankfully, this is where starches come into play. Depending on whether or not I care to keep something gluten-free, I usually thicken up sauces with cornstarch, tapioca flour, whole wheat flour, or brown rice flour. Yes, I could drag you through the contents of one of my university food science textbooks and explain the unique culinary properties of each. But honestly, my recipes usually call for so little, so just use whichever you've got. I keep starches in the pantry to add a luscious glossy texture to my Cherry Amaretto Sauce (page 251) and to help hold all the flavour together in my Golden Pork Wontons (page 225).

Sweeteners

Let's set the record straight once and for all. All sugar is ultimately sugar. While honey, maple, and coconut sugars may offer *minutely* different nutritional properties, our body doesn't see them much differently than the demonized white stuff. So let's just agree that sweet things taste good and whatever we choose, let's make it count. While all sugars add sweetness, I specifically choose honey, maple syrup, agave nectar, or coconut sugar when I want to add specific subtle flavour to a dressing, sauce, or dessert. For instance, the tropical aroma of coconut sugar is the best thematic choice for my Veggie Noodle Pad Thai (page 71), while the floral notes of a good-quality honey make it a perfect choice for candying the tangy kumquats on my Creamsicle Granita Parfait (page 261). In some cases, white, brown, and icing sugar just work better than their liquid counterparts, so make sure you always have a bag of each on hand.

My Staple Recipes

Now that you've got the tools and ingredients to rock the kitchen like a boss, here are some awesome techniques to put them to use. I make a big batch of these staple recipes once a week to save myself oodles of time during the weeknight dinner dash.

Cauliflower Rice

I love real rice but I also adore cauliflower rice as a fantastic way to add fibre, texture, and cancer-fighting antioxidants to a meal. A lot of stores and brands sell it pre-made, but it's easy to make yourself. Simply pulse cauliflower florets into small rice-like pieces in your food processor. Cauliflower rice is a great way to stretch out your grains, like in my Asparagus, Pea, and Tomato Quinotto (page 65) and my Brown Butter and Orange Cauli-Couscous Salad with Beets and Goat Cheese (page 117). It's also a perfect base to add sweet, subtle flavour to recipes like Cheese-Explosion Cauliflower Tots (page 211).

Cashew Cream

I love the sweet, nutty, subtle flavour of rich cashew cream and use it as a richer, thicker plant-based alternative to yogurt, cream, and even cheese. To get it super smooth, you have to soak your raw cashews overnight in water in the fridge, then purée the drained cashews in a high-speed blender with a little liquid. It usually takes ¼ cup (60 mL) of liquid and a bit of patience for the oils to really start to break down some of the tougher fibres, but if you want a lighter, thinner cream, you can add more liquid to reach your desired consistency. Use it to make a vegan "cream cheese" dip in my Layered Everything Bagel Dip (page 201), to add richness to my Buckwheat Blintzes with Wild Blueberry

Sauce (page 35), and for a luxurious sour–cream–like topper for my Beet Tartare with Cashew Caper Cream and Crispy Kasha (page 199).

Cottage Cheese Cream

I adore cottage cheese because it has a whopping 28 grams of satisfying protein per cup and is a tabula rasa for sweet or savoury flavours. It's a snacking staple for me in its unadulterated state, but if the lumpy texture puts you off, I've got a wicked hack. Puréeing it in a high-speed blender transforms cottage cheese into something smooth, thick, and unapologetically luscious. It's a great substitute for Greek yogurt if you're not a fan of yogurt's biting tang but still need a protein-rich vessel for my Morning Perk Espresso Granola (page 27). I use this technique in my Peach Melba Sweet Potato Toast with Whipped Cottage Cheese (page 24), Buckwheat Blintzes with Wild Blueberry Sauce (page 35), Two-Ingredient Protein "Ice Cream" (page 173), Carrot "Cake" Protein Parfait (page 174), Chewy Crackle Almond Apple Cookies (page 162), and PB and J Protein Pancakes (page 33).

DIY Gluten-Free Oat Flour

I always have gluten-free oats in the cupboard for quick, fibre-rich breakfasts, so rather than going out to track down specialty oat flour or paying a premium for a gluten-free flour, I make my own by processing oats in the food processor until they turn into a fine, smooth flour. It takes about 1¼ cups (300 mL) of old-fashioned or quick oats to yield about 1 cup of oat flour, so I make a huge batch and keep it in the pantry for baking. Oats are technically naturally gluten-free, but they're often grown alongside gluten-containing grains, so there are concerns about cross-contamination during growing and harvesting. For that reason, only use oats labelled "gluten-free" if you're making flour for those with celiac disease or gluten intolerance. I use oat flour in my Pomegranate-Glazed Apples Stuffed with Turkey Pistachio Meatloaf (page 89), Stuffed Hawaiian Burgers with Grilled Pineapple, Peameal, and Teriyaki Ketchup (page 91), Peanut Butter Banana Chocolate Chip Muffins (page 165), and my Ultimate Sticky Toffee Puddings (page 239).

Mushroom Meat

Mushrooms are loaded with umami (a.k.a. the fifth taste sensation), and when minced to a ground meat–like consistency, they have a deliciously beefy texture and flavour. It's a great way to stretch your meat budget while also adding moisture and is as easy as pulsing mushrooms in a food processor a few times. Try it in my Stuffed Hawaiian Burgers (page 91), my Chocolate Stout Veggie Chili (page 148), and my Golden Pork Wontons (page 225).

Spiralized Vegetables

Okay, so you put up with me waxing poetic about my spiralizer. Here's my trick to help you use it. Line a baking sheet with a few layers of paper towel or a kitchen towel. Lay the veggie noodles on the paper and sprinkle with kosher salt. Top with another few layers of paper towel, a cutting board, and some heavy books or pots, and let the veggies sit for 10 minutes. After 10 minutes, transfer the noodles to a colander and rinse thoroughly with cold water to remove the salt. Gently squeeze and shake the noodles and lay them down on fresh paper towel, covering with another dry layer. Top with those heavy items and let the noodles dry for 10 minutes before adding to your recipe. While zucchini is my go-to, most spiralizers work well with cucumbers, carrots, parsnips, beets, and sweet potatoes. Try out my Zucchini Noodle Carbonara (page 67) and Veggie Noodle Pad Thai (page 71).

Rise and Shine

ABBEY'S TIP Mornings can get crazy, so I often prepare the tomatoes and avocado smash the night before and just pop the bread in the toaster for a speedier morning assembly. To prevent the avocado from browning, pack it into an airtight container, drizzle a thin layer of room-temperature water on top, cover, and refrigerate for up to 3 days. When you're ready to eat, carefully pour off the water, give the smash a stir, and assemble.

Avocado Protein Smash with Balsamic Roasted Tomatoes

Dairy-free • Healthy fats • High fibre • No added sugar • Nut-free • Vegan • Vegetarian

Serves 6

Avocado toast is kinda like wearing three-inch pumps at the office. You feel pretty cool rockin' them for the first forty-five minutes, but before you know it, you're tackling your office mates for their sensible sneakers or ballet flats. I'm all for enjoying something that's trendy and super tasty, but this girl needs protein to get through a tough morning at work. My version sneaks in staying power with some cannellini beans and hearty Ezekiel bread and sexes it up with candy-like tomatoes. It's practicality with style—every girl's shoe fantasy in food.

Balsamic Roasted Tomatoes
6 Roma tomatoes, cut in half lengthwise and seeded
4½ teaspoons (22 mL) extra-virgin olive oil
3 small cloves garlic, thinly sliced
1 tablespoon (15 mL) balsamic vinegar
Sea salt and cracked black pepper

Avocado Protein Smash
1 can (15 ounces/425 g) cannellini beans, drained
 and rinsed
2 ripe avocados, pitted, peeled, and diced
3 tablespoons (45 mL) fresh lemon juice, more to taste

¼ cup (60 mL) fresh parsley leaves
¼ cup (60 mL) fresh basil leaves
1 small clove garlic, finely minced
Sea salt and cracked black pepper
6 slices Ezekiel bread or your favourite sprouted bread
4½ teaspoons (22 mL) extra-virgin olive oil

Garnish
Fresh basil leaves
Fleur de sel
Extra-virgin olive oil

1. Preheat the oven to 450°F (230°C). Line a baking sheet with parchment paper or a silicone baking mat.

2. **Make the Balsamic Roasted Tomatoes** In a medium bowl, toss the tomato halves with the olive oil and spread out on the baking sheet cut side up. Sprinkle the garlic over the tomatoes, drizzle with balsamic vinegar, and season with a pinch each of salt and pepper. Roast until the tomatoes soften and begin to caramelize slightly (be careful that they don't burn, so keep an eye on them), 15 to 25 minutes, depending on their size.

3. **Make the Avocado Protein Smash** Meanwhile, in a food processor or high-speed blender, combine the cannellini beans, avocados, lemon juice, parsley, basil, and garlic; process until smooth. Season with salt, pepper, and additional lemon juice to taste.

4. Once the tomatoes are roasted, carefully transfer them to a plate along with any juices and caramelized bits, and set aside. Wipe the baking sheet dry with a bit of paper towel, then drizzle both sides of the bread with olive oil. Place on the baking sheet and bake until lightly golden brown, about 5 minutes, rotating halfway through.

5. To assemble, divide the Avocado Protein Smash among the toast slices, top each serving with 2 pieces of roasted tomato, and garnish with fresh basil, a sprinkle of fleur de sel, and a drizzle of olive oil.

Peach Melba Sweet Potato Toast with Whipped Cottage Cheese

Gluten-free • Healthy fats • High fibre • High protein • Vegetarian

Serves 2

Truth bomb: sweet potato "toast" is not a substitute for real toast. We don't need a replacement for bread. It's perfectly nourishing all on its own, and frankly, it's often a satisfying start to my day. But sweet potato toast really is its own kind of wonderful. Turns out the internet has taught us that you can stick all kinds of things into your toaster and they'll come out as delicious "toast." Throw a few slices of raw sweet potato in, and out pops a totally portable hand-held treat. With its golden-brown exterior and a supple, sweet centre, sweet potato toast is the perfect vehicle for delicate whipped cottage cheese, caramelized peaches, and sweet raspberries. Dessert has nothing on this peach Melba brekkie. No ice cream required.

1 peach, sliced into 16 thin wedges

1 teaspoon (5 mL) pure liquid honey, more to taste, divided

¾ cup (175 mL) 2% or 4% cottage cheese

1 sweet potato, scrubbed and sliced lengthwise into 4 slices (each ¼ inch/5 mm thick)

½ cup (125 mL) fresh raspberries

3 tablespoons (45 mL) sliced unsalted natural almonds, toasted

1. Preheat the broiler to high. Lay the peach slices on a baking sheet and drizzle with 1 teaspoon (5 mL) honey. Broil just until bubbly and caramelized but not overcooked and mushy (we're not making peach jam here—though that would be delicious, too), about 5 minutes.

2. In a small food processor or blender, purée the cottage cheese. Coarsely chop 4 of the caramelized peach slices and add them to the food processor. Process until smooth. Add honey to taste.

3. Place the sweet potato slices in the toaster and toast until tender and golden, 3 to 4 toaster rounds each, depending on your toaster settings.

4. To assemble, smear a generous dollop of the cottage cheese mixture onto each sweet potato slice. Top with slices of broiled peach, a few raspberries, and a sprinkle of almonds.

ABBEY'S TIP Sweet potatoes are rich in fibre and antioxidants like carotenoids, which not only give these taters their gorgeous orange hue but also have been linked to a reduced risk for stomach, kidney, and breast cancers. Unlike bread toast, sweet potato toast holds up beautifully in an airtight container in the fridge for up to 5 days, or in the freezer, wrapped individually in wax or parchment paper, for up to 6 months.

ABBEY'S TIP This granola will keep for up to 3 weeks in an airtight container at room temperature. Since I don't usually like to share, I make a double batch, then portion it into cute mason jars to give away as gifts. In my experience, my sleep-deprived new momma friends are particularly appreciative.

Morning Perk Espresso Granola

Dairy-free • Gluten-free • Healthy fats • High fibre • Vegetarian

Serves 8

Coffee. It's the secret of high-powered executives, rock stars, stay-at-home moms, and as far as I can tell, everyone else who's killing it at life. It gets my butt on a stationary bike at 6 a.m., keeps me going when I need that extra burst of energy, and tastes like sweet liquid manna after a late night out. The best part is it's just as good for the body as it is the soul. In fact, coffee is actually the greatest source of antioxidants in the Western diet—greater than fruits and veggies combined! Not surprising, considering that research suggests regular coffee drinkers may have a lower risk of depression, Type 2 diabetes, and even early death. Because all the good things in life deserve to be savoured, I skip the drive-through, making a point to sit down and sip my morning java, thus setting the right tone for my long day ahead. When a single latte just isn't enough, the extra hit in this espresso granola does the trick. Sweet and bitter yet spicy and nutty, this is basically legal crack for adults. Caffeinated and motivated, that's my motto.

1 large pasteurized egg white

2 tablespoons (30 mL) pure maple syrup

2 tablespoons (30 mL) unsulphured molasses

2 tablespoons (30 mL) virgin coconut oil, melted

4½ teaspoons (22 mL) instant espresso powder

1 teaspoon (5 mL) pure vanilla extract

2 cups (500 mL) old-fashioned rolled oats
   (gluten-free, if required)

½ cup (125 mL) sliced unsalted natural almonds

½ cup (125 mL) coarsely chopped unsalted natural
   hazelnuts

2 tablespoons (30 mL) black or white chia seeds

1½ teaspoons (7 mL) cinnamon

½ teaspoon (2 mL) ground ginger

½ teaspoon (2 mL) fleur de sel

3 tablespoons (45 mL) minced pitted Medjool dates

3 tablespoons (45 mL) minced crystalized ginger

2 tablespoons (30 mL) cacao nibs

To Serve (optional)

Unsweetened almond milk

Almond yogurt or coconut yogurt

1. Preheat the oven to 300°F (150°C). Line a baking sheet with parchment paper or a silicone baking mat.

2. In a small ramekin, whisk the egg white until it looks white and frothy.

3. In another small ramekin, stir together the maple syrup, molasses, coconut oil, espresso powder, and vanilla.

4. In a large bowl, mix the oats, almonds, hazelnuts, chia seeds, cinnamon, and ginger. Pour the espresso syrup over the oats and stir to coat. Add the frothed egg white and stir until well coated.

5. Spread the granola evenly on the lined baking sheet and sprinkle with fleur de sel. Bake for 15 minutes. Remove from the oven and stir in the minced dates. Flip the baking sheet around and bake for an additional 10 to 15 minutes, or until golden brown and toasty. Remove from the oven.

6. Stir the crystalized ginger and cacao nibs into the granola and let cool on the baking sheet to room temperature.

7. Great on its own, or serve with unsweetened almond milk or almond or coconut yogurt.

Tropical Coconut Smoothie Bowl

Gluten-free • Healthy fats • High fibre • High protein • Vegetarian

Serves 4

Let's be honest. We often opt for smoothies because they're a fast and easy breakfast. But that's exactly why I avoid them. When we mindlessly chug our breakfast on the run, we can easily blast past our satiety signals instead of savouring every bite or sip. So, instead of gulping my smoothie on the go, I've turned it into a dish worth craving. I was eating smoothie bowls well before they became an edible art form on social media. Creamy and crunchy, sweet and tangy, this antioxidant-rich power bowl lets you skip the brain freeze and just slow down. Taking a picture may make it last longer, but savouring every spoonful is the real key to smoothie-eating success.

½ cup (125 mL) vanilla protein powder
2 frozen peeled ripe bananas, diced
1 cup (250 mL) finely diced frozen pineapple
2 cups (500 mL) coconut 2% Greek yogurt
2 teaspoons (10 mL) lime zest
Juice of 2 limes

Garnish
1 kiwi, peeled and thinly sliced
½ mango, peeled, pitted, and thinly sliced
1 small banana, thinly sliced
⅓ cup (75 mL) coarsely chopped Chili and
    Chocolate Nut Mix (page 183)
½ cup (125 mL) unsweetened flaked coconut,
    toasted
2 teaspoons (10 mL) lime zest

1. In a high-speed blender, combine the protein powder, bananas, pineapple, yogurt, lime zest, and lime juice. Blend until smooth. Divide among 4 wide, shallow bowls.

2. Garnish each bowl with sliced kiwi, mango, and banana, a sprinkle of Chili and Chocolate Nut Mix, toasted coconut, and lime zest.

ABBEY'S TIP Smoothie bowls are best when they're frothy, thick, and cold, so I like to chill my bowls in the freezer for a few minutes before filling and serving. If you want to make a big batch without compromising the creamy-cool consistency, you can pour the mixture into ice cube trays and freeze for later. When you're ready to serve, tip the frozen cubes into your blender and give it a quick buzz until smooth.

Chai Chia Pudding with Warm Maple Cinnamon Apples

Dairy-free • Gluten-free • Healthy fats • High fibre • Vegan • Vegetarian

Serves 4

Chai tea is my hatha yoga. It breathes energy into me with its spicy aromas and centres my focus with a gentle hit of caffeine. But truth be told, one too many downward dogs and I get a wee bit antsy—this girl needs to move! Chai Chia Pudding, in contrast, is the power yoga I crave. Chia seeds bloom in a bowl of steeped chai tea, yielding a thick, luxurious pudding, loaded up with a mountain of caramelized apple ribbons. This bowl gives you the protein, fibre, and healthy fats to conquer a wicked morning, while totally nourishing your mind and soul. Warrior pose optional.

Chai Chia Pudding
1½ cups (375 mL) unsweetened vanilla almond milk
4 chai tea bags
½ cup (125 mL) chia seeds
½ teaspoon (2 mL) cinnamon
2 teaspoons (10 mL) pure maple syrup, or to taste

Warm Maple Cinnamon Apples
2 crisp red apples (such as Empire)
1 tablespoon (15 mL) fresh lemon juice
2 teaspoons (10 mL) virgin coconut oil
2 teaspoons (10 mL) pure maple syrup
Generous pinch of cinnamon
Unsweetened coconut or almond yogurt,
    for serving (optional)
¼ cup (60 mL) pecans, toasted and crushed

1. **Make the Chai Chia Pudding** In a small saucepan, bring the almond milk to a simmer over medium heat. Add the tea bags, turn off the heat, cover the pot, and steep the tea until it reaches room temperature. Once it reaches room temperature, squeeze the tea bags gently to release as much flavour as possible, then discard the bags.

2. Transfer the almond milk tea to a 24-ounce (750 mL) container with a lid and stir in the chia seeds and cinnamon. Refrigerate for at least 3 hours or ideally overnight.

3. The next morning, stir in the maple syrup.

4. **Make the Warm Maple Cinnamon Apples** Spiralize the apples into ribbons using one of the thicker spiralizer blades. (The super-skinny blades just turn apples to mush, and no one likes mush.) In a medium bowl, very gently toss the apple ribbons with lemon juice.

5. Melt the coconut oil in a large nonstick skillet over medium-high heat. Add the maple syrup and apple ribbons and very gently toss until slightly softened and golden brown. Remove from the heat and sprinkle with cinnamon.

6. To assemble, divide the Chai Chia Pudding among 4 glasses and top with the apple ribbons, yogurt (if using), and crushed pecans.

ABBEY'S TIP Always keep the skins on your apples. Not only does that skin almost double the fibre content but it also stains the ribbons a pretty pink. As for the ribbons themselves, if you don't own a spiralizer, you can totally dice, slice, or even just randomly chop the apples up and still rock this dish.

PB and J Protein Pancakes

Gluten-free • Healthy fats • High protein • Vegetarian

Serves 4

This may sound a bit dramatic, but I owe my life to PB and J. Though I'm now much more adventurous (foie gras, anyone?), as a child, "expanding my palate" meant just being cool with the crusts left on. While PB and J is no longer my every-single-day go-to dish, I have to admit that I still crave that sweet, salty combination of rich nuts and fruity jam. I don't believe in denying myself anything, never mind life essentials, so I take my cravings to the next level with a stack of these pancakes. Layers of my naturally sweet chia seed grape jam, a creamy mousse whipped from protein-packed cottage cheese, and fluffy pancakes so hearty you'll be satisfied until lunch. More grown-up? Maybe not, but the best part of adulthood is breaking the rules.

Grape Chia Jam

1½ cups (375 mL) seedless Coronation grapes

1 to 2 teaspoons (5 to 10 mL) fresh lemon juice, depending on the sweetness of the grapes

4½ teaspoons (22 mL) white or black chia seeds

Peanut Butter Mousse

1 cup (250 mL) 2% cottage cheese

4½ teaspoons (22 mL) natural peanut butter

Protein Pancakes

1½ cups (375 mL) 2% cottage cheese

1½ cups (375 mL) quick-cooking rolled oats
  (gluten-free, if required)

2 tablespoons (30 mL) natural peanut butter

1 tablespoon (15 mL) pure vanilla extract

2½ teaspoons (12 mL) baking powder
  (gluten-free, if required)

¼ teaspoon (1 mL) cinnamon

Pinch of sea salt

1 cup (250 mL) pasteurized egg whites

2 tablespoons (30 mL) unsalted butter

1 cup (250 mL) seedless Coronation grapes

2 tablespoons (30 mL) finely chopped salted peanuts

1. **Make the Grape Chia Jam** In a medium saucepan over medium-high heat, cook the grapes until they are bubbling, syrupy, and soft. Remove the pot from the heat, and mash the grapes with a potato masher or a large fork until the mixture is jammy and loose but still has some visible pieces of fruit. Stir in 1 teaspoon (5 mL) lemon juice, taste, and add more lemon juice depending on how sweet or tart you like your jam.

2. Transfer the mixture to a heatproof container. Stir in the chia seeds. Refrigerate the jam for at least 20 minutes, until it thickens.

3. **Make the Peanut Butter Mousse** Meanwhile, in a food processor, process the cottage cheese with the peanut butter until very creamy and smooth. Scrape the mousse into a bowl and set aside. Return the food processor bowl to the base.

4. Preheat the oven to 200°F (100°C). Line a baking sheet with parchment paper or a silicone baking mat.

continues

5. **Make the Protein Pancakes** In the food processor, process the cottage cheese, oats, and peanut butter until thick and fairly smooth but still with visible pieces of oats. Add the vanilla, baking powder, cinnamon, and salt and process until well combined. Add the egg whites and give them a quick whiz to combine but don't let them fluff up to soufflé status.

6. Melt the butter in a large nonstick skillet over medium-high heat. Add ¼ cup (60 mL) of the batter for each pancake. Sprinkle a few grapes onto each pancake. Cook until gentle bubbles start forming on the surface and the bottom is golden brown, 3 to 4 minutes. Flip and continue to cook until golden brown on the bottom, 2 to 3 minutes. Transfer to the baking sheet and keep warm in the oven while you cook the remaining pancakes.

7. Serve the pancakes with a few dollops of Peanut Butter Mousse, Grape Chia Jam, and a pinch of chopped peanuts.

ABBEY'S TIP Coronation grapes are a Canadian hybrid with the sweetness of Concords but without the seeds. Second only to wine, they're my favourite way to load up on heart-healthy antioxidants. Feel free to make a double batch of the jam. It will keep for at least a week in an airtight jar in the refrigerator.

Buckwheat Blintzes with Wild Blueberry Sauce

Gluten-free • High fibre • Healthy fats • Vegetarian

Serves 4

I may be Jewish, but blintzes are secretly the only Jewish food I actually get excited about. They're basically dessert masquerading as a meal, so what's not to like? Usually I have no qualms about eating my sweets first, but an hour later, I'm likely to be caught red-handed rifling through a co-worker's string cheese stash in a hangry snacking spree. Not after this morning meal. My blintzes start with homemade buckwheat crêpes, giving them a gluten-free fibre boost and a flavour like rich toasted nuts. You could just stop there, but the filling and sauce are where the magic happens. Packed with a protein-rich cream made with whipped cashews and cottage cheese, these completely blur the line between breakfast and dessert. And to make Bubbie proud, just go to town with that blueberry sauce!

Buckwheat Crêpes

1 cup (250 mL) unsweetened vanilla almond milk
¼ cup (60 mL) filtered water
1 cup (250 mL) light buckwheat flour
2 large eggs
3 tablespoons (45 mL) unsalted butter, melted,
    more for cooking
2 tablespoons (30 mL) pure maple syrup
1 teaspoon (5 mL) pure vanilla extract
½ teaspoon (2 mL) sea salt

Blintz Filling

¼ cup (60 mL) unsalted natural cashews,
    soaked in water in the fridge overnight
1 cup (250 mL) 2% cottage cheese
¼ cup (60 mL) mashed very ripe banana
    (about ½ banana)
1½ teaspoons (7 mL) pure maple syrup
1 teaspoon (5 mL) pure vanilla extract
¼ teaspoon (1 mL) lemon zest
½ teaspoon (2 mL) fresh lemon juice
Pinch of sea salt

Wild Blueberry Sauce

4 cups (1 L) frozen or fresh wild blueberries
4 teaspoons (20 mL) pure maple syrup
¼ cup (60 mL) fresh lemon juice
2 teaspoons (10 mL) tapioca starch or cornstarch
1 teaspoon (5 mL) lemon zest
Pinch of sea salt

1. **Make the Buckwheat Crêpe Batter** In a food processor or blender, combine the almond milk, water, buckwheat flour, eggs, melted butter, maple syrup, vanilla, and salt. Process until smooth. Cover and refrigerate for at least 1 hour or up to 1 day.

2. **Make the Wild Blueberry Sauce** Combine the wild blueberries and maple syrup in a small saucepan over medium-high heat. When the mixture begins to boil, whisk together the lemon juice and tapioca starch in a small ramekin until smooth, then pour into the sauce. Reduce the heat to medium and simmer until the sauce reduces to a glossy, syrup-like consistency, 6 to 7 minutes. Stir in the lemon zest and salt, remove from the heat, cover, and keep warm.

continues

3. **Make the Blintz Filling** Drain the cashews. In a high-speed blender, purée the cashews until they reach a fine, grainy consistency. Add the cottage cheese, banana, maple syrup, vanilla, lemon zest and juice, and salt. Blend until very smooth. Set aside.

4. **Cook the Buckwheat Crêpes** Heat an 8-inch (20 cm) nonstick skillet over medium heat. Brush the pan lightly with melted butter. Pour a scant ¼ cup (60 mL) of the crêpe batter into the pan, tilting the pan so the batter covers the whole bottom. Cook until the bottom looks dry, is light golden, and easily lifts from the pan, 1 to 2 minutes. Using a spatula, very carefully lift up the crêpe and flip it over. Continue to cook until it easily lifts from the pan, another minute or so. Carefully slide the crêpe onto a plate. Repeat with the remaining batter, brushing the pan lightly with melted butter before cooking each crêpe. Set aside the skillet.

5. **Assemble the Blintzes** Spoon 3 tablespoons (45 mL) of filling down the centre of each crêpe. Fold the bottom over the filling, fold in the sides, and roll up the blintz. Repeat with the remaining crêpes and filling.

6. Heat the skillet over medium heat, and brush the pan with butter. Lay the blitzes seam side down in the pan. Cook until golden brown on the bottom, about 2 minutes, then turn and continue to cook until the other side is golden brown. Serve topped with warm Wild Blueberry Sauce.

ABBEY'S TIP Buckwheat is a naturally gluten-free grain, rich in antioxidants and fibre. While dark buckwheat flour is more satiating than the light version, it can also be difficult to work with. So if you're going to use it, I recommend making a little extra batter to account for a few accidents.

Parmesan Garlic French Toast with Creamy Mushroom Sauce

High protein • No added sugar • Nut-free

Serves 8

This local Italian joint we go to serves the most irresistible complimentary garlic bread—it's honestly so good I've doggy-bagged my entire meal because I "accidentally" inhaled a whole loaf. But when the free food is better than what you pay for, I say cut to the chase and turn it into the main course at home. This Parmesan Garlic French Toast gives you the goods in the first meal of the day, because life is just too short to have to wait. Salty, cheesy, thickly cut toast gets soaked in a rich eggy custard and pan-fried to a garlicky golden brown. Finished off with dreamy mushroom cream sauce, it's a classy way to get what you really want without doggy-bagging the rest.

Parmesan Garlic French Toast

4 large eggs

1 cup (250 mL) 1% or 2% milk

1 clove garlic, minced

¼ cup (60 mL) finely grated Parmigiano-Reggiano cheese

2 tablespoons (30 mL) finely minced fresh flat-leaf parsley

1 tablespoon (15 mL) minced fresh chives

1 teaspoon (5 mL) herbes de Provence

½ teaspoon (2 mL) kosher salt

¼ teaspoon (1 mL) cracked black pepper

Butter and extra-virgin olive oil, for cooking

8 thick slices whole-grain or Ezekiel bread

Creamy Mushroom Sauce

1 pound (450 g) cremini mushrooms, thinly sliced (about 5½ cups/1.375 L)

1 tablespoon (15 mL) balsamic vinegar

2 teaspoons (10 mL) unsalted butter

1 teaspoon (5 mL) herbes de Provence

1 can (12 ounces/354 mL) 1% or 2% evaporated milk

1 teaspoon (5 mL) tapioca starch or cornstarch

1 tablespoon (15 mL) minced fresh chives

Kosher salt and cracked black pepper

Garnish (optional)

Shaved Parmigiano-Reggiano cheese

Finely chopped fresh flat-leaf parsley

1. Preheat the oven to 200°F (100°C). Line a baking sheet with parchment paper or a silicone baking mat.

2. **Make the Parmesan Garlic French Toast** In a medium bowl, whisk together the eggs, milk, garlic, Parmesan, parsley, chives, herbes de Provence, salt, and pepper until well combined.

3. Heat 1 or 2 teaspoons (5 or 10 mL) each of butter and olive oil in a large nonstick skillet over medium heat until the pan is thinly coated. Working with a few slices at a time, dip the bread into the egg mixture, pushing it down to generously coat on both sides. Fry until golden brown, 1 to 3 minutes per side. Transfer to the baking sheet and keep warm in the oven while you cook the rest of the French toast.

4. **Make the Creamy Mushroom Sauce** Wipe out the skillet and return it to medium-high heat. Add the mushrooms and cook, stirring, until they release all their water and they begin to turn golden brown, about 5 minutes. Stir in the balsamic vinegar, butter, and herbes de Provence and reduce the heat to medium.

5. In a small bowl, whisk together the evaporated milk and tapioca starch, then stir into the mushroom mixture. Simmer the sauce, stirring occasionally, until it thickens and starts to bubble. Stir in the chives, season to taste with salt and pepper, and remove from the heat.

6. Serve the French toast topped with the Creamy Mushroom Sauce and extra Parmesan and parsley (if using).

ABBEY'S TIP This may surprise you, but putting "multigrain" or "whole wheat" on a package doesn't necessarily make it "whole-grain." Outsmart those sneaky marketers: ignore the health halos on the packaging and look for the words "whole-grain" at the top of the ingredient list. Although any bread would work in this recipe, I love a good, rich, whole-grain bread for its natural hearty texture and nutty flavour, as well as its fibre and nutrients. In fact, studies suggest eating more whole grains may help reduce the risk of cardiovascular disease and Type 2 diabetes.

Almond-Crusted French Toast with Tart Cherry Sauce

Dairy-free • High fibre • Healthy fats • Vegan • Vegetarian

Serves 8

Blame the Real Housewives TV show, but I've never aspired to be one of those "ladies who brunch." I'm all for hanging with my girls, and I love me some brunch, but that show suggests it's more about what everyone's not eating than what they are eating. This French toast provides just the remedy to quell that needless diet chatter. The satiating almond crust gives way to the soft, marshmallowy centre, with a tart cherry sauce sure to cause a bit of a stir. The fact that it's dairy-free, egg-free, and packed with omega-3s from a vegan "flaxseed egg" is truly beside the point. Its deliciousness makes dining with the worst diet Debbies totally drama-free. It doesn't make for great television, but it makes a hell of a brunch.

Almond-Crusted French Toast

1½ cups (375 mL) unsweetened vanilla almond milk

¼ cup + 2 tablespoons (90 mL) ground flaxseed

3 tablespoons (45 mL) pure maple syrup

2 teaspoons (10 mL) pure vanilla extract

1 cup (250 mL) almond meal (see Tip)

3 tablespoons (45 mL) light brown sugar

1½ teaspoons (7 mL) cinnamon

½ teaspoon (2 mL) nutmeg

¼ teaspoon (1 mL) sea salt

Virgin coconut oil, for cooking

8 thick slices whole-grain bread

Tart Cherry Sauce

3 cups (750 mL) fresh or thawed frozen pitted sour cherries

2 tablespoons (30 mL) pure maple syrup, or to taste

¼ cup (60 mL) freshly squeezed orange juice

2 teaspoons (10 mL) tapioca starch or cornstarch

¼ teaspoon (1 mL) orange zest

Pinch of sea salt

To Serve

Coconut yogurt

¼ cup (60 mL) sliced unsalted natural almonds, toasted

Additional pure maple syrup, if desired

1. Preheat the oven to 200°F (100°C). Line a baking sheet with parchment paper or a silicone baking mat.

2. **Make the Almond-Crusted French Toast** In a shallow bowl, make a flaxseed egg by whisking the almond milk with the flaxseed until well combined. Refrigerate for 20 minutes, until thickened and slightly goopy (kind of like an egg). Stir in the maple syrup and vanilla.

3. In another shallow bowl, stir together the almond meal, brown sugar, cinnamon, nutmeg, and salt.

4. Heat a large griddle or nonstick skillet over medium heat and grease with a light coating of coconut oil.

5. Working with a few slices at a time, dip the bread into the flaxseed egg mixture, letting it soak for a few seconds on each side, then dip both sides into the almond meal mixture. Fry until golden brown, 2 to 3 minutes per side. Transfer to the baking sheet and keep warm in the oven while you cook the rest of the French toast.

6. **Make the Tart Cherry Sauce** Combine the cherries and maple syrup in a small saucepan over medium-high heat. While the mixture begins to boil, whisk together the orange juice and tapioca starch in a small ramekin until smooth, then pour into the sauce. Reduce the heat to medium and simmer until the sauce reduces to a glossy, syrup-like consistency, 6 to 7 minutes. Remove from the heat and stir in the orange zest and salt.

7. Serve the Almond-Crusted French Toast with a dollop of Tart Cherry Sauce, coconut yogurt, a sprinkle of almonds, and maple syrup, if desired.

ABBEY'S TIP This French toast recipe calls for almond meal, which is a little coarser than almond flour, and usually includes the skins. It adds the wicked crunch factor to the crust to juxtapose the pillowy interior, but in a pinch, you can easily swap one for the other. This is the perfect post-run snack, not only because it's packed with refuelling carbs as well as protein and fibre from the almond crust, but those sour cherries boast serious recovery benefits, too. Tart cherries are packed with antioxidants, anti-inflammatory compounds, and melatonin, which research suggests may help reduce muscle soreness and promote a more restful sleep after a good sweat session. 5 a.m. spin class? Bring. It. On.

Prosciutto, Pear, and Goat Cheese Egg Cups

Gluten-free • High fibre • High protein • No added sugar • Nut-free

Serves 6

San Francisco is my favourite city to be a tourist. On my last visit, I popped into a wee hole in the wall with a sandwich board outside advertising "bacon-wrapped eggs." Even next to the magnificent California sites, the B-word always excites. Apparently, I'm not the only one: when I placed my order, my server told me I got the last one. A nearby diner groaned in disappointment. I turned around to look at him. His needy eyes pleaded with me. I quickly turned away. Inspired by my moral fail, my version combines candy-like onions, sweet pear, tangy goat cheese, and dainty strips of flavourful prosciutto. You get the full-on bacon experience without the grease factor, and to me, that's key for hand-held eats!

Caramelized Onions
1 teaspoon (5 mL) extra-virgin olive oil

1 teaspoon (5 mL) unsalted butter

½ small Vidalia onion, finely diced

1 teaspoon (5 mL) balsamic vinegar

1 teaspoon (5 mL) minced fresh thyme leaves

Sea salt and cracked black pepper

Egg Cups
Extra-virgin olive oil in an oil atomizer

12 very thin slices prosciutto

⅓ cup (75 mL) finely diced red pear

6 large eggs

Sea salt and cracked black pepper

1 ounce (28 g) goat cheese, crumbled (about ¼ cup/60 mL)

Fresh thyme leaves, for garnish (optional)

1. **Make the Caramelized Onions** In a large nonstick skillet, heat the olive oil and butter over medium-low heat. Add the onions and stir to coat them in the oil and butter. Stirring every 5 minutes, cook the onions until they reach a caramelized, amber colour, 45 to 60 minutes. Stir in the balsamic vinegar and thyme and season with salt and pepper. Remove from the heat.

2. Preheat the oven to 375°F (190°C). Coat 6 muffin cups with olive oil from the oil atomizer.

3. **Make the Egg Cups** Lay a slice of prosciutto in a muffin cup, then cover with another slice going in the other direction, so you have 2 criss-crossed slices that cover all the sides. Allow the prosciutto to peek out about ½ inch (1 cm) above the muffin cup, but if it's longer, tuck the ends into the cup. Repeat with the remaining prosciutto.

4. Divide half of the pear and half of the caramelized onions among the cups. Carefully break an egg into each cup and season with a pinch each of salt and pepper.

5. Top with the rest of the pear and onions as well as a few pieces of goat cheese.

6. Bake for 20 to 25 minutes, or until the egg whites are opaque and the prosciutto is crispy. Garnish with thyme leaves (if using).

ABBEY'S TIP These are the perfect on-the-go breakfast for busy mornings when cutlery is not going to happen. Simply store in an airtight container in the fridge for up to 5 days, rewarm in the microwave for 20 seconds, and enjoy them hand-held in a napkin.

Caprese Frittata

Gluten-free • High protein • No added sugar • Nut-free • Vegetarian

Serves 4

Full confession: I can't flip an omelette to save my life. I've tried many times, but the results are never pretty. That's why I adore the carefree, rustic frittata. If you can throw a few veggies in a pan with a bunch of eggs, you can make a frittata. Also, it's a fun word to say. FRI-TA-TA. The key to rocking your frittata is to add just a few high-quality seasonal ingredients and to let each one really shine. When my husband and I went to Italy, we ate Caprese salad every day—now a favourite flavour combo for us. Juicy, sweet tomatoes, herbaceous basil, and luscious, creamy cheese were the epitome of culinary perfection, so when you combine them with eggs, you get a dazzling breakfast. Buon appetito, lovelies!

8 large eggs
½ cup (125 mL) 1% milk
1 tablespoon (15 mL) thinly sliced fresh basil
½ teaspoon (2 mL) sea salt
¼ teaspoon (1 mL) cracked black pepper
1 tablespoon (15 mL) extra-virgin olive oil
½ cup (125 mL) finely diced yellow onion

1 clove garlic, minced
1¼ cups (300 mL) halved or quartered (depending on size) grape or cherry tomatoes
2 ounces (55 g) bocconcini (about ½ cup/125 mL), thinly sliced
Pinch of fleur de sel, for garnish
4 to 6 fresh basil leaves, gently torn, for garnish

1. Preheat the oven to 350°F (180°C).

2. In a small bowl, lightly beat the eggs with the milk until the yolks mix well with the whites, being careful not to overmix. Add the basil, salt, and pepper and stir until well combined.

3. Heat the olive oil in a 10-inch (25 cm) ovenproof skillet over medium-high heat. Add the onion and sauté until softened, 3 to 4 minutes. Add the garlic and stir for 30 seconds, until fragrant.

4. Spread the onions and garlic evenly over the bottom of the skillet. Pour the egg mixture on top, then reduce the heat to medium. Sprinkle the eggs with the tomatoes, then top with the sliced cheese. Cook until the edges start to set and pull away gently from the pan, about 5 minutes.

5. Transfer the skillet to the oven and bake for 15 to 17 minutes, until the frittata pulls slightly away from the edges and is set throughout.

6. Sprinkle the frittata with fleur de sel and fresh basil. Slice into wedges and serve warm or at room temperature.

ABBEY'S TIP Friends don't let friends use fat-free or low-fat cheese. While cheeses like bocconcini may be high in saturated fat, new research is suggesting that enjoying full-fat dairy may actually be better for metabolic and heart health than the diet stuff. More importantly, it tastes better, and in a recipe with a handful of ingredients, each and every one counts.

Spicy Chickpea Shakshuka with Silky Eggplant and Runny Eggs

Gluten-free • Healthy fats • High fibre • High protein • Nut-free • Vegetarian

Serves 6

When we travelled in Israel, my now-hubby and I made it our mission to eat shakshuka at least every other day. Lapping up all of its fresh, fragrant, and filling goodness, we ate a lot of saucy eggs, but the best bowl came from a charming venue in Jaffa called Dr. Shakshuka. Now, I don't know how the University of Israel awards honorary doctorates, but this guy deserves his title. I studied his exemplary teachings (in other words, I ate. A lot), and then I brought home my own take on this all-day, any-day staple. Silky eggplant melts into a hearty pool of rich, spicy tomatoes, bulked up with chickpeas and runny eggs. Finished off with a sprinkle of salty feta and a pinch of lemony za'atar, this dish starts any day with a healthy dose of saucy sass. Yep, this doctor is definitely in.

1 tablespoon (15 mL) extra-virgin olive oil
½ Vidalia onion, thinly sliced
2 Japanese eggplants, diced into ½-inch (1 cm) cubes
   (about 3½ cups/875 mL)
2 cloves garlic, finely minced
Sea salt and cracked black pepper
1 can (28 ounces/796 mL) crushed tomatoes
1 can (28 ounces/796 mL) diced tomatoes
1 tablespoon (15 mL) harissa paste
1 tablespoon (15 mL) ground cumin
1 tablespoon (15 mL) sweet smoked paprika
1 tablespoon (15 mL) pure liquid honey, or to taste
¼ teaspoon (1 mL) cayenne pepper, or to taste
1 can (19 ounces/540 mL) chickpeas, drained and rinsed
6 large eggs

Garnish
¼ cup (60 mL) crumbled feta cheese
¼ teaspoon (1 mL) za'atar
Fresh whole cilantro leaves (optional)

1. In a large cast-iron skillet, heat the olive oil over medium-high heat. Add the onion and sauté until softened and lightly golden, about 5 minutes.

2. Add the eggplant and sauté until it starts to caramelize, 10 to 12 minutes.

3. Stir in the garlic and continue to stir until fragrant, about 30 seconds. Season everything with a generous pinch each of salt and pepper.

4. Add the crushed and diced tomatoes, harissa, cumin, paprika, honey, cayenne, and chickpeas. Reduce the heat to medium, cover, and simmer until the eggplant starts to soften, 10 to 15 minutes. If you find the shakshuka has reduced too much and is starting to scorch on the bottom, simply add a splash of water.

continues

5. Reduce the heat to low. Make 6 little wells in the mixture around the edge of the pan, and carefully crack an egg into each well. Spoon a little of the sauce over the egg whites to completely submerge them. Season the eggs with a pinch each of salt and pepper, cover the pan, and cook until the whites are set but the yolks are still runny, another 6 to 8 minutes. Remove from the heat.

6. Adjust the seasoning of the sauce with salt and pepper. Garnish with crumbled feta, za'atar, and cilantro (if using). Serve in the skillet family style, or dish out into individuals bowls with a big spoon and a piece of crusty bread for dipping.

ABBEY'S TIP Harissa is a North African and Middle Eastern red chili paste that packs some serious Scoville power, so a little goes a really long way. Different regions have different recipes, but the standard version includes smoked chilies, garlic, oil, tomatoes, cumin, coriander, caraway, and mint. You can often find it in Middle Eastern markets or in the international section in the grocery store, but if you're struggling to track it down, you could easily swap in berbere, chili paste, tabil, or even any standard hot sauce. Regardless of what you choose, make sure you wash your hands well after handling any chili products and avoid touching your eyes (or any other body part, for that matter).

Whipped Proats (Protein Oatmeal) Three Ways

Dairy-free • Gluten-free • Healthy fats • High fibre • High protein • No added sugar • Vegetarian

Serves 2

Egg whites and oats? I know, the combination sounds like something a drunken college kid might concoct in the frat house at 3 a.m., but actually, it's a fitness-industry secret. When I first saw my trainer put the two together, I assumed either he had dulled down his palate with too many boiled chicken breasts or his turbo-charged workout just made him too ravenous to care. It was hard to tell, really. In any case, I just had to transform this post-workout pick-me-up into something tasty. This protein oatmeal, affectionately nicknamed "proats," whips the egg whites seamlessly into oats to yield the creamiest, lightest bowl of oatmeal you've ever face-planted into. I've included my three favourite combinations to inspire your new go-to morning meal.

Whipped Proats

½ cup (125 mL) old-fashioned rolled oats (gluten-free, if required)

1½ cups (375 mL) filtered water

½ teaspoon (2 mL) cinnamon

Generous pinch of sea salt

1 cup (250 mL) pasteurized egg whites

1 very ripe banana, mashed

1 teaspoon (5 mL) pure vanilla extract

1. In a small saucepan, combine the oats with water, cinnamon, and salt. Bring to a simmer over medium-high heat, then reduce the heat to medium and cook, stirring occasionally, until the oats have absorbed almost all the water but are still very moist and thick, 3 to 5 minutes.

2. In a small bowl, beat the egg whites until white and foamy, then whisk them into the oats. Cook, whisking constantly, until the mixture looks creamy and light, about 3 minutes.

3. Add the banana and vanilla and stir until well combined. Remove from the heat, cover the pot with a lid, and let the oats sit for another 3 minutes, until they puff up slightly and get super creamy and rich.

Passion Fruit Berry

2 small passion fruits, flesh only

½ cup (125 mL) fresh blackberries

½ cup (125 mL) fresh raspberries

1 teaspoon (5 mL) hemp hearts

2 tablespoons (30 mL) coarsely chopped unsalted natural cashews

Pure liquid honey (optional)

1. Pour the Whipped Proats into 2 bowls. Top each serving with passion fruit, blackberries, raspberries, hemp hearts, cashews, and a drizzle of honey, if desired.

continues

Almond Joy

2 teaspoons (10 mL) unsweetened cocoa powder, sifted

2 tablespoons (30 mL) natural almond butter

¼ cup (60 mL) unsweetened flaked coconut, toasted

2 tablespoons (30 mL) unsalted sliced natural almonds, toasted

2 teaspoons (10 mL) cacao nibs

Pure liquid honey (optional)

1. Whisk the cocoa powder into the Whipped Proats in the final moment of cooking.

2. Pour the mixture into 2 bowls. Top each serving with a swirl of almond butter, toasted coconut, almonds, cacao nibs, and a drizzle of honey, if desired.

Fig Pomegranate

¼ cup (60 mL) plain 2% Greek yogurt

1 large fresh fig, trimmed and thinly sliced

¼ cup (60 mL) pomegranate arils

2 tablespoons (30 mL) coarsely chopped unsalted natural pistachios

1 teaspoon (5 mL) white or black chia seeds

Pure liquid honey (optional)

1. Pour the Whipped Proats into 2 bowls. Top each serving with a dollop of Greek yogurt, fig slices, pomegranate, pistachios, chia seeds, and a drizzle of honey, if desired.

ABBEY'S TIP Normally I'm for eating whole eggs in all their runny, yolky glory, but here, pure egg whites are the key to getting a bowl of creamy, dreamy, fluffy oats. The whites also account for almost 70 percent of the protein in eggs, so this breakfast is my go-to for nourishing sore muscles after the gym. Save the yolks for my Macerated Balsamic Pepper Strawberries with Rosé Sabayon (page 267).

Kale, Apple, and Pumpkin Savoury Oats

Gluten-free • Healthy fats • High fibre • No added sugar • Nut-free • Vegetarian

Serves 4

For some reason, society has settled on certain rules about which foods can be eaten for breakfast and which foods are for dinner. Unsurprisingly, breaking those rules is one of my favourite pastimes. I know I'm not the only adult that gets an adrenaline rush from a plate of late-night pancakes, but being a morning person, I get equally jazzed about savoury breakfast fare. This bowl of savoury oats is an absolutely wicked way to fight taste-bud fatigue, and it's the yummiest way I know to get more vegetables in the first half of your day. Crunchy pepitas and tangy apple nod to the usual oatmeal suspects, while fibre-rich kale, pumpkin, caramelized onions, and an unexpected bite from blue cheese offer a decadent grown-up touch. Talk about tasty cheap thrills!

Caramelized Onions

2 teaspoons (10 mL) unsalted butter
2 teaspoons (10 mL) extra-virgin olive oil
2 medium sweet yellow onions, thinly sliced
Sea salt and cracked black pepper

Oatmeal

3 cups (750 mL) low-sodium vegetable stock
1 cup (250 mL) old-fashioned rolled oats
   (gluten-free, if required)
1 Granny Smith apple, cored and finely diced
2 cups (500 mL) thinly sliced stemmed kale
⅓ cup (75 mL) pure pumpkin purée
Sea salt and cracked black pepper

To Serve

1 teaspoon (5 mL) extra-virgin olive oil
4 large eggs
Sea salt and cracked black pepper
¼ cup + 2 tablespoons (90 mL) pepitas, toasted
1 ounce (28 g) blue cheese, crumbled
   (about ¼ cup/60 mL)

1. **Make the Caramelized Onions** In a large nonstick skillet, heat the butter and olive oil over medium-low heat. Add the onions and stir to coat them in the oil and butter. Stirring every 5 minutes, cook the onions until they reach a caramelized, amber colour, 45 to 60 minutes. Season with salt and pepper and remove from the heat.

2. **Make the Oatmeal** In a medium saucepan, heat the stock until it comes to a boil. Stir in the oats, cover, and reduce the heat to medium-low. Simmer until most of the liquid has evaporated, 5 to 6 minutes.

3. Reduce the heat to low. Add the apple, kale, and pumpkin purée and stir until the kale begins to wilt. Cover the pot and cook gently for another 5 minutes. If the oat mixture starts looking too dry, just add a splash of water to loosen it up. Once the kale has softened, stir in the Caramelized Onions and season with salt and pepper. Keep warm.

4. Wipe out the skillet, add the olive oil, and heat over medium-low heat. Fry the eggs until the whites are set but the yolks are still runny, about 2½ minutes. Season with a pinch each of salt and pepper.

5. To serve, divide the oatmeal among 4 bowls and top with a sunny-side-up egg, a sprinkle of pepitas, and crumbled blue cheese.

ABBEY'S TIP Rolled oats are packed with a unique fibre that's consistently been shown to help reduce bad cholesterol, prevent blood sugar spikes, and help head off the hangry monster. Add in a few handfuls of vegetables and a fried egg, and you'll be satisfied for hours.

Raspberry Limeade Overnight Oats

Gluten-free • High fibre • Healthy fats • No added sugar • Nut-free

Serves 4

In the summer, when I'm too hot for a bowl of oats and too busy for anything else, these overnight oats fill the bill. When I was a kid we used to call this breakfast "muesli," and it was considered something only hippies forced their kids to eat. (Trust me, I was one of those kids!) But Instagram made this make-ahead morning meal cool again, so as usual I'm going to make it cooler. With a hearty combination of oats, flax, and protein-rich Greek yogurt and a flavour profile reminiscent of those cups of reconstituted juice you sold on the lawn for ten cents, this is a breakfast the whole family will love.

4 Medjool dates, pitted and minced
1 small ripe banana, mashed
1½ cups (375 mL) fresh or frozen raspberries
¾ cup (175 mL) plain 2% Greek yogurt
¾ cup (175 mL) unsweetened vanilla soy milk
2 teaspoons (10 mL) ground flaxseed
1 teaspoon (5 mL) lime zest
1 teaspoon (5 mL) fresh lime juice
1 teaspoon (5 mL) pure vanilla extract
½ teaspoon (2 mL) cinnamon
¼ teaspoon (1 mL) ground ginger
Pinch of sea salt
1½ cups (375 mL) old-fashioned rolled oats
  (gluten-free, if required)

Garnish (optional)
¼ cup (60 mL) plain 2% Greek yogurt
¼ cup (60 mL) fresh raspberries
¼ cup (60 mL) unsweetened flaked coconut, toasted
1 teaspoon (5 mL) lime zest
Pure liquid honey

1. In a blender or food processor, process the dates until they reach a coarse, paste like consistency. Add the banana, raspberries, yogurt, soy milk, flaxseed, lime zest, lime juice, vanilla, cinnamon, ginger, and salt. Blend until smooth.

2. Transfer the fruit-yogurt mixture to a large container or jar. Stir in the oats, cover, and set in the fridge to soften overnight.

3. The next morning, divide the mixture among 4 bowls and garnish, if desired, with a dollop of yogurt, fresh raspberries, toasted coconut, lime zest, and honey to taste.

ABBEY'S TIP Steel-cut oats are awesome simmered low and slow for porridge, and quick-cooking oats are ideal for a speedy fix, but for overnight oats you want the supple bite of the old-fashioned, or large-flake, variety. Feel free to make a big batch for a few morning meals; they should last in the fridge for up to 3 days.

Sweet Potato and Black Bean Scramble Breakfast Taco with Tomatillo Salsa

Gluten-free • Healthy fats • High fibre • Nut-free • Vegetarian

Makes 8 tacos; Serves 4

Scientific research suggests that if you make vegetarian dishes delicious enough, carnivores will gobble them up with abandon. Okay, so the sample size of this particular study was exactly two—the hubs and me—but as far as I'm concerned, our results can be extrapolated, and easily applied to, well, tacos. Everything tastes better in a taco. That's also in a scientific study. Seriously, though, a million trendy taco and margarita bars can't be wrong. Smoky sweet potatoes, sprightly tomatillo salsa, and creamy scrambled eggs find absolute perfection in a toasty breakfast tortilla. And just like that, without opening a single book (aside from this one, of course), you're officially a science nerd. With a major in tacos, of course.

Tomatillo Salsa

½ jalapeño pepper, halved lengthwise

4 large tomatillos, husks removed, halved lengthwise

2 tablespoons (30 mL) coarsely chopped green onions (white and light green parts only)

2 tablespoons (30 mL) coarsely chopped fresh cilantro leaves

4 teaspoons (20 mL) fresh lime juice

Sea salt

Sweet Potato Black Bean Scramble

2 cups (500 mL) peeled and finely diced sweet potato (about 1 large)

1 tablespoon (15 mL) + 1½ (7 mL) teaspoons extra-virgin olive oil, divided

1 can (19 ounces/540 mL) black beans, drained and rinsed

1 teaspoon (5 mL) pure maple syrup

1 teaspoon (5 mL) minced chipotle pepper in adobo sauce, more if you like it spicy

1 teaspoon (5 mL) ground cumin

½ teaspoon (2 mL) cinnamon

4 large eggs

Sea salt and cracked black pepper

To Serve

8 small corn tortillas, toasted

½ avocado, pitted, peeled, and thinly sliced or finely diced

½ cup (125 mL) fresh cilantro leaves

1 ounce (28 g) Cotija cheese, crumbled

1 lime, cut into wedges

1. Preheat the broiler to high and line a baking sheet with foil.

2. **Make the Tomatillo Salsa** If you don't want your salsa to be too spicy, remove the seeds and veins from the jalapeño, but I like a little kick. Place the tomatillos and jalapeño cut side down on the baking sheet. Broil until lightly charred and shrivelled, about 5 minutes.

3. Transfer the tomatillos, jalapeño, green onions, cilantro, and lime juice to a high-speed blender or food processor and blend until smooth. Season with salt and set aside.

4. **Make the Sweet Potato Black Bean Scramble** Add the sweet potatoes to a pot of water with a pinch of salt, and bring to a boil. Boil until they are crisp-tender, 3 to 4 minutes. Drain and dry well.

continues

5. In a medium nonstick skillet, heat 1 tablespoon (15 mL) of the olive oil over medium-high heat. Add the sweet potatoes and toss until well coated in the oil. Add the black beans, maple syrup, chipotle pepper, cumin, and cinnamon. Cook, stirring, until the beans and potatoes are well coated in the spices and the potato is caramelized and cooked through, 6 to 7 minutes. Transfer to a bowl and cover to keep warm.

6. Whisk the eggs in a bowl and season with a generous pinch each of salt and pepper. Return the skillet to medium-low heat and add the remaining 1½ teaspoons (7 mL) olive oil. Pour the eggs into the skillet and slowly stir with a wooden spoon or spatula, bringing the eggs from the sides of the pan towards the middle. Continue to cook and gently stir until the eggs look silky and runny.

7. To serve, divide the eggs and the sweet potato bean mixture among the tortillas, top with a generous spoonful of Tomatillo Salsa, some avocado, a sprinkling of cilantro, and some Cotija cheese. Serve with lime wedges for an extra zing.

ABBEY'S TIP I love shaking things up occasionally, so I sometimes swap out the eggs for tofu. Tofu is packed with natural plant compounds called isoflavones, which research suggests may reduce the risk of cancer, insulin resistance, and bone loss. To make this recipe with tofu, replace the eggs with 12 ounces (340 g) of crumbled extra-firm tofu and add ¼ teaspoon (1 mL) turmeric and 1 tablespoon (15 mL) nutritional yeast for extra flavour. Simply "scramble" them in the pan like you would with the egg, and enjoy your taco vegan style!

Beet, Celeriac, and Brussels Sprout Holiday Hash

Gluten-free • Healthy fats • High fibre • High protein • No added sugar • Vegetarian

Serves 4

Growing up, hash wasn't just for breakfast. Frozen taters, some random bits from the deli drawer, a few eggs, and a swimming pool's worth of ketchup made a welcome meal morning, noon, and night. I still keep a bag of precooked potatoes in my freezer for speedy everyday meals, but this colourful root-veggie version upgrades the original into something more festive. Nutty celeriac (or celery root), sweet, earthy beets, and hearty Brussels sprouts are dressed with tangy goat cheese and perfectly runny eggs for a white, red, and green centrepiece for a holiday brunch.

1 tablespoon (15 mL) + 2 teaspoons (10 mL) fresh lemon juice, divided

2 cups (500 mL) peeled celeriac diced into ½-inch (1 cm) cubes

2 cups (500 mL) peeled red beets diced into ½-inch (1 cm) cubes

2 tablespoons (30 mL) extra-virgin olive oil

½ small yellow onion, finely diced

2 cloves garlic, finely minced

1 tablespoon (15 mL) fresh thyme leaves

4 cups (1 L) Brussels sprouts, trimmed and finely shredded

2 cups (500 mL) stemmed, cleaned, and chopped beet greens

1 tablespoon (15 mL) lemon zest

Sea salt and cracked black pepper

1 tablespoon (15 mL) seasoned rice vinegar

4 large eggs

To Serve

2 ounces (55 g) goat cheese, crumbled

⅓ cup (75 mL) natural unsalted shelled pistachios, coarsely chopped

1. Line a baking sheet with paper towel (or a kitchen towel you don't mind staining).

2. Add a few cups of water to a medium saucepan with 1 teaspoon (5 mL) of the lemon juice and a pinch of salt, and bring to a boil over high heat. Add the celeriac, reduce the heat to medium, cover, and simmer for 8 to 10 minutes, until the celeriac is tender enough to stick a fork through but still firm enough to hold its shape. Using a slotted spoon, transfer the celeriac to one half of the lined baking sheet.

3. Top up the pot with a bit more water if a lot evaporated, and add another 1 teaspoon (5 mL) lemon juice. Turn the heat up to high and bring to a boil. Add the beets, reduce the heat to medium, cover, and simmer for 8 to 10 minutes, until the beets are tender enough to stick a fork through but still firm enough to hold their shape. Transfer with a slotted spoon to the other half of the lined baking sheet.

4. Heat a large nonstick or cast-iron skillet over medium-high heat and add the olive oil. Add the onion and sauté until it begins to soften, 5 to 6 minutes. Add the garlic and stir until fragrant, about 30 seconds. Then add the cooked celeriac and beets and the thyme. Cook, stirring frequently, until the vegetables are caramelized, 8 to 9 minutes. Stir in the Brussels sprouts, beet greens, lemon zest, and the remaining 1 tablespoon (15 mL) lemon juice. Reduce the heat to medium and cook, stirring every minute or so, until the greens have wilted. Remove from the heat, season with salt and pepper, and keep warm.

continues

5. Meanwhile, replace the paper towel on the baking sheet with fresh sheets.

6. Rinse out the saucepan and fill two-thirds full with water. Bring to a boil, then reduce the heat to a very gentle simmer—you should just see small bubbles coming to the surface. Stir in the rice vinegar.

7. Crack one egg into a small measuring cup. Use a spoon to create a whirlpool in the water, to help the egg white wrap around the yolk, then gently tip the egg into the middle of the whirlpool. Repeat with the remaining 3 eggs. Cook the eggs for about 3 minutes, until the white is opaque but the yolk still feels runny. Carefully remove them, one by one, with a slotted spoon and transfer them to the lined baking sheet. Sprinkle the eggs with a pinch each of salt and pepper.

8. To serve, divide the hash among 4 plates. Top each serving with a poached egg, goat cheese, and pistachios.

ABBEY'S TIP Okay, guys, let's get something straight. Beet greens (the foliage at the tops of your beet bulbs) aren't kitchen scraps to be thrown in the bin, nor are they second fiddle to their roots. They're rock stars in their own right, loaded with vitamins K, A, C, and E, plus calcium, folate, magnesium, and fibre. If your beets don't come with greens, you can easily substitute Swiss chard, kale, spinach, or use a few cups more Brussels sprouts.

Power Meals

Asparagus, Pea, and Tomato Quinotto

Gluten-free • Healthy fats • High fibre • High protein • No added sugar • Nut-free • Vegetarian

Serves 4

When I went to Italy, I had a bucket list of foods that I had to have, and risotto was right at the top. Creamy, comforting, and blessedly cheesy! I've had some pretty graphic dreams about the stuff. My version skips the starchy rice and starts instead with a mixture of protein-packed quinoa and fibre-rich cauliflower pulsed into rice-like "grains." Mixed with sweet, juicy tomatoes, supple peas, tender spring asparagus, and a luscious swirl of ricotta cheese, trust me, even Nonna will approve.

1 head cauliflower, cut into florets

6 cups (1.5 L) low-sodium vegetable stock

1 tablespoon (15 mL) +1 teaspoon (5 mL) extra-virgin olive oil, divided

1 pound (450 g) asparagus, trimmed and cut into 1-inch (2.5 cm) pieces

1½ cups (375 mL) halved cherry tomatoes

2 cloves garlic, finely minced

2 tablespoons (30 mL) fresh thyme leaves, more for garnish

Sea salt and cracked black pepper

1 cup (250 mL) quinoa (any colour), rinsed and drained

½ cup (125 mL) dry white wine

½ cup (125 mL) frozen peas

¼ cup + 2 tablespoons (90 mL) ricotta cheese

¼ cup + 2 tablespoons (90 mL) finely grated Parmigiano-Reggiano cheese, more for garnish

1 teaspoon (5 mL) lemon zest, more for garnish

1. In a food processor, pulse the cauliflower florets until they reach a rice-like consistency. Measure out 2 cups (500 mL) and set aside for another dish (see Tip).

2. Heat the vegetable stock in a small saucepan over medium-low heat. Cover and keep warm.

3. In a medium saucepan, heat 1 tablespoon (15 mL) of the oil over medium-high heat. Add the asparagus and fry until it begins to soften and lightly caramelize, 1½ to 3 minutes, depending on how thick your asparagus spears are. Stir in the cherry tomatoes and fry for 2 minutes. Finally, reduce the heat to medium and add the garlic and thyme. Stir until fragrant, about 30 seconds. Season with a pinch each of salt and pepper. Scoop all the vegetables into a bowl.

4. Return the pan to medium heat and add the remaining 1 teaspoon (5 mL) olive oil. Add the quinoa and the reserved cauliflower rice. Stir until the quinoa and cauliflower are coated in the oil, about 2 minutes. Pour in the white wine and scrape up any of the flavourful bits that found their way onto the bottom of the pan. Cook, stirring, until the wine is fully absorbed.

5. Add about ½ cup (125 mL) of the warm vegetable stock and cook, stirring, until the stock has been almost totally absorbed, 3 to 5 minutes. Continue adding stock ½ cup (125 mL) at a time, continuing to stir, until the quinoa is tender but still a bit wet—neither soupy nor dry—about 20 minutes. You're not looking for that super-dry, fluffy consistency you normally aim for when you whip up a batch of quinoa. This usually takes 4 to 5 cups (1 to 1.25 L) of stock, but yours could take the full 6 cups (1.5 L).

continues

6. Stir in the frozen peas, ricotta cheese, Parmigiano-Reggiano, lemon zest, and the reserved cooked vegetables. Stir until the peas have thawed through, then season with sea salt and a generous helping of cracked black pepper.

7. Divide the quinotto among 4 bowls or plates. Top each serving with additional Parmesan, lemon zest, and thyme leaves, if desired, and serve.

ABBEY'S TIP Whereas traditional risotto has a strict "à la minute" serving protocol, quinotto can be made ahead, refrigerated for up to 3 days, and reheated. It will thicken as it sits in the fridge, so if you want to loosen it up again, just swirl in another dollop of ricotta or a splash of vegetable stock. Any leftover cauliflower rice can be used to make my Brown Butter and Orange Cauli-Couscous Salad (page 117) or Cheese-Explosion Cauliflower Tots (page 211).

Zucchini Noodle Carbonara

Gluten-free • Healthy fats • High fibre • High protein • No added sugar • Nut-free

Serves 2

Want to know what real food porn is? Put a bowl of carbonara in front of me, and get ready to censor the hell out of what you see—things are bound to get a little R-rated. Swapping in a vegetable masquerading as a noodle isn't traditional, but it's far more refreshing on the palate, it eliminates my urge to make a side salad, and ultimately lets me focus on the sauce. Rich egg meets salty pancetta meets nutty Parmigiano-Reggiano. Then I just load it up with my hubby's favourite veg— sweet peas, lots and lots of sweet peas. A good carbonara is as simple as it is luxurious. Ultimately, it's just a tasty way to sex up eating a big bowl of vegetables for dinner.

4 medium zucchini, ends sliced off, spiralized into noodles
½ teaspoon (2 mL) kosher salt
3 teaspoons (15 mL) extra-virgin olive oil, divided
2 slices pancetta (¼ inch/5 mm thick), diced
1 shallot, minced
1 clove garlic, minced

1 cup (250 mL) frozen peas
2 large eggs, beaten
1 large egg yolk, beaten
⅓ cup (75 mL) finely grated Parmesan cheese,
    more for garnish if desired
Sea salt and cracked black pepper

1. Line a baking sheet with a few layers of paper towel. Lay the zucchini noodles on top and sprinkle with the salt. Top with another few layers of paper towel, a cutting board, and some heavy items like books or pots. Let sit for 10 minutes.

2. After 10 minutes, transfer the noodles to a colander and rinse thoroughly with cold water to remove the salt.

3. Replace the paper towels on the baking sheet with a few new layers. Gently squeeze and shake the zucchini noodles, then lay them out on the paper towels. Top with a few more layers of paper towel, the cutting board, and the heavy items, and let dry for 10 minutes.

4. Heat a large cast-iron skillet over medium heat and add 1 teaspoon (5 mL) of the olive oil. Add the pancetta and cook until crisp. Using a slotted spoon, transfer the pancetta to a small dish and set aside.

5. Return the skillet to medium heat and add the remaining 2 teaspoons (10 mL) olive oil. Add the shallot and cook, stirring, for 2 minutes. Add the garlic and stir for 1 minute. Then add the peas and cook, stirring frequently, until thawed, about 2 minutes.

6. Finally, add the dry zucchini noodles, increase the heat to medium-high, and sauté for 2 to 3 minutes, or until the noodles are warmed through. Remove from the heat.

7. In a medium bowl, beat together the eggs, egg yolk, and Parmesan. Add the egg mixture to the zucchini noodles and toss gently until coated, about 2 minutes. Add the reserved pancetta, toss gently again, and season with pepper.

8. Divide the zucchini noodles between 2 bowls. Top with more Parmesan, if desired, and season with salt.

continues

ABBEY'S TIP I'm all for "real" pasta, but I also love switching things up with zucchini. Packed with vitamin C, vitamin A, B vitamins, folate, and potassium, it's an antioxidant-rich staple that's available all year round. It also contains a fibre called pectin which has been linked to reduced risk of heart disease, high cholesterol, Type 2 diabetes, and inflammation. You can whip up a large batch of zoodles ahead of time and keep them in a sealed container in the fridge for up to 3 days.

Veggie Noodle Pad Thai

Dairy-free • Gluten-free • Healthy fats • High fibre • High protein

Serves 4

In grad school, I hung out with people from all over the world, each with diverse upbringings, cultures, interests, and beliefs. We may have been different, but one thing we could all agree on was that a double order of No. 3 Pad Thai was the key to study session success. Sure, we were adults, we could have made a noodle bowl at home, but do you know how many ingredients are in restaurant pad Thai? No starving student has the time (or budget) for that! Graduate from dorm-room delivery with my veggie-loaded pad Thai. This zoodly meal simplifies the often laborious ingredient list while retaining that authentic tangy tamarind punch. Sweet, sour, spicy, and fresh, it's the student-friendly staple all grown up.

Pad Thai Sauce

¼ cup (60 mL) tamarind paste

4½ teaspoons (22 mL) coconut sugar

4½ teaspoons (22 mL) low-sodium tamari (gluten-free, if required)

1 tablespoon (15 mL) fresh lime juice

2 teaspoons (10 mL) Sriracha

½ cup (125 mL) low-sodium chicken stock

Zucchini Noodle Pad Thai

4 large zucchini, spiralized into noodles

2 large carrots, peeled and spiralized into noodles

½ teaspoon (2 mL) kosher salt

2 teaspoons (10 mL) extra-virgin olive oil, divided

2 large eggs, beaten

Sea salt and cracked black pepper

2 large skinless, boneless chicken breasts, thinly sliced

3 cups (750 mL) bean sprouts

Garnish

¼ cup (60 mL) fresh cilantro leaves

⅓ cup (75 mL) finely chopped unsalted natural peanuts

Thinly sliced Thai red chilies (optional)

Sriracha (optional)

Lime wedges

1. **Make the Pad Thai Sauce** In a small food processor, combine the tamarind paste, coconut sugar, tamari, lime juice, Sriracha, and chicken stock. Process until fairly smooth. Set aside.

2. **Make the Zucchini Noodle Pad Thai** Line 2 baking sheets with a few layers of paper towel or a kitchen towel. Spread the zucchini noodles on one baking sheet and the carrot noodles on the other and sprinkle with kosher salt. Cover with another few layers of paper towel (or another kitchen towel), then place a cutting board and some heavy items like books or pots on top. It may look a little crazy, but just trust me, this will force the excess liquid out of the veg. Leave the zoodles alone for 10 minutes.

3. Transfer the zucchini noodles to a colander and rinse thoroughly with cold water to remove the salt. Replace the paper towels on the baking sheet with a few new layers of paper towel (or a kitchen towel). Gently squeeze and shake the noodles and spread them on the baking sheet. Top with a few more layers of paper towel (or a kitchen towel), the cutting board, and the heavy items and let dry for another 10 minutes. Repeat with the carrot noodles.

4. Heat 1 teaspoon (5 mL) of the olive oil in a large nonstick skillet over medium heat. Add the eggs, season with a pinch each of salt and pepper, and scramble the eggs gently until cooked through. Transfer the eggs to a bowl and set aside.

continues

5. In the same pan, heat the remaining 1 teaspoon (5 mL) olive oil over medium-high heat. Add the chicken breasts, season with a pinch each of salt and pepper, and stir-fry until golden and cooked through, 5 to 6 minutes. Transfer to the bowl with the eggs.

6. To assemble, return the pan to medium heat and add the reserved Pad Thai Sauce. When it begins to bubble, add the carrot noodles and toss in the sauce for 1 minute. Add the zucchini noodles and toss in the sauce for 1 minute. Finally, add the eggs, chicken, and bean sprouts and cook for an additional 1 minute, or until the veggies are al dente and everything is warmed through.

7. To serve, divide the Veggie Noodle Pad Thai among 4 bowls. Garnish with cilantro, peanuts, chilies (if using), Sriracha (if using), and lime wedges.

ABBEY'S TIP I love ketchup on my french fries, but please don't crush my foodie heart by putting it in pad Thai like some cheap, Westernized restaurants do. The real deal is all about tamarind paste. Grown in long, brown pods like peanut shells, and popular in Asian, Indian, Mexican, and African cuisines, tamarind's characteristic sticky, tangy pulp is rich in fibre, B vitamins, calcium, and iron. It's also the key to making badass pad Thai, so do not leave it out. You can find tamarind paste at any Asian market or in the international section of major grocers.

Autumn Butternut Squash Mac and Cheese with Sage Panko

Healthy fats • High fibre • High protein • No added sugar • Nut-free • Vegetarian

Serves 6

I could pretend I gave up the blue-boxed, orange-powdered noodle habit in university, but let's be honest, where's the fun in that? And while I admit there's definitely a time and place for convenience, my adult palate often leaves me craving something more. If mac and cheese is your spirit animal, then let me introduce you to the king of the spirit animal jungle. My mac and cheese features a satiny squash and cauliflower cream as a fibre-rich alternative to the classic flour-based roux most sauces require, and I add just a sprinkle of flaxseed to give the crispy panko crust a hit of heart-healthy omega-3s. If you use the right cheese, a little goes a long way, and that's why I adore the combination of high-quality Parmigiano-Reggiano and well-aged cheddar. The result is a melty, creamy, bubbly, cheesy, crackly dish that's a hit at any age.

Autumn Butternut Squash Mac and Cheese

10 ounces (280 g) whole-grain short-cut pasta
 (such as macaroni, fusilli, or penne)
1 tablespoon (15 mL) extra-virgin olive oil
2 teaspoons (10 mL) unsalted butter
2 cups (500 mL) thinly sliced sweet onion (about 1 large)
Sea salt and cracked black pepper
2 cloves garlic, minced
1½ cups (375 mL) low-sodium chicken stock
2 cups (500 mL) frozen diced butternut squash
2 cups (500 mL) frozen diced cauliflower
1 cup (250 mL) 2% milk
⅛ teaspoon (0.5 mL) freshly grated nutmeg

8 ounces (225 g) well-aged (3 to 5 years) white cheddar
 cheese, finely shredded (about 2 cups/500 mL), divided
1 ounce (28 g) Parmigiano-Reggiano cheese, finely grated
 (about ¼ cup/60 mL)

Sage Panko

3 cloves garlic, minced
½ cup (125 mL) whole wheat panko breadcrumbs
1 tablespoon (15 mL) minced fresh sage
2½ teaspoons (12 mL) ground flaxseed
1 ounce (28 g) Parmesan cheese, finely grated
 (about ¼ cup/60 mL)
4½ teaspoons (22 mL) extra-virgin olive oil
Fleur de sel

1. Preheat the oven to 375°F (190°C). Lightly grease an 8-inch (2 L) square baking dish.

2. **Make the Autumn Butternut Squash Mac and Cheese** Bring a large pot of generously salted water to a boil. Add the pasta and cook until very al dente, about 2 minutes shy of the recommended cooking time. Drain, and set aside.

3. Return the pot to the stove and heat the olive oil and butter over medium-low heat. Add the onions and stir to coat them in the oil and butter. Stirring every 5 minutes, cook the onions until they reach a caramelized, amber colour, 45 to 60 minutes. Season with salt and pepper and remove from the heat. Remove three-quarters of the onions to a small bowl or plate and set aside.

4. Return the pot with the remaining caramelized onions to the medium-low heat and add the garlic. Cook, stirring, for 1 to 2 minutes, or until fragrant. Then stir in the chicken stock, squash, cauliflower, and a pinch each of salt and pepper. Cover the pot with a lid, increase the heat to medium-high, and cook for 6 to 8 minutes, or until the squash and cauliflower are fork-tender.

continues

5. Stir in the milk and nutmeg, then transfer the mixture to a high-speed blender or food processor. Blend until very smooth. Return the mixture to the pot.

6. Heat the sauce over medium heat. Stir in ¾ of the cheddar and the Parmesan. Gently stir until fully melted.

7. Add the cooked pasta and the reserved caramelized onions and stir until all the noodles are well coated. Season with salt and pepper, to taste.

8. Transfer half of the mixture to the prepared baking dish and spread it in a single layer. Top with the remaining cheddar, and then add the remaining mac and cheese mixture. Set aside.

9. **Make the Sage Panko** In a small bowl, mix together the garlic, panko, sage, flaxseed, Parmesan, and olive oil. Sprinkle over the mac and cheese.

10. Bake, uncovered, for 20 to 22 minutes, or until bubbling, the breadcrumbs are lightly brown, and you get those amazing golden cheese bits around the edges. Finish with a generous sprinkle of fleur de sel and serve.

ABBEY'S TIP Feeling the not-so-sexy effects of "that time of the month"? Pass the cheese, please! Research suggests that dairy products, like our BFF cheese, may help reduce some of the most common symptoms of PMS, such as fatigue, depression, swelling, pain, and that relentless, raging appetite. Not that you need a fancy research paper to remind you of the absolute pleasure mac and cheese brings. If you want to make this ahead, you can layer the cheesy mac mixture into the dish, cover, and refrigerate for up to 2 days. When you need your cheese fix, just add the breadcrumbs and bake.

Lemon Cumin Grilled Eggplant with Tahini Yogurt Drizzle

Gluten-free • Healthy fats • High fibre • Vegetarian

Serves 4

For years I was convinced that eggplant was just a sneaky sub-edible sponge that people breaded, deep-fried, and topped with a crippling amount of cheese to disguise its true identity. I was happy to continue living with that lie, until I went to Israel and had eggplant done right. If you take the time to "sweat" out your eggplant, you get a supple sweet vegetable ready to be glazed in warm cumin and zesty lemon before being kissed on the grill. Draped with a nutty tahini cream and a sprinkle of pomegranate arils, the inherent deliciousness of eggplant is exposed. And all without a single shred of mozzarella.

Lemon Cumin Grilled Eggplant
8 Japanese eggplants, halved lengthwise
2 teaspoons (10 mL) kosher salt
¼ cup (60 mL) extra-virgin olive oil
2 teaspoons (10 mL) lemon zest
2 tablespoons (30 mL) fresh lemon juice
2 teaspoons (10 mL) ground cumin
1 teaspoon (5 mL) pure liquid honey
Sea salt and cracked black pepper

Tahini Yogurt Drizzle
½ cup (125 mL) plain 2% Greek yogurt
2 tablespoons (30 mL) tahini
2 tablespoons (30 mL) fresh lemon juice
2 tablespoons (30 mL) extra-virgin olive oil
½ teaspoon (2 mL) ground cumin
Sea salt and cracked black pepper

Garnish
⅓ cup (75 mL) pomegranate arils
3 tablespoons (45 mL) pine nuts, toasted
1 tablespoon (15 mL) sesame seeds, toasted
½ teaspoon (2 mL) za'atar
Fleur de sel
¼ cup (60 mL) fresh cilantro leaves (optional)

1. **Make the Lemon Cumin Grilled Eggplant** Arrange the eggplants cut side up on a cutting board or baking sheet. With a knife, score the cut sides of the eggplants in a diamond pattern about ¼ inch (5 mm) deep. Sprinkle with the kosher salt, then let them sit for 30 minutes to sweat out the excess moisture and bitterness. Lightly rinse the eggplants and gently pat them very dry with a paper towel or kitchen towel.

2. In a small bowl, mix together the olive oil, lemon zest, lemon juice, cumin, and honey. Brush the eggplants on both sides with the mixture.

3. Preheat a grill to high heat. Place the eggplants cut side down on the grate and grill, with the lid closed, for 4 to 5 minutes, or until well charred. Turn over and grill, covered, for another 3 minutes, or until soft and cooked through. Transfer the eggplants cut side up to a platter or plate and sprinkle with a pinch each of sea salt and pepper.

4. **Make the Tahini Yogurt Drizzle** In a food processor, combine the yogurt, tahini, lemon juice, olive oil, cumin, and a pinch each of salt and pepper. Process until smooth. Transfer to a squeeze bottle, piping bag, or plastic bag with a tiny hole cut out of one corner.

5. Drizzle the eggplants with the tahini sauce. Garnish with pomegranate arils, pine nuts, sesame seeds, za'atar, a pinch of fleur de sel, and cilantro (if using).

ABBEY'S TIP We eat with our eyes first, making the pretty purple hue of eggplant an appealing asset, but this colour is also a great indicator of its heart-healthy anthocyanin antioxidants. Any eggplant will technically work here, but I like the long, sweet, melt-in-your-mouth Japanese variety. Feel free to make a double batch of the tahini sauce, and save it for up to 3 days in the fridge for drizzling on chicken, beef, or skewered vegetables.

Chicken, Sweet Potato, and Cauliflower Curry

Dairy-free • Gluten-free • Healthy fats • High fibre • High protein • No added sugar

Serves 4

Forget Kim K's fabulous nude behind. This curry recipe has single-handedly broken the internet more than once. Okay, so it just crashed my personal server from the volume of traffic, but hey, that's saying something, right? Thankfully, the next time the World Wide Web goes down, you'll have everything you'll need right here. Hearty sweet potato, tender cauliflower, pretty rainbow chard, and protein-packed edamame add flavour and colour to tender, juicy chicken thighs. This one's not a publicity stunt, folks—it's the number one recipe on the *Abbey's Kitchen* blog, and you'll quickly figure out why.

1 tablespoon (15 mL) + 2 teaspoons (10 mL)
   extra-virgin olive oil, divided
8 skinless, boneless chicken thighs, trimmed of
   excess fat
Sea salt and cracked black pepper
1 small yellow onion, finely diced
3 cloves garlic, finely minced
4 teaspoons (20 mL) finely grated fresh ginger
3 tablespoons (45 mL) curry powder
1 tablespoon (15 mL) ground cumin
1 tablespoon (15 mL) ground coriander
¼ teaspoon (1 mL) cayenne pepper
¼ teaspoon (1 mL) sea salt
1 bottle (23 ounces/680 mL) tomato passata
   or tomato purée

1 medium sweet potato, peeled and diced into ⅓-inch
   (8 mm) cubes (2 to 2½ cups/500 to 625 mL)
1 can (14 ounces/400 mL) light coconut milk
1 medium head cauliflower, cut into small florets
   (6 to 8 cups/1.5 to 2 L)
1 bunch rainbow Swiss chard, stalks and ribs cut into
   ¾-inch (2 cm) pieces and leaves thinly sliced
½ cup (125 mL) frozen shelled edamame

Garnish

¼ cup (60 mL) unsalted natural pistachios, crushed
¼ cup (60 mL) golden raisins (optional)
Fresh cilantro leaves

1. Heat 1 tablespoon (15 mL) of the olive oil in a large nonstick skillet over medium-high heat.

2. Season the chicken thighs with salt and pepper, and place them in the skillet boned side up. Cook until browned on both sides, about 3 minutes per side. Once browned (but not cooked through), transfer to a plate.

3. Add the remaining 2 teaspoons (10 mL) olive oil to the skillet and reduce the heat to medium. Add the onion and cook, stirring often, until it begins to soften, about 5 minutes. Add the garlic, ginger, curry powder, cumin, coriander, cayenne, and salt. Cook, stirring, until fragrant, 30 to 60 seconds.

4. Add the tomato passata and the sweet potatoes, cover the skillet with a lid, and simmer for 10 minutes, or until the sweet potato is almost fork-tender.

5. Stir in the coconut milk, then nestle in the chicken thighs and cauliflower. Sprinkle the Swiss chard stalks and ribs on top. Cover and cook, stirring every few minutes to ensure the cauliflower and chicken reach the heat at the bottom, until the cauliflower and sweet potato soften and the chicken thighs reach an internal temperature of 165°F (74°C), 10 to 14 minutes.

6. Stir in the Swiss chard leaves and frozen edamame and cook just until the edamame are warmed through and the leaves wilt, about 2 minutes. Taste and season with salt and extra cayenne, if desired.

7. Serve garnished with pistachios, raisins (if using), and cilantro.

ABBEY'S TIP A cocktail of powerful antioxidants, curry powders vary based on region, but they usually include a combination of coriander, sweet basil, cumin, turmeric, cardamom, and red pepper. This recipe is even tastier after the flavours have had time to meld, so make a big batch on the weekend for the week ahead.

ABBEY'S TIP Prosciutto is one of my favourite ingredients for adding a huge amount of flavour from a single paper-thin slice. Unlike traditional strip bacon, prosciutto is often sold nitrate-free and made simply with pork, salt, and spices. When shopping for prosciutto, take the opportunity to get a free snack and sample a few varieties on offer. You want to choose a prosciutto that is silky, pliable, and soft, and not leathery, dry, or greasy. Store yours in an airtight storage bag in the fridge with pieces of parchment or plastic wrap between the slices for up to 2 months.

Prosciutto-Wrapped Chicken Breasts Stuffed with Pear and Gouda

Gluten-free • Healthy fats • High protein • No added sugar • Nut-free

Serves 4

My husband married me largely in part because I make "the best chicken ever." His words, not mine. Good chicken-making skills rates high on his Bubbe's list of what makes a good Jewish wife, but my penchant for prosciutto might earn me a naughty look or two. Well, that is, until they taste it. Bacon does make everything better—especially when it comes to a lean protein like chicken. Add to that sweet pears, earthy mushrooms, and creamy Gouda cheese and serve it with my Balsamic Roasted Brussels Sprouts, Grapes, and Figs (page 133), and I'm back in Bubbe's good graces.

2 teaspoons (10 mL) extra-virgin olive oil

¼ cup (60 mL) minced Vidalia onion (about ½ onion)

1 cup (250 mL) minced mushrooms

1 tablespoon (15 mL) minced fresh rosemary

1 red pear, finely diced

½ teaspoon (2 mL) balsamic vinegar

Sea salt and cracked black pepper

8 thin slices prosciutto

4 skinless, boneless chicken breasts (about 6 ounces/170 g each)

½ cup (125 mL) finely shredded Gouda cheese

Olive oil in an oil atomizer

1. Preheat the oven to 400°F (200°C).

2. Heat the olive oil in a small nonstick skillet over medium heat. Add the onions and cook, stirring from time to time, until they are translucent and start to caramelize, about 10 minutes. Add the mushrooms and rosemary and cook for an additional 5 minutes, until the mushrooms begin to brown and release their juices.

3. Add the pear and balsamic vinegar and stir until warmed through. If your pear is very hard, cook for an additional 3 minutes, until it softens slightly. Season with salt and pepper and remove from the heat.

4. Lay 2 slices of prosciutto on a cutting board, overlapping them slightly along a long edge. Repeat with the remaining prosciutto, making 4 rectangles.

5. Butterfly a chicken breast by cutting a deep slit horizontally into the thicker side and cutting almost all the way through the breast. Repeat with the remaining chicken. Season the chicken with salt and pepper on top and inside the slit.

6. Lay each chicken breast in the middle of a prosciutto rectangle, rounded side down and crosswise to the prosciutto. Carefully open up each slit and divide the Gouda and the pear mixture among the breasts. Carefully wrap the prosciutto around the breasts, enclosing the filling on the one side, and "sealing" the prosciutto edges on the bottom of the breasts. Turn the chicken over to be presentation side up.

7. Lightly grease a baking sheet with olive oil in an oil atomizer and heat the sheet in the oven for 5 minutes.

8. Place the chicken breasts seam side down on the hot baking sheet and bake the chicken until the prosciutto crisps up and a meat thermometer inserted into the thickest part of the breast and stuffing reads 165°F (74°C), 18 to 20 minutes.

Sweet Tea Bourbon Chicken Breasts

Dairy-free • Healthy fats • High protein • Nut-free

Serves 4

I'm Canadian, not some dainty Southern belle, but hand me a boozy sweet tea and a plate of finger-lickin'-good chicken, and I can be as sweet as pecan pie. For a taste of Southern hospitality (without the humidity), these boozy chicken breasts fit the bill. While the Deep South certainly isn't known for its light fare, this dish channels a hot summer tailgate party into a lean piece of otherwise pedestrian poultry. The secret here is an overnight cocktail bath for the ol' gal, and out she comes tender and sweet, with just enough liquor to make any Georgia peach blush.

1 cup (250 mL) boiling water

2 orange pekoe tea bags

3 tablespoons (45 mL) bourbon

3 tablespoons (45 mL) low-sodium soy sauce

3 tablespoons (45 mL) extra-virgin olive oil, divided

2 tablespoons (30 mL) + 4½ teaspoons (22 mL) pure liquid honey, divided

1½ teaspoons (7 mL) minced fresh rosemary

Juice and rind (cut in wide strips) of 1 orange

Juice and rind (cut in wide strips) of 1 lemon

4 boneless, skinless chicken breasts (about 6 ounces/170 g each)

Sea salt and cracked black pepper

Fleur de sel

1. **Make the Sweet Tea Bourbon Marinade** Combine the boiling water and tea bags in a cup and steep for 5 to 6 minutes. Remove the tea bags and let the tea cool until warm. In a large resealable plastic bag, combine the tea, bourbon, soy sauce, 2 tablespoons (30 mL) of the olive oil, 2 tablespoons (30 mL) of the honey, rosemary, orange juice and rind, and lemon juice and rind. Add the chicken breasts, seal the bag, and turn to coat the chicken. Marinate in the fridge for at least 4 hours or overnight.

2. Preheat the oven to 400°F (200°C). Line a baking sheet with parchment paper.

3. **Cook the Chicken Breasts** Remove the chicken breasts from the marinade, reserving the marinade. Pat the chicken with paper towel to remove any excess moisture, and season with a generous pinch each of sea salt and pepper.

4. In a large ovenproof nonstick skillet, heat the remaining 1 tablespoon (15 mL) olive oil over medium-high heat. Lay the breasts in the skillet presentation side down. Sear on each side until golden brown, 2 to 4 minutes per side, then transfer the skillet to the oven and continue cooking for 10 to 12 minutes, or until the internal temperature is 145°F to 150°F (63°C to 65°C). (You are not cooking it completely at this point.)

5. **Make the Glaze** Meanwhile, strain the marinade through a piece of cheesecloth, discarding the solids. In a small nonstick skillet, combine ½ cup (125 mL) of the marinade and the remaining 4½ teaspoons (22 mL) honey. Bring to a boil, then immediately reduce the heat to a moderate simmer and cook until the glaze reduces to about 3 tablespoons (45 mL), about 15 minutes. You'll see the colour has also changed from light brown to dark brown. Remove from the heat.

6. Remove the chicken from the oven and brush with the sticky glaze. Return the glazed chicken to the oven to cook for an additional 5 to 7 minutes, or just until they reach 165°F (74°C).

continues

7. If there's any residual sauce in the pan, rinse your brush (it touched undercooked chicken) and give the chicken one last lacquer. Sprinkle with a pinch of fleur de sel and serve.

ABBEY'S TIP I'm not sure if it's the bourbon, the fried chicken, or the black tea, but Southern guys and gals know how to live—literally. Studies have suggested that people who drink three or more cups of tea a day have a 21 percent lower risk of stroke than those who drink only one cup. Packed with polyphenol antioxidants, tea has also been linked to a reduced risk of cancer, Type 2 diabetes, and bone fractures. Make a double batch of tea while you're at it, and serve it over ice with a shot of bourbon, a healthy splash of lemon juice, and a little honey.

Apple Cider Can Chicken with Maple Mustard Glaze

Dairy-free • Gluten-free • High protein • Nut-free

Serves 4

Beer can chicken might not exactly be a French culinary classic, but I think even the great Julia Child would love this one. I like to pretend this maple mustard and apple cider version is a little more sophisticated, but let's be honest: you're still putting a can up a chicken carcass, and there's nothing classy about that. Posh or not, this chicken boasts the sweetest, spiciest, tangiest skin and the juiciest, most aromatic meat ever. Pair it with my Brussels Sprout, Apple, and Apricot Slaw with Beer Vinaigrette (page 129) for an unapologetically delicious way to sass up Julia's iconic roast bird.

Maple Mustard Glaze

3 tablespoons (45 mL) pure maple syrup

3 tablespoons (45 mL) spicy brown mustard

2 teaspoons (10 mL) low-sodium tamari (gluten-free, if required)

2 teaspoons (10 mL) Worcestershire sauce

Apple Cider Can Chicken

4½ teaspoons (22 mL) minced fresh thyme

4½ teaspoons (22 mL) lemon zest

1 teaspoon (5 mL) sweet smoked paprika

1 teaspoon (5 mL) kosher salt

1 teaspoon (5 mL) cracked black pepper

2 tablespoons (30 mL) virgin olive oil

1 chicken (3 to 4 pounds/1.35 to 1.8 g)

1 can (16 ounces/473 mL) alcoholic dry apple cider

4 fresh thyme sprigs

1. Preheat a grill to medium-high heat (about 375°F/190°C) using the burners on only one side of the grill.

2. **Make the Maple Mustard Glaze** In a small bowl, stir together the maple syrup, mustard, tamari, and Worcestershire sauce. Set aside.

3. **Make the Apple Cider Can Chicken** In another small bowl, stir together the thyme, lemon zest, paprika, salt, pepper, and olive oil. Set aside.

4. Remove the neck and giblets from the chicken and discard. Pat the chicken dry with paper towels.

5. Empty about half of the apple cider (ideally into your mouth), and insert the sprigs of thyme into the can. Place the can on a flat surface.

6. Gently massage the chicken all over with the thyme rub, then manoeuvre the chicken cavity over the cider can. I know, it feels wrong, but it will be so right.

7. Place the chicken on the centre of the grill grate on the side where the burners are off (indirect heat), balancing the chicken a bit like a tripod on the can and two legs.

continues

8. Close the lid and cook the chicken for about 50 minutes before checking on it. When it gets close to 155°F (68°C) on a meat thermometer inserted into the meaty part of the leg and breast, use a heatproof brush to gingerly (yet generously) brush the chicken with the Maple Mustard Glaze. Be careful not to be too aggressive with your brushing, or you may knock the bird over, and that can be messy. Close the lid and continue to cook the chicken a little longer. When the thermometer reads 165°F (74°C), it's done. Remove the chicken (still on the can) from the grill, gently lift it off the cider can, and throw out the can. Loosely cover the chicken with foil and let rest for about 10 minutes before carving and serving.

ABBEY'S TIP Red wine tends to get all the glory when it come to heart health, yet boozy apple cider also comes packed with a ton of polyphenol antioxidants that have been associated with reducing the risk of heart disease. Now hold on, that is not a prescription to go on a bender on Saturday night. A drink a day for women is really the sweet spot for getting those benefits without the associated questionable decisions. If you're finding your chicken-cider tripod is a bit tipsy, you can place it on a small barbecue-safe tray to catch any drips or spills.

Pomegranate-Glazed Apples Stuffed with Turkey Pistachio Meatloaf

Dairy-free • Gluten-free • Healthy fats • High fibre • High protein

Serves 4

My nickname growing up was Abbey Apple Seed, my alter ego moniker chosen for my superhero ability to eat all the fruit. Brisk autumn weekends were spent at the orchard selecting the best ruby-red apples for pie, though admittedly I ate more just sitting there than I picked. But apples aren't just for casual snacking or sugar-soaked pastries. My namesake fruit can easily elevate humdrum savoury meals as well. A mix of lean ground turkey, rich pistachios, sweet apricots, warm cinnamon, and fiery ginger gets packed into an edible apple bowl, transforming a 1950s staple into an elegant entertaining-worthy meal. Apples are packed with fibre, vitamin C, and antioxidants that may help protect against Type 2 diabetes and heart disease. I find the varieties that hold up best in baking are Empire, Cortland, Gala, and Pink Lady. Pair this main with my Roasted Za'atar Radishes with Feta Pea Purée (page 130), and you're armed and ready to take on dinner. Nickname: accepted. Mission: accomplished.

Pomegranate-Glazed Apples Stuffed
with Turkey Pistachio Meatloaf

3 teaspoons (15 mL) extra-virgin olive oil, divided

¼ cup (60 mL) very finely minced shallot (about 1 medium)

1 clove garlic, finely minced

3 tablespoons (45 mL) very finely minced peeled fresh ginger (about a 1-inch/2.5 cm piece)

½ cup (125 mL) unsalted natural pistachios

½ cup (125 mL) old-fashioned rolled oats (gluten-free, if required)

1 pound (450 g) extra-lean ground turkey

1 large egg, lightly beaten

⅓ cup (75 mL) lightly packed minced dried apricots (about 8 apricots)

½ teaspoon (2 mL) cinnamon

1 teaspoon (5 mL) sea salt

½ teaspoon (2 mL) cracked black pepper

4 large baking apples (such as Empire, Cortland, Gala, or Pink Lady)

2 teaspoons (10 mL) fresh lemon juice

1 teaspoon (5 mL) pomegranate molasses, room temperature

Apple Pistachio Salsa

Reserved apple scraps (about 1½ cups/375 mL)

¼ cup (60 mL) lightly packed minced dried apricots, lightly packed (about 6 apricots)

¼ cup (60 mL) minced unsalted natural pistachios

¼ cup (60 mL) pomegranate arils (optional)

Sea salt and cracked black pepper

1. Preheat the oven to 425°F (220°C). Lightly grease a deep 11- x 7-inch (2 L) baking dish.

2. **Make the Pomegranate-Glazed Apples Stuffed with Turkey Pistachio Meatloaf** In a medium skillet, heat 1 teaspoon (5 mL) of the olive oil over medium heat. Add the shallots and cook, stirring often, for 2 minutes, or until softened. Add the garlic and ginger and stir for another minute, until fragrant. Scrape the mixture into a large bowl.

3. In a food processor, combine the pistachios and rolled oats. Process until the oats reach a flour-like consistency and the pistachios are very finely chopped. Add the oat mixture to the shallot mixture.

continues

4. Add the turkey, egg, apricots, cinnamon, salt, and pepper. Gently mix until everything is evenly distributed.

5. Cut the apples in half lengthwise, then cut a tiny sliver off the rounded side so the apples sit flat without wobbling over. Use a melon baller (or a small metal spoon) to remove the core and the stem from each apple and discard. Then hollow out the apple halves, leaving about ¼ inch (5 mm) of flesh around the edges, saving the apple scraps in a small bowl. Working quickly, toss the apple scraps with the lemon juice and remaining 2 teaspoons (10 mL) olive oil. Set aside.

6. Arrange the hollowed-out apple halves cut side up in the baking dish and season with a pinch each of salt and pepper. Fill the apple halves with the turkey mixture, packing it right to the edges to cover the apple flesh. Drizzle with pomegranate molasses. Cover the baking dish with foil and bake for 18 minutes. Remove the foil and continue to bake until the tops are caramelized and brown and an instant-read thermometer inserted in the centre of a stuffed apple reads 165°F (74°C), another 12 to 15 minutes.

7. **Make the Apple Pistachio Salsa** When ready to serve, transfer the reserved apple scraps to a food processor and pulse about 5 times, until they are coarsely minced but not puréed. Transfer to a medium bowl and stir in the apricots, pistachios, pomegranate arils (if using), and salt and pepper to taste.

8. Serve the meatloaves with the Apple Pistachio Salsa.

ABBEY'S TIP Pomegranate molasses is a Middle Eastern staple made of reduced pomegranate juice with a bit of added sugar. It's in the international section of most grocery stores, but with a little patience you can easily make it yourself. Simply bring 4 cups (1 L) pomegranate juice, ½ cup (125 mL) honey, and 1 tablespoon (15 mL) lemon juice to a boil until the honey is dissolved, then reduce the heat to medium-low and cook for 1 hour, or until reduced to a thick syrup. Store in an airtight container in the fridge for up to 1 month. It's not-too-sweet character is perfect for glazing these meatloaves, but you'll also love it drizzled on fruit salad, roasted vegetables, and vanilla ice cream.

Stuffed Hawaiian Burgers with Grilled Pineapple, Peameal, and Teriyaki Ketchup

Healthy fats • High fibre • High protein • Nut-free

Serves 4

My mom always says that in today's age of overplanning and micromanaging, the only real surprise we have is when we meet our maker. I hate surprises—especially morbid ones—unless, of course, that surprise happens to be a mouthful of unexpected cheese. Sign. Me. Up. Umami-rich mushrooms are finely minced and mixed with a delicious duo of pork and beef, yielding a patty that could only be made more perfect with a surprise explosion of cheese. Topped with lean Canadian bacon and candy-like pineapple just kissed on a fiery grill, this heavenly burger towers over basic beefy stacks. Mom says the higher the burger, the closer to God, and I say amen to that.

Stuffed Hawaiian Burgers

6 ounces (170 g) cremini mushrooms, stemmed and quartered

6 tablespoons (90 mL) old-fashioned rolled oats

6 ounces (170 g) extra-lean ground beef

6 ounces (170 g) extra-lean ground pork

1 large egg, lightly beaten

4½ teaspoons (22 mL) finely minced jalapeño pepper

1 tablespoon (15 mL) finely minced green onion

2 teaspoons (10 mL) teriyaki sauce

1 teaspoon (5 mL) cracked black pepper

¾ teaspoon (4 mL) kosher salt

¼ cup (60 mL) finely shredded Monterey Jack cheese

4 whole-grain burger buns

Toppings

2 tablespoons (30 mL) ketchup

6 teaspoons (30 mL) teriyaki sauce, divided

4 lean slices peameal (Canadian) bacon

4 slices fresh pineapple (¼ inch/5 mm thick)

1 cup (250 mL) tightly packed arugula (optional)

¼ cup (60 mL) pickled sliced jalapeño peppers (optional)

1. **Make the Stuffed Hawaiian Burgers** Pulse the mushrooms in a food processor until they are finely minced—they should look like ground meat. Remove from the food processor and use all of your strength to squeeze out any residual liquid. Transfer to a large bowl.

2. Add the oats to the food processor and pulse into a powder-like consistency. Add the oat flour to the bowl with the mushrooms. Add the ground beef, ground pork, egg, jalapeños, green onions, teriyaki sauce, pepper, and salt. Delicately combine the ingredients just until mixed through, being careful not to overwork or squeeze the burger mixture.

3. Portion the meat into 4 equal balls. Make a hole in the centre of each ball and pack about 1 tablespoon (15 mL) of the cheese (squished into a ball) into each hole. Form the meat around it, then squish the patties down to form epic stuffed burgers about 1 inch (2.5 cm) thick. Refrigerate for 10 to 30 minutes to firm up.

continues

4. Meanwhile, in a small bowl, stir together the ketchup and 4 teaspoons (20 mL) of the teriyaki sauce. Set aside.

5. Preheat a grill to medium-high heat and lightly grease the grate. Grill the burgers, with the lid closed, for 4 to 6 minutes per side, or until the internal temperature is 160°F (70°C).

6. **Prepare the Toppings** Meanwhile, grill the bacon for about 2 minutes per side, or until fully opaque and cooked through. Brush the pineapple with the remaining 2 teaspoons (10 mL) teriyaki sauce and grill until charred, about 2 minutes per side. Hollow out both sides of the buns and lightly toast on the grill for 30 to 60 seconds.

7. To assemble, on each bun, layer a slice of peameal bacon, a pineapple ring, arugula (if using), and a burger. Top with a dollop of the teriyaki ketchup and a few pickled jalapeños (if using), and finish with the bun top.

ABBEY'S TIP I have nothing against bread or fluffy, doughy buns, but I also like being able to fit my food into my mouth without someone cracking an inappropriate joke or losing half my meal down my blouse. Hollowing out some of the bun leaves more room for stacking my burger high with fillings, and saves me the dry cleaning bill from a messy lunch. But don't throw those goodies out! If you're not going to eat those little scraps, freeze them for when you're ready to make croutons. Toss them in a few teaspoons of olive oil and bake them in a 375°F (190°C) oven for 7 to 10 minutes, until crispy.

Grilled Chili Lime Steak with Creamy Corn Sauce and Corn and Tomato Salad

Dairy-free • Gluten-free • Healthy fats • High protein • Nut-free

Serves 4

Nothing says summer like a family and friends barbecue, and despite my love for grilled zucchini and butter-rubbed corn, let's get real—steaks are the real superstars of the buffet. I admittedly get a little territorial about which piece of steak is mine on the grill, but serving this lean flank steak family style is one of the best ways I know to make and keep good friends. A tangy, fiery marinade imparts a ton of Mexican flavour. This is complemented beautifully by the fresh summer corn that's both whizzed into a creamy, spicy sauce and mixed into a light and bright tomato salad. It's the best of summer on a plate. Get ready to have a lot of new friends.

Grilled Chili Lime Steak

2 cloves garlic, finely minced
¼ cup (60 mL) chopped fresh cilantro
3 tablespoons (45 mL) virgin olive oil
3 tablespoons (45 mL) fresh lime juice
2 tablespoons (30 mL) low-sodium tamari (gluten-free, if required)
4 teaspoons (20 mL) pure liquid honey
2 teaspoons (10 mL) chili powder
1 teaspoon (5 mL) ground cumin
½ teaspoon (2 mL) sweet smoked paprika
¼ teaspoon (1 mL) cayenne pepper

1 flank or skirt steak (1½ pounds/675 g), trimmed of excess fat
Sea salt and cracked black pepper
¼ cup (60 mL) fresh cilantro leaves, for garnish (optional)

Corn Sauce and Corn and Tomato Salad

4 corn cobs, shucked
½ jalapeño pepper, cut in half lengthwise
¼ cup (60 mL) light coconut milk
4 teaspoons (20 mL) fresh lime juice, divided
Kosher salt and cracked black pepper
1 cup (250 mL) grape tomatoes, quartered
2 teaspoons (10 mL) extra-virgin olive oil

1. **Make the Grilled Chili Lime Steak** In a small food processor, combine the garlic, cilantro, olive oil, lime juice, tamari, honey, chili powder, cumin, paprika, and cayenne; process until smooth. Transfer the marinade to a large resealable plastic bag. Add the flank steak, seal the bag, and turn to coat the steak. Marinate in the refrigerator for at least 4 hours or overnight.

2. Preheat a grill for direct cooking over high heat. Lightly grease the grate.

3. Remove the steak from the marinade and wipe off any excess marinade. Place the steak on the grill and cook, with the lid closed, until the outside gets deliciously caramelized and the internal temperature is 125°F (51°C) for medium-rare, about 2 minutes per side, depending on the thickness. Transfer the steak to a cutting board or plate, cover it with foil, and let rest for 10 minutes.

4. **Make the Corn Sauce** While the steak rests, place the corn cobs and the jalapeño (cut side down) on the grill. Cook the jalapeño for just 1 to 2 minutes on each side, until lightly charred. Cook the corn, turning every few minutes, until charred on all sides, about 10 minutes total.

continues

5. Finely mince the jalapeño (including the seeds if you like a bit of heat). Remove the corn from the cobs by standing them upright in a large bowl and running a knife down the sides. Place half of the corn kernels and half of the jalapeño in a blender and add the coconut milk and 2 teaspoons (10 mL) of the lime juice. Blend until super smooth, then season with kosher salt and pepper. Keep warm.

6. **Make the Corn and Tomato Salad** In a medium bowl, toss together the remaining corn kernels and jalapeños, the grape tomatoes, olive oil, and the remaining 2 teaspoons (10 mL) lime juice. Season with kosher salt and pepper.

7. Slice the steak very thinly against the grain (that is, look for the long fibres of the meat and cut across them) and ideally on a diagonal (so the slices are wider and have more surface area). Sprinkle with a pinch each of sea salt and cracked black pepper.

8. To serve, smear the Corn Sauce across individual plates or a serving platter, top with the slices of steak, and garnish with a few cilantro leaves, if desired. Serve with the Corn and Tomato Salad on the side.

ABBEY'S TIP Lean beef is some of nature's tastiest fuel. Not only does it offer a wicked hit of high-quality protein to nourish muscles, but it's also one of the absolute best sources of easily absorbed iron, zinc, and energizing B vitamins. Flank and skirt steak are easily exchangeable lean cuts of beef that pack a ton of rich, beefy flavour, but they will get tough if they're overcooked. Limit yourself to a cool medium-rare or rare, and slice the beef thinly against the grain for the most succulent bite.

Cider-Braised Sausages and Cabbage with Fresh Apple Salsa

Dairy-free • Gluten-free • Healthy fats • High fibre • High protein • Nut-free

Serves 4

"Babe, can we have cabbage for dinner?" It would have been an unusual request before I had invented this dish. If done right, cabbage is addictive. So much so that my husband got a little stressed when he learned I was going to include this recipe in my book. "No! Not our cabbage!" he cried out, as if letting our "secret" out of the bag would cause a nationwide cabbage shortage. I think we'll be all right. Sweet strands of snappy, purple cabbage, aromatic fennel, and tangy green apple provide a light yet undeniably fulfilling bed for protein-packed sausage. Yes, it may seem like a lot of cabbage per person (hint, it's fantastic as leftovers), but my hubby and I usually eat the whole thing, so I wouldn't presume that you won't, too.

Cider-Braised Sausages and Cabbage

2 slices pancetta (⅛ inch/3 mm thick), diced

2 tablespoons (30 mL) extra-virgin olive oil, divided

8 lean turkey or chicken sausages (2 to 3 ounces/ 55 to 85 g each)

2 shallots, diced

¾ bulb fennel, finely shredded (reserve remainder for Fresh Apple Salsa)

1 head red cabbage, finely shredded

½ Granny Smith apple (reserve remainder for Fresh Apple Salsa), cut into matchsticks

1 cup (250 mL) alcoholic dry apple cider

2 tablespoons (30 mL) unpasteurized apple cider vinegar

2 tablespoons (30 mL) whole-grain mustard

2 tablespoons (30 mL) pure maple syrup

Sea salt and cracked black pepper

Fresh Apple Salsa

½ Granny Smith apple, finely diced

¼ bulb fennel, finely diced

1 teaspoon (5 mL) fennel fronds

3 tablespoons (45 mL) pomegranate arils

1 tablespoon (15 mL) extra-virgin olive oil

2 teaspoons (10 mL) unpasteurized apple cider vinegar

1 teaspoon (5 mL) minced crystallized ginger

½ teaspoon (2 mL) whole-grain Dijon mustard

½ teaspoon (2 mL) pure maple syrup

Sea salt and cracked black pepper

1. **Make the Cider-Braised Sausages and Cabbage** Heat a large pot over medium-high heat. Add the diced pancetta and sauté until crispy, 5 to 6 minutes. Transfer to a dish or plate.

2. Add 1 tablespoon (15 mL) of the olive oil to the pot. Prick the sausages a few times with a fork and add them to the oil. Brown them on each side, 2 to 3 minutes per side. Transfer to the dish with the pancetta.

3. Reduce the heat to medium and add the shallots and the fennel. Sauté for 3 minutes, or until they begin to soften. Add the cabbage, apples, apple cider, apple cider vinegar, mustard, maple syrup, and a generous pinch each of salt and pepper. Stir until the cabbage begins to wilt, about 10 minutes. Cover with a lid and cook for 12 to 15 minutes, until the apples begin to melt into the cabbage, and the cabbage and fennel start to soften.

continues

4. Return the sausages and pancetta to the pot, nestling them under the cabbage, and cook, covered, until the sausages are cooked through and the internal temperature is 165°F (74°C), about 10 more minutes. Season with salt and pepper.

5. **Make the Fresh Apple Salsa** Meanwhile, in a medium bowl, combine the apple, fennel, fennel fronds, pomegranate arils, olive oil, cider vinegar, ginger, mustard, maple syrup, and a pinch each of salt and pepper. Stir well.

6. Divide the cabbage among 4 bowls or plates. Top each serving with 2 sausages and a generous spoonful of Fresh Apple Salsa.

ABBEY'S TIP Brassica vegetables such as cabbage are known for their anticancer properties, while packing in a ton of flavonoid and phenolic antioxidants. Although any cabbage (even Brussels sprouts!) would work in this recipe, I like the crunchy texture of the purple variety. Plus, that pretty colour comes from a megadose of anthocyanin antioxidants, which research suggests may help protect against heart disease, cancer, and cognitive decline.

Cumin Pork Tenderloin with Rhubarb Orange Sauce

Dairy-free • Gluten-free • Healthy fats • High protein • Nut-free

Serves 4

If your childhood played out anything like mine, pork was often served dry, grey, and with a mountain of potatoes under which to bury the ashen meat. Today I know that when cooked right, there's no need to waste perfectly good mash on hiding this mild, lean "other white meat." A beautiful pork tenderloin is a lovely protein for piling on loads of sprightly flavour, like this springtime rhubarb, orange, and cumin sauce. Sweet and tangy oranges complement the bright acidity of fresh rhubarb, smoothed over with an aroma of smoky, warm spice. No sneaky meat guise required.

Cumin Pork Tenderloin

1 tablespoon (15 mL) extra-virgin olive oil

1 pork tenderloin (1½ pounds/675 g), trimmed of silver skin and excess fat

1 teaspoon (5 mL) ground cumin

¼ teaspoon (1 mL) sea salt

¼ teaspoon (1 mL) cracked black pepper

Rhubarb Orange Sauce

1 teaspoon (5 mL) extra-virgin olive oil

½ shallot, minced

1½ teaspoons (7 mL) grated fresh ginger

¼ teaspoon (1 mL) ground cumin

⅛ teaspoon (0.5 mL) cinnamon

1 tablespoon (15 mL) Cointreau or other orange liqueur

½ pound (225 g) rhubarb, cut into ¼-inch (5 mm) dice (about 2 cups/500 mL)

½ cup (125 g) freshly squeezed orange juice, divided

1 teaspoon (5 mL) tapioca starch or cornstarch

1 tablespoon (15 mL) pure liquid honey

1 navel orange, segmented and cut into small pieces

Sea salt and cracked black pepper

¼ cup (60 mL) fresh cilantro leaves, coarsely chopped

1. Preheat the oven to 425°F (220°C). Line a baking sheet with foil.

2. **Cook the Cumin Pork Tenderloin** Heat the olive oil in a large nonstick skillet over medium-high heat. Pat the pork dry, then sprinkle it liberally with cumin, salt, and pepper. Fry until nicely browned all over, 6 to 8 minutes total. Transfer to the baking sheet and roast until the internal temperature is 145°F (63°C), about 20 minutes. Remove from the oven, tent the pork with foil, and let rest for 5 minutes before slicing.

3. **Make the Rhubarb Orange Sauce** Meanwhile, return the skillet to medium-high heat and heat the olive oil. Add the shallot, ginger, cumin, and cinnamon and stir until fragrant. Add the Cointreau and cook until it evaporates. Then add the rhubarb and ¼ cup (60 mL) of the orange juice. Reduce the heat to medium and simmer for about 5 minutes, until most of the juice has evaporated and the rhubarb is tender when pricked with a fork.

4. In a small bowl, stir together the remaining ¼ cup (60 mL) orange juice and the tapioca starch, and add that to the skillet along with the honey. Stir until the sauce thickens slightly and coats the rhubarb, then stir in the orange segments. Remove from the heat and season with salt and pepper.

5. Slice the rested pork into ½-inch (1 cm) medallions, top with a sprinkle of cilantro, and serve with the Rhubarb Orange Sauce on the side.

ABBEY'S TIP Bright red and pleasantly tangy, rhubarb is a forgotten vegetable (yes, it's a vegetable) that packs a heart-healthy, mouth-puckering punch of goodness—it's packed with anthocyanin polyphenols and satisfying fibre. In fact, one study found that eating rhubarb stalk fibre daily for a month reduced bad LDL cholesterol by 9 percent! If you can't find fresh rhubarb (in season April to June), frozen works just fine.

Ginger Turmeric Shrimp

Dairy-free • Gluten-free • Healthy fats • High protein • No added sugar

Serves 4

Light, lean, and packed with protein, shrimp are the tabula rasa of the ocean. That's a nice way of saying they need a helping hand in the flavour department to transform them from belly-filler to happy dance—inducer. Thankfully, this zesty marinade bridges the gap. Nutty cumin, spicy ginger, savoury garlic, and fresh cilantro play nice together in this flavour-bath for our shrimp. Belly filled and dancing? This main really does it all.

½ cup (125 mL) minced fresh cilantro

3 tablespoons (45 mL) chopped peeled fresh ginger

2 tablespoons (30 mL) chopped garlic

2 teaspoons (10 mL) ground cumin

1 teaspoon (5 mL) ground turmeric

3 tablespoons (45 mL) extra-virgin olive oil

1 tablespoon (15 mL) fresh lemon juice

Sea salt and cracked black pepper

Cinnamon

1 pound (450 g) large shrimp, peeled and deveined

Fleur de sel

To Serve

Cooked whole-grain brown rice or quinoa (optional)

3 tablespoons (45 mL) sliced unsalted natural almonds, toasted

3 tablespoons (45 mL) golden raisins

Fresh whole cilantro leaves, for garnish

1. In a food processor, combine the cilantro, ginger, garlic, cumin, turmeric, olive oil, lemon juice, and a pinch each of salt, pepper, and cinnamon. Purée the marinade. Place the shrimp in a large resealable plastic bag, add the marinade, seal the bag, and toss until the shrimp are coated. Refrigerate for ideally 30 minutes, or up to an hour and a half.

2. Have a bed of your favourite whole-grain rice or grain (if using) ready on a platter or plates. Cover with foil to keep warm.

3. Heat a large nonstick skillet over medium-high heat. Add the marinated shrimp (along with the marinade) and sauté until the spices caramelize on both sides, just about 1 minute per side. Remove from the heat (make sure those shrimp don't overcook), sprinkle with a pinch of fleur de sel, and arrange over the rice.

4. Serve topped with almonds, raisins, and cilantro.

ABBEY'S TIP If you're about to turn the page thinking you have the notorious "cilantro-hating gene" and so you're genetically determined to hate this dish, think again. Although research has identified a gene responsible for making cilantro taste like soap, some studies suggest genetics likely play only a small role that can easily be overcome. Research has shown that crushing the leaves, as done in this marinade, helps release enzymes that convert the soapy aromatic compounds into more mild aromas. And ta-da, science wins (and so do your taste buds).

Rum-and-Lime-Glazed Ahi Tuna Tacos with Pineapple Avocado Salsa

Dairy-free • Gluten-free • Healthy fats • High fibre • High protein • Nut-free

Serves 4

While the thought of "island time," a.k.a. "late for life," gives me Type A night terrors, the sun-soaked cuisine of the islands makes me want to slow down and savour. My one visit to Jamaica can be summed up as me double-fisting the rum punch while I waited for the jerk chicken stall to open, a consistent hour past its scheduled time. I'm neurotic about being punctual, but some things are just worth the wait. This recipe channels my lazy-vacation vibes into boozy, sweet, and tangy fish tacos. They're basically an island party in your hand. A simple jerk seasoning, a splash of rum, and a drizzle of honey glaze beautify quick-cooking ahi tuna steaks. Topped off with a sweet and buttery pineapple avocado salsa, it's got the flavour of a Caribbean all-inclusive holiday, but without the hangover—or the annoying wait.

Rum-and-Lime-Glazed Ahi Tuna

2 teaspoons (10 mL) garlic powder

2 teaspoons (10 mL) onion powder

2 teaspoons (10 mL) kosher salt

2 teaspoons (10 mL) ground allspice

1 teaspoon (5 mL) cinnamon

½ teaspoon (2 mL) nutmeg

½ teaspoon (2 mL) cayenne pepper

3 tablespoons (45 mL) pure liquid honey

2 tablespoons (30 mL) virgin olive oil

2 tablespoons (30 mL) fresh lime juice

2 tablespoons (30 mL) light rum

4 ahi (yellowfin) or young albacore tuna steaks
(5 to 6 ounces/140 to 170 g each and at least
1 inch/2.5 cm thick, but the thicker the better)

Pineapple Avocado Salsa

1½ cups (375 mL) finely diced fresh pineapple

1 tablespoon (15 mL) minced seeded jalapeño pepper

½ red bell pepper, finely diced

1 avocado, pitted, peeled, and finely diced

1 green onion (white and light green parts only), minced

4½ teaspoons (22 mL) fresh lime juice, or to taste

1 teaspoon (5 mL) pure liquid honey, or to taste

Sea salt and cracked black pepper

To Serve

8 corn tortillas (6 inches/15 cm each)

1½ cups (375 mL) finely shredded red cabbage

⅓ cup (75 mL) fresh cilantro leaves, for garnish

1. Prepare a grill for direct cooking over high heat. Lightly grease the grates.

2. **Make the Rum-and-Lime-Glazed Ahi Tuna** In a small bowl, combine the garlic powder, onion powder, salt, allspice, cinnamon, nutmeg, cayenne, honey, olive oil, lime juice, and rum. Stir well and set aside.

3. **Make the Pineapple Avocado Salsa** In a medium bowl, combine the pineapple, jalapeño, red pepper, avocado, green onion, lime juice, and honey. Season with salt and pepper, stir well, and set aside.

4. When the grill is screaming hot, brush the tuna steaks on all sides with the glaze. Quickly sear the tuna, turning once, until the glaze caramelizes but the inside stays rare, 1 to 2 minutes per side. If the tuna steaks are thicker than 1 inch (2.5 cm), you can also quickly sear the sides as well (about 30 seconds max). Transfer the tuna to a plate or cutting board and let rest for 5 minutes.

5. While the tuna rests, quickly grill the tortillas on each side until lightly charred, about 30 seconds maximum per side.

6. To serve, thinly slice the tuna against the grain (the direction of the fibres). Sprinkle the shredded cabbage onto the bottom of each tortilla. Top with the Pineapple Avocado Salsa and slices of the tuna. Garnish with cilantro.

ABBEY'S TIP Tuna's a big boy in the ocean, so it naturally carries more mercury than its smaller, leaner brothers. Compared with bigeye tuna, however, yellowfin (a.k.a. ahi) and young albacore tuna contain about half the amount and are safe to eat in moderation. To reduce your mercury exposure, ask your fishmonger for the youngest sushi-grade tuna. Fresh tuna should smell, well, fresh—like a gusty ocean breeze—and I recommend having your steaks cut to order and eating them within 1 day. Also, you probably won't use all of the Pineapple Avocado Salsa for your fish tacos. I like to eat it like a salad all on its own, or use it to top grilled vegetables or greens.

ABBEY'S TIP Okay, while those celebrity-diet gurus might not be that creative in the kitchen, they're onto something by suggesting we eat more fish. Fatty fish like salmon is packed with vitamins A and D as well as one of the best food sources of omega-3 fatty acids. Often overlooked, these essential fats have been linked to a reduced risk of depression, macular degeneration, fetal brain disorders, inflammation, heart disease, ADHD, and so much more. So yeah, it's good stuff. Before you buy your salmon, always check a sustainability app such as SeaChoice, Ocean Wise, or Seafood Watch to double-check that your choice is still healthy and safe for the environment.

Orange Honey Salmon with Pistachio, Olive, and Herb Relish

Gluten-free • Healthy fats • High protein

Serves 4

I admit I've been suckered into reading those gossip magazines while at the nail salon. You know, the ones where they describe the daily diets of those svelte celebrity women, and both the diets and the women look the same. Why is everyone eating the same plain baked salmon and steamed broccoli for lunch? Are the mags just limited in stock photos, or are celebs actually that mundane? And whose mediocre recipe is this? Salmon doesn't have to taste like a dry, chalky omega-3 supplement on a plate. No, it can be supple, sweet, and brimming with flavour. I glaze my salmon with a combination of spicy mustard, sticky honey, and bittersweet orange, and serve it with a herbaceous, briny pistachio and olive relish. While I'm definitely tired of keeping up with those celebs, I never tire of this dish.

Pistachio, Olive, and Herb Relish

½ cup (125 mL) coarsely chopped unsalted natural pistachios

¼ cup (60 mL) pitted and finely chopped Kalamata olives

¼ cup (60 mL) cherry tomatoes, seeded and finely diced

½ cup (125 mL) finely chopped fresh flat-leaf parsley

2 tablespoons (30 mL) finely chopped fresh basil

1 tablespoon (15 mL) finely grated Parmesan cheese

½ clove garlic, minced

½ teaspoon (2 mL) orange zest

4½ teaspoons (22 mL) freshly squeezed orange juice

1 teaspoon (5 mL) extra-virgin olive oil

½ teaspoon (2 mL) pure liquid honey

¼ teaspoon (1 mL) herbes de Provence

Cracked black pepper

Orange Honey Salmon

2 teaspoons (10 mL) whole-grain Dijon mustard

2 teaspoons (10 mL) pure liquid honey

¼ teaspoon (1 mL) orange zest

2 teaspoons (10 mL) freshly squeezed orange juice

¼ teaspoon (1 mL) herbes de Provence

Sea salt and cracked black pepper

4 skinless salmon fillets (4 ounces/115 g each)

1. Preheat the oven to 450°F (230°C). Line a baking sheet with parchment paper.

2. **Make the Pistachio, Olive, and Herb Relish** In a small bowl, combine the pistachios, olives, tomatoes, parsley, basil, Parmesan, garlic, orange zest, orange juice, olive oil, honey, herbes de Provence, and a pinch of pepper. Stir well.

3. **Make the Orange Honey Salmon** In a small bowl, combine the mustard, honey, orange zest, orange juice, herbes de Provence, and a pinch each of salt and pepper. Stir well. Lay the salmon on the parchment paper skinned side down and brush with a layer of the glaze. Bake for 8 to 10 minutes, or until the flesh is opaque but not quite at the point of flaking apart.

4. Serve the Orange Honey Salmon topped with a generous few spoonfuls of the Pistachio, Olive, and Herb Relish.

Salads,
Sidekicks,
and Soups

Avocado Watermelon Salad with Pickled Shallots and Lime Chili Dressing

Gluten-free • Healthy fats • High fibre • Nut-free • Vegetarian

Serves 4

Sometimes I overestimate my tolerance to spicy food. Bad move. A few years ago, I was dining at a trendy taco joint in London and enjoying a heavenly watermelon salad with an aromatic chili oil. It hit that perfect spicy-sweet-spot ratio—you know, the one where you get a sizzling rush of endorphins but not enough to sweat through your silk shirt? Love it. But that love affair ended when I decided to bite into the red chili garnish. Tongue violently wagging, hands uncontrollably flailing, and mascara running down my tear-soaked cheeks, I was living my own version of culinary hell (and it was not the hot you want). Thankfully, I trusted my instinct and quelled the burn with a mouthful of guacamole. So it wasn't my most ladylike moment, but my intuition was spot on. Not only did the avocado temper the overwhelming fire, but damn, it was good! Here's my fork-friendly version that will keep you safely in the sexy sizzle zone. Pink and green, tangy and sweet, and perfectly spicy and cool. Serve alongside my Rum-and-Lime-Glazed Ahi Tuna Tacos (page 104).

Pickled Shallots

2 small shallots, sliced lengthwise into thin strips
½ cup (125 mL) fresh lime juice
2 tablespoons (30 mL) filtered water
4 teaspoons (20 mL) pure liquid honey
½ teaspoon (2 mL) sea salt

Lime Chili Dressing

¼ cup (60 mL) fresh lime juice
2 teaspoons (10 mL) Dijon mustard
2 teaspoons (10 mL) pure liquid honey
1½ teaspoons (7 mL) minced seeded hot red chili pepper
¼ cup (60 mL) extra-virgin olive oil
Sea salt and cracked black pepper

Avocado Watermelon Salad

1 avocado, pitted, peeled, and cubed
3 cups (750 mL) cubed seedless watermelon
3 cups (750 mL) peeled, seeded, and cubed
   English cucumber
2 tablespoons (30 mL) thinly sliced fresh mint
3 ounces (85 g) feta cheese, crumbled, for garnish

1. **Make the Pickled Shallots** Fill a small saucepan with water and bring to a boil over high heat. Add the shallots and blanch for 20 seconds. Drain.

2. In a small bowl, whisk together the lime juice, water, honey, and salt. Add the blanched shallot and refrigerate for 1 hour.

3. **Make the Lime Chili Dressing** Meanwhile, in a small bowl, stir together the lime juice, mustard, honey, and chili pepper. Whisking constantly, slowly add the olive oil, whisking until completely emulsified. Season with salt and pepper.

4. **Make the Avocado Watermelon Salad** In a large serving bowl, toss together the avocado, watermelon, cucumber, mint, and drained Pickled Shallots. Immediately drizzle with the dressing. Enjoy chilled or at room temperature, garnished with the feta.

ABBEY'S TIP Onions, including the milder shallots, are loaded with antioxidants and have been studied for their potential antimicrobial, anticancer, and bone-building properties. I love fancy flavonoids and stuff, but it doesn't change my strong opinion about eating onions raw. I'm that girl who will pick every last onion shard out of her Greek salad with absolutely no shame. Raw-onion-phobes will appreciate these pretty pickled shallots. The "quickle" technique helps mellows the sulphurous onion bite, and it adds a lovely citrusy note—perfect for adding a kick to salads, burgers, cheese plates, and more. I keep these in the fridge for up to 2 weeks for last-minute garnishes, or make a big batch to pack into a pretty jar for an easy hostess gift.

Crispy Chickpea, Fennel, and Cherry Salad with Tarragon Citronette

Gluten-free • Healthy fats • High fibre • Nut-free • Vegetarian

Serves 4

No one eats salad to let it dissolve in their mouth into a satiny coating on their tongue—that's what ice cream is for! Salads, my friends, are all about the crunch. So when I'm craving a salad that hits a high note on the Richter scale, I bust out this crazy crunchy chickpea and fennel combination. Aromatic crisp fennel is the base for a beaming midday meal, with the added support of protein-loaded chickpea "croutons." Balanced out by buttery lettuce, sweet summer stone fruit, and a tangy tarragon citronette, it's a perfect partner to my Asparagus, Pea, and Tomato Quinotto (page 65)—and the tastiest way to crunch.

Crispy Chickpea, Fennel, and Cherry Salad

1 can (19 ounces/540 mL) chickpeas, drained, rinsed, and dried

1 tablespoon (15 mL) extra-virgin olive oil

¼ teaspoon (1 mL) sea salt, more to taste

6 cups (1.5 L) gently torn butter lettuce

1 small bulb fennel, thinly sliced crosswise on a mandoline (reserve fronds for serving, if desired)

2 cups (500 mL) pitted and halved dark cherries

1 red plum, cut into thin wedges

¼ cup (60 mL) crumbled feta cheese

Tarragon Citronette

2 tablespoons (30 mL) minced shallot

2 teaspoons (10 mL) minced fresh tarragon

2 teaspoons (10 mL) Dijon mustard

2 teaspoons (10 mL) pure liquid honey

⅓ cup (75 mL) light olive oil

¼ cup (60 mL) fresh lemon juice

Sea salt and cracked black pepper

1. Preheat the oven to 425°F (220°C). Line a baking sheet with parchment paper.

2. **Make the Crispy Chickpea, Fennel, and Cherry Salad** Spread the chickpeas on a clean kitchen towel. Top with another towel and gently rub the chickpeas until they start to pop out of their thin, translucent skins. The skins hold a lot of moisture, so getting rid of as many as you can will help keep them crispier longer. Don't worry about getting each and every one, just remove any that easily slip off.

3. Transfer the chickpeas to the baking sheet and toss with the olive oil and salt. Bake, stirring at least once, for 20 to 22 minutes, or until golden brown and crispy.

4. Turn the oven off and leave the chickpeas in the oven (with the oven door closed) for at least an hour or until the pan is no longer hot.

5. **Make the Tarragon Citronette** In a small bowl or mason jar, combine the shallot, tarragon, mustard, honey, olive oil, lemon juice, and a pinch each of salt and pepper. Whisk (or shake the jar) until well combined.

6. To assemble, in a large serving bowl, combine the lettuce, fennel, cherries, plum, and Tarragon Citronette. Toss well. Sprinkle with the feta, the crispy chickpeas, and some of the reserved fennel fronds (if using).

ABBEY'S TIP Please, watch your little knuckles on the mandoline! Veggies have a way of jumping off the blade and sacrificing your precious fingers, and without them, it's really hard to like and comment on Instagram #foodporn! Pro tip: always use the blade protector, go slowly, and discard the little fennel end when it gets too small. You can totally eat the stub as a snack, but shaving it further is just not worth your digits!

Shaved Cauliflower, Apple, and Burrata Salad with Apple Cider Vinaigrette

Gluten-free • Healthy fats • High fibre • Vegetarian

Serves 4

I really like cheese, so the idea of building a meal around the stuff gets me pretty jazzed. And while I would happily eat a cheese platter topped with a few lettuce leaves and call it "salad" absolutely guilt-free, this version with luscious burrata offers a more balanced approach. Stringy, mild curds mingle in a pool of thick, spreadable, oozy cream that's so sensual, you'll lap up every veggie it touches on the plate. And speaking of vegetables, this combination gives my cheesy dream-lover much more than just a snuggly bed of leaves. Crunchy, thinly sliced cauliflower, juicy red apple, chewy, sweet dates, spicy arugula, and rich hazelnuts fill out the all-star cast. This salad accompanies my Autumn Butternut Squash Mac and Cheese with Sage Panko (page 73) beautifully. Cheese . . . helping people eat their salad (and everything else) since, well, forever.

Apple Cider Vinaigrette

1½ teaspoons (7 mL) minced shallot
¼ cup (60 mL) unpasteurized apple cider vinegar
1 tablespoon (15 mL) pure liquid honey
1½ teaspoons (7 mL) whole-grain Dijon mustard
¼ cup (60 mL) extra-virgin olive oil
Sea salt and cracked black pepper

Shaved Cauliflower, Apple, and Burrata Salad

8 cups (2 L) loosely packed arugula
2 cups (500 mL) thinly sliced cauliflower
    (using a mandoline)
1 large red apple (such as Empire, Red Delicious, or
    Cortland), cored and thinly sliced
4 Medjool dates, pitted and thinly sliced
½ cup (125 mL) toasted and coarsely chopped hazelnuts
½ cup (125 mL) burrata cheese pulled into pieces

1. **Make the Apple Cider Vinaigrette** In a small bowl, mix together the shallot, apple cider vinegar, honey, and mustard. Constantly whisk as you add in the olive oil until incorporated. Season with salt and pepper.

2. **Make the Shaved Cauliflower, Apple, and Burrata Salad** In a large serving bowl, layer the arugula, cauliflower, apple, and dates. Toss with ¾ of the Apple Cider Vinaigrette. Sprinkle with the hazelnuts and burrata, and drizzle with the remaining vinaigrette.

ABBEY'S TIP Burrata means "buttered" in the language of love, and although I can't speak a lick of Italian, I definitely understand that. Like all cheese, burrata is a good source of bone-supporting calcium and an excellent source of pleasure. As a fresh cheese, it's definitely best served within 48 hours of purchase, so if you buy a big ball and have extra, throw it onto crostini or melt it into pasta.

Brown Butter and Orange Cauli-Couscous Salad with Beets and Goat Cheese

High fibre • No added sugar • Vegetarian

Serves 4

They need to stop writing Disney stories about handsome princes and start writing them about the lifelong companionship a lady can have with good butter. Rich, creamy, and beautifully smooth, butter never disappoints. Nor does it select gardening gear as Valentine's Day gifts, forget your mom's name, or leave dirty dishes right beside the sink. (WHY!!) But if we're talking royalty, brown butter is truly the pleasure king. Cooking butter low and slow allows the moisture to evaporate and the milk proteins to caramelize, leaving behind a nutty, toasty liquid gold that elevates even the humblest fare. Here it transforms humdrum couscous and its doppelgänger, cauli-couscous, into an elegant side with jewel-like beets, juicy oranges, crisp almonds, and tangy goat cheese. Serve it with my Cumin Pork Tenderloin with Rhubarb Orange Sauce (page 100), because some couples are just meant for a happily ever after.

Cauli-Couscous Salad

3 small red beets
1 tablespoon (15 mL) fresh lemon juice
2 cups (500 mL) cauliflower florets
¼ cup + 2 tablespoons (90 mL) low-sodium vegetable stock
¼ cup (60 mL) freshly squeezed orange juice (about 1 small orange)
1 tablespoon (15 mL) unsalted butter
½ cup (125 mL) whole wheat couscous
1 teaspoon (5 mL) orange zest
Sea salt and cracked black pepper

To Serve

2 large oranges, peeled and segmented (reserve any excess juice)
3 tablespoons (45 mL) sliced unsalted natural almonds, toasted
3 tablespoons (45 mL) crumbled goat cheese
2 tablespoons (30 mL) torn fresh mint leaves

1. **Make the Cauli-Couscous Salad** Place the beets in a medium saucepan and add enough water to cover and the lemon juice to prevent their pretty colour from bleeding. Bring to a boil over high heat, then reduce the heat to medium-low and simmer, uncovered, for 30 to 45 minutes, until tender. Drain the beets. When cool enough to handle, peel, and slice the beets into wedges (about 8 wedges per beet). Set aside.

2. In a small food processor, pulse the cauliflower until it reaches a rice-like consistency. Set aside.

3. Pour the vegetable stock and orange juice into a small saucepan and bring to a boil over medium-high heat. Once it begins to bubble, reduce heat to low, cover, and keep warm.

4. Meanwhile, heat the butter in a medium saucepan with a light-coloured bottom (so that you can see the colour change) over medium heat. Swirl the pan fairly frequently to make sure the butter cooks evenly. As it melts, it will

continues

begin to foam and will progress from yellow to golden to a toasted-brown colour. This should take 2 to 3 minutes. As soon as you see the brown colour and smell a nutty aroma, strain the butter through cheesecloth or simply remove the white bits (milk solids) with a spoon, leaving behind the beautiful nutty oils. Whatever you do, do not wash out the saucepan! Those little caramelized bits on the bottom are culinary gold!

5. Return the strained butter to the saucepan over medium-low heat. Immediately add the couscous and stir to coat it in the butter. Stir in the warm orange juice mixture and the orange zest. Turn off the heat, cover the pan, and let stand until the liquid has been completely absorbed, about 5 minutes.

6. Add the pulsed cauliflower, cover again and allow the residual heat to warm the cauliflower through for an additional 5 minutes. Fluff the couscous and cauliflower with a fork and season with salt and pepper.

7. To serve, transfer the couscous mixture to a large serving bowl. Top with the beet wedges, the orange segments, and any orange juice you collected when segmenting the oranges. Sprinkle with a pinch each of salt and pepper and garnish with toasted almonds, goat cheese, and mint.

ABBEY'S TIP Contrary to what our moms were likely taught, new research suggests there is no strong association between saturated fats and cardiovascular disease, and that butter actually increases our "good" HDL cholesterol. Butter's fatty acid profile includes an anti-inflammatory short-chain fatty acid called butyrate, plus antioxidants, fat-soluble vitamins, and even omega-3 fats! To get the most nutrient bang for your buttery buck, look for grass-fed butter in the store.

Grilled Togarashi Cauliflower Steaks with Sesame Chermoula

Dairy-free • Healthy fats • High fibre • Nut-free • Vegetarian

Serves 4

I'm well aware that cauliflowers don't make steaks. Let's get something clear here—nothing can, or should ever, replace steak. But sliced thickly and seared on a hot grill, this modest white vegetable becomes something even most diehard carnivores adore. My cauli-steaks get their next-level addictiveness from a generous coating of Japanese spices and a bright, fragrant, and refreshing herb sauce. They're meaty, delicious, and packed with antioxidant power—a tasty way to get your steak and veggie fix in one go.

Sesame Chermoula

1 cup (250 mL) chopped fresh cilantro
1 cup (250 mL) chopped fresh flat-leaf parsley
1 clove garlic, coarsely chopped
2 tablespoons (30 mL) fresh lime juice
2 teaspoons (10 mL) grated fresh ginger
1 teaspoon (5 mL) sesame seeds, toasted
   (or shichimi togarashi for extra heat)
1 teaspoon (5 mL) low-sodium soy sauce
1 teaspoon (5 mL) sesame oil
1 teaspoon (5 mL) pure liquid honey
¼ cup (60 mL) extra-virgin olive oil

Grilled Togarashi Cauliflower Steaks

⅓ cup (75 mL) hoisin sauce
4 teaspoons (20 mL) fresh lime juice
1 tablespoon (15 mL) shichimi togarashi
2 teaspoons (10 mL) grated fresh ginger
2 teaspoons (10 mL) fish sauce
2 medium heads cauliflower
Extra-virgin olive oil in an oil atomizer

Garnish

Generous pinch of sesame seeds, toasted
   (or shichimi togarashi for extra heat)
2 tablespoons (30 mL) nori cut into thin strips (optional)

1. **Make the Sesame Chermoula** In a food processor or high-speed blender, combine the cilantro, parsley, garlic, lime juice, ginger, sesame seeds, soy sauce, sesame oil, and honey. Pulse until finely minced. Add the olive oil and process until fairly smooth but with visible bits of herbs. Set aside.

2. **Make the Grilled Togarashi Cauliflower Steaks** In a small bowl, stir together the hoisin sauce, lime juice, shichimi togarashi, ginger, and fish sauce. Set aside.

3. Cut one of the cauliflowers in half through the core, then cut one 1-inch (2.5 cm) steak from the cut side of one half, and another 1-inch (2.5 cm) steak from the cut side of the other half. Repeat with the second cauliflower. Keep any remaining cauliflower bits for another dish (see Tip).

4. Preheat a grill for direct cooking over medium-high heat. Spritz the cauliflower steaks with olive oil in an oil atomizer and grill, with the lid closed, for 6 to 9 minutes on each side, or until fork-tender and lightly charred. If the cauliflower is charring faster than it is cooking through, transfer to indirect heat on the grill, and cover with the lid to finish cooking through. Once fork-tender, transfer to a baking sheet and brush the hoisin sauce mixture generously on both sides.

5. Return the glazed cauliflower to the grill over direct heat for 1 minute per side, or until the glaze just caramelizes.

continues

6. To serve, drizzle a few spoonfuls of the Sesame Chermoula over each cauliflower steak. Sprinkle with sesame seeds and strips of nori (if using).

ABBEY'S TIP Shichimi togarashi is a tasty Japanese spice mix made of red chili, black and white sesame seeds, poppy seeds, orange zest, wasabi, and nori seaweed. It's dangerously addictive and increasingly easy to find in Asian markets and the spice aisle at major grocers, but in a pinch, can be replaced by equal parts red chili flakes and sesame seeds. While preparing your cauliflower steaks with this togarashi glaze, you'll likely have some rogue florets that pop off on either side—don't throw these out! These little runaways are perfect for pulsing into cauliflower rice for recipes like my Brown Butter and Orange Cauli-Couscous Salad (page 117) and Cheese-Explosion Cauliflower Tots (page 211).

Wild Rice and Bok Choy Salad with Creamy Cashew Dressing

Dairy-free • Gluten-free • Healthy fats • High fibre • Vegan • Vegetarian

Serves 4 to 6

Green fatigue is very real. Sometimes, you just can't take another forkful of kale, spinach, or romaine. And while occasionally we all need a judgment-free vacation from vegetables altogether (and that's totally cool), more often a little salad shake-up will do the trick. Salads don't have to start with traditional lettuce. I created this beauty with nutty wild rice, protein-packed edamame, and shredded crisp bok choy. Satisfying all by itself, but it's even more next-level goodness when tossed in my Creamy Cashew Dressing with a handful of crunchy nuts. Anticipate office envy with this one; it's going to need full-time refrigerator supervision.

Wild Rice and Bok Choy Salad
½ cup (125 mL) wild rice, rinsed and drained

1 red bell pepper, cut into thin strips and each strip cut in half

3 cups (750 mL) finely shredded bok choy

1 cup (250 mL) frozen shelled edamame, thawed

¼ cup (60 mL) coarsely chopped toasted unsalted natural cashews, more for garnish

¼ cup (60 mL) coarsely chopped fresh cilantro, more for garnish

Sea salt and cracked black pepper

Creamy Cashew Dressing
¼ cup (60 mL) natural cashew butter

¼ cup (60 mL) light coconut milk

½ clove garlic, finely minced

1 teaspoon (5 mL) lime zest

3 tablespoons (45 mL) fresh lime juice

½ teaspoon (2 mL) curry powder

½ teaspoon (2 mL) Sriracha, or to taste, more for garnish if desired

¼ teaspoon (1 mL) sea salt, or to taste

1. **Make the Wild Rice and Bok Choy Salad** In a medium saucepan, combine the wild rice, a pinch of salt, and about 3 cups (750 mL) of water. Bring to a boil over high heat. Reduce the heat, cover the pan, and simmer for 35 to 45 minutes, or until the rice is chewy with burst kernels, but not dry and brittle. Drain, transfer to a large serving bowl, and let cool to room temperature.

2. Add the red peppers, bok choy, edamame, cashews, and cilantro. Season with a pinch each of salt and pepper and stir to combine.

3. **Make the Creamy Cashew Dressing** In a blender or small food processor, combine the cashew butter, coconut milk, garlic, lime zest, lime juice, curry powder, Sriracha, and salt; blend until smooth. Adjust the seasoning, if needed, and toss with the salad.

4. To serve, sprinkle the salad with additional crunchy cashews, cilantro, and a squirt of Sriracha, if desired.

ABBEY'S TIP Despite its confusing moniker, wild rice isn't actually rice at all. It's a naturally gluten-free grass whose seeds simply resemble rice. With more fibre, protein, and antioxidant capacity than regular rice, wild rice adds a hearty, fulfilling base to salads, soups, and stir-fries. If you can't find wild rice, feel free to substitute a nice nutty whole grain like rice, barley, or wheat berries.

Miso Cucumber, Avocado, and Toasted Sesame Salad

Dairy-free • Gluten-free • Healthy fats • High fibre • Nut-free • Vegan • Vegetarian

Serves 4

For my bachelorette party, a few of my chef friends treated my gal pals and me to an amazing lunch at the cottage. I may have been the bride-to-be, but the star of the day was definitely the chefs' cucumber avocado salad. I may have already been two or three drinks in, but I made a mental note (as best as a tipsy bachelorette could) to make my own version at home. The key to making this salad super snappy to contrast with the buttery avocado is to draw some of the liquid out of the cucumbers with a simple pinch of salt. Finish the whole thing off with a generous drizzle of umami-rich miso dressing and a sprinkle of crackly sesame, and it's the perfect no-lettuce salad for any time of the year. Bachelorettes, bridal parties, and drinkie drinks optional.

Miso Dressing

¼ cup (60 mL) light olive oil

3 tablespoons (45 mL) white miso

2 tablespoons (30 mL) seasoned rice vinegar

2 tablespoons (30 mL) fresh lime juice

2 teaspoons (10 mL) coconut sugar

2 teaspoons (10 mL) low-sodium tamari
   (gluten-free, if required)

1 teaspoon (5 mL) thinly sliced Thai red chili

1 teaspoon (5 mL) toasted sesame oil

Sea salt and cracked black pepper

Cucumber and Avocado Salad

12 mini cucumbers

1 teaspoon (5 mL) kosher salt

1 avocado, pitted, peeled, and thinly sliced

½ teaspoon (2 mL) white sesame seeds, toasted

½ teaspoon (2 mL) black sesame seeds

2 tablespoons (30 mL) torn fresh mint leaves

2 tablespoons (30 mL) fresh cilantro leaves

½ to 1 teaspoon (2 to 5 mL) minced red Thai chili
   (depending on heat preference)

1. **Make the Miso Dressing** In a small food processor, combine the olive oil, miso, rice vinegar, lime juice, coconut sugar, tamari, chili, and sesame oil; process until smooth. Taste and season with sea salt and pepper, if needed.

2. **Make the Cucumber and Avocado Salad** Cut the cucumbers in half lengthwise and use a spoon to remove the seeds. Cut the cucumber halves on a diagonal into pieces 1½ inches (4 cm) long. In a large bowl, toss the cucumbers with the kosher salt, and let sit in the fridge for 20 to 30 minutes. Transfer to a colander, rinse with cold water, and pat dry with paper towel or a kitchen towel. Tumble the cucumbers onto a platter.

3. To serve, arrange the avocado slices among the cucumber pieces, then drizzle with the Miso Dressing. Sprinkle with the sesame seeds, mint, cilantro, and chili. Serve at room temperature.

ABBEY'S TIP Don't throw out those cucumber innards! I like adding them to a pitcher of water with a few lime wedges and mint leaves or adding them to a smoothie for a hydrating post-workout snack.

Charred Broccoli, Quinoa, and Hazelnut Crunch Salad

Dairy-free • Gluten-free • Healthy fats • High fibre • Vegan • Vegetarian

Serves 4

Every once in a while, a salad comes along that gets you more excited than a gooey poutine. This is that salad. I was inspired by a food truck in Los Angeles that had me crushing on their quinoa and nut salad. As much as I was loving the sea-salted air of the West Coast, I couldn't wait to go home and make my own version in my kitchen. Crunchy, rich hazelnuts, tangy cranberries, sweet maple, toasty caramelized broccoli, and sprightly pickled shallots will help you nail your salad game. Don't get me wrong—poutine always has a special place in my heart, but this salad is so swoon-worthy, even the salad-skeptics will be going in for more.

Quick Pickled Shallots
1 shallot, thinly sliced
¼ cup (60 mL) unpasteurized apple cider vinegar
1 tablespoon (15 mL) filtered water
2 teaspoons (10 mL) pure maple syrup
¼ teaspoon (1 mL) salt

Charred Broccoli, Quinoa, and Hazelnut Crunch Salad
1 large bunch broccoli
1 tablespoon (15 mL) extra-virgin olive oil

Sea salt and cracked black pepper
1 cup (250 mL) cooked multicoloured quinoa
6 tablespoons (90 mL) toasted coarsely chopped hazelnuts
6 tablespoons (90 mL) dried cranberries

Maple Dijon Dressing
4 teaspoons (20 mL) whole-grain Dijon mustard
4 teaspoons (20 mL) pure maple syrup
4 teaspoons (20 mL) extra-virgin olive oil
Sea salt and cracked black pepper

1. **Make the Quick Pickled Shallots** Bring 2 cups (500 mL) water to a boil in a small saucepan. Add the sliced shallot and blanch for 30 seconds. Drain, then transfer to a small bowl. Add the apple cider vinegar, filtered water, maple syrup, and salt. Refrigerate for 1 hour.

2. Place a baking sheet in the oven and preheat the oven to 450°F (230°F).

3. **Make the Charred Broccoli, Quinoa, and Hazelnut Crunch Salad** Remove the thick stem from the broccoli, leaving 1 to 2 inches (2.5 to 5 cm) beyond the base of each floret. Reserve the thick stem for another use (see Tip). Cut the broccoli florets into thin pieces 2 to 3 inches (5 to 8 cm) long and ¼ inch (5 mm) thick. Toss with olive oil and a pinch each of salt and pepper. Spread on the baking sheet and roast for 8 to 10 minutes, until golden brown and tender.

4. **Make the Maple Dijon Dressing** In a small bowl, stir together the mustard, maple syrup, olive oil, and salt and pepper to taste.

5. To serve, in a large serving bowl, mix the charred broccoli with the quinoa, hazelnuts, cranberries, drained Quick Pickled Shallots, and Maple Dijon Dressing. Season with salt and pepper, toss well, and serve at room temperature.

ABBEY'S TIP Like other cruciferous vegetables, broccoli contains a unique cancer-fighting plant compound called isothiocyanate. Use up the bottom ends of those broccoli stems by shredding them on a mandoline for slaws, adding them to puréed soups, thinly slicing for stir-fries, or whirling them into pestos or sauces.

Brussels Sprout, Apple, and Apricot Slaw with Beer Vinaigrette

Healthy fats • High fibre • Vegetarian

Serves 4

They say you can't make friends with salad, but I've figured out how—beer! No, this isn't a frat party prank, this is ice-cold hard fact. Trust me, I have a lot of friends. Beer makes a damn good vinaigrette that not only tastes really really awesome but is amazingly good for you, too. Like wine, beer packs over fifty heart-healthy antioxidants, and studies suggest it may help reduce the risk of heart disease when consumed in moderation (that is, one or two beers a day, not a Saturday night bender). My go-to brew gets tossed with salty cheese, pungent Brussels sprouts, crunchy apple, and sweet apricots to yield a salad you'll be proud to serve. So go ahead, crack open a cold one, and share your favourite liquid sidekick with your greens.

Beer Vinaigrette

¼ cup (60 mL) light fruity beer (see Tip)
¼ cup (60 mL) fresh lemon juice
4 teaspoons (20 mL) pure liquid honey
¼ cup (60 mL) virgin or light olive oil
Sea salt

Brussels Sprout, Apple, and Apricot Slaw

1¼ pounds (565 g) Brussels sprouts, trimmed
1 small bulb fennel, trimmed
1 large Granny Smith apple
8 dried apricots, finely minced
Sea salt
⅓ cup (75 mL) sliced unsalted natural almonds, toasted, for garnish
¼ to ½ cup (60 to 125 mL) finely grated Parmigiano-Reggiano cheese, for garnish

1. **Make the Beer Vinaigrette** In a small bowl, stir together the beer, lemon juice, and honey. Whisking constantly, add in the olive oil until combined and season with salt to taste.

2. **Make the Brussels Sprout, Apple, and Apricot Slaw** Using a mandoline, finely shred the Brussels sprouts, fennel, and apple into a large bowl. Mix in the apricots and season with a pinch of salt.

3. Add the Beer Vinaigrette to the slaw and gently massage the Brussels sprout greens to coax more flavour into each bite. Garnish with the almonds and Parmesan, and enjoy at room temperature.

ABBEY'S TIP Notice the recipe only calls for ¼ cup (60 mL) of beer—that was intentional, of course. So please don't cook with beer you wouldn't drink because the flavour in the beer will influence the flavour of the dressing. In this recipe, I like a light, fruity Belgian white ale or saison, but if you like a bit more spice, a tripel works nicely with Brussels sprouts, too.

Roasted Za'atar Radishes with Feta Pea Purée

Gluten-free • Healthy fats • High fibre • No added sugar • Vegetarian

Serves 4

For most of culinary history, radishes have been added to salads as that token red thing or been carved into decorative "roses" on the crudité platters at Chinese buffets. But thanks to trendy chefs and their Instagram accounts, this spring staple is now Kale 2.0. Crunchy, peppery, and piquant when fresh, these cruciferous babes take on a mildly sweet taste when roasted in a scorching oven. And with a healthy dose of fibre, antioxidants, and anticancer compounds, they're no slouch in the nutrition department either. Seasoned with some citrusy za'atar, then plunked onto a purée of sweet peas, these radishes deserve their own social media account.

Roasted Za'atar Radishes

3 cups (750 mL) trimmed and halved (or quartered, depending on the size) red radishes

4½ teaspoons (22 mL) extra-virgin olive oil

1½ teaspoons (7 mL) za'atar

1 teaspoon (5 mL) lemon zest

Pinch each of kosher salt and cracked black pepper

Feta Pea Purée

1 teaspoon (5 mL) extra-virgin olive oil

1 small clove garlic, minced

1 small shallot, minced

1½ cups (375 mL) frozen or fresh green peas

½ cup (125 mL) low-sodium vegetable stock (gluten-free, if required)

2 tablespoons (30 mL) crumbled Greek feta cheese

1 tablespoon (15 mL) plain 4% Greek yogurt

1½ teaspoons (7 mL) chopped fresh mint

1 teaspoon (5 mL) lemon zest

Kosher salt and cracked black pepper

Garnish

¼ cup (60 mL) thawed frozen or cooked fresh green peas

2 tablespoons (30 mL) pine nuts, toasted

2 tablespoons (30 mL) golden raisins

2 tablespoons (30 mL) thinly sliced fresh mint

3 tablespoons (45 mL) crumbled Greek feta cheese

Pinch of sumac or more za'atar

Pinch of fleur de sel

1. Place a baking sheet in the oven and preheat the oven to 450°F (230°C).

2. **Make the Roasted Za'atar Radishes** In a medium bowl, toss the radishes in the olive oil. Place the radishes cut side down on the heated baking sheet and roast for 18 minutes, or until crisp-tender, turning once about halfway through. Remove from the oven and immediately sprinkle with za'atar, lemon zest, salt, and pepper. Set aside.

3. **Make the Feta Pea Purée** Meanwhile, in a large nonstick skillet, heat the olive oil over medium heat. Add the garlic and shallots and cook, stirring often, until they're soft and aromatic, about 5 minutes. Stir in the peas and vegetable stock and bring to a simmer over medium-high heat. Reduce the heat to medium-low, cover with the lid, and cook until the peas are tender but still green, 3 to 4 minutes for frozen peas and 5 to 7 minutes for fresh peas.

4. Transfer the pea mixture to a blender or food processor and add the feta, yogurt, mint, lemon zest, and salt and pepper to taste. Blend until very smooth.

5. To serve, smear the Feta Pea Purée on a platter or plate and pile the radishes on top. Garnish with fresh peas, pine nuts, raisins, mint, feta, sumac, and fleur de sel. Serve at room temperature.

ABBEY'S TIP Za'atar is a Middle Eastern seasoning blend with an irresistible fresh, nutty, and lemony flavour. You can often find it in the spice section of major grocers, but you can also easily whip it up yourself with equal parts dried thyme, dried sumac, and toasted sesame seeds. Make a big batch to add a burst of flavour to bread, fish, meat, fish, and vegetables.

Balsamic Roasted Brussels Sprouts, Grapes, and Figs

Dairy-free • Gluten-free • Healthy fats • No added sugar • Vegan • Vegetarian

Serves 4

Brussels sprouts, which used to occupy the outskirts of your dinner plate, are now officially the hottest vegetable to eat. Not only are they loaded with fibre, antioxidants, and heart-healthy potassium, but as a member of the cruciferous family, they pack a serious anticancer punch. If you're still warming up to them, consider this an essential step on your way to permanent Brussels sprout bliss. Ripe, jammy figs and juicy, shrivelled grapes add natural sweetness to caramelize the sprouts, yielding a sweet, tangy, crispy vegetable side. Forget the outskirts of the plate: you'll want these gems covering the entire thing.

2 cups (500 mL) trimmed and halved Brussels sprouts

1 cup (250 mL) seedless red grapes

4 fresh figs, halved

1 teaspoon (5 mL) fresh thyme leaves

4½ teaspoons (22 mL) extra-virgin olive oil

Sea salt and cracked black pepper

1 tablespoon (15 mL) aged balsamic vinegar

¼ cup (60 mL) coarsely chopped toasted pecans

1. Preheat the oven to 400°F (200°C). Line a baking sheet with parchment paper or a silicone baking mat.

2. In a medium bowl, combine the Brussels sprouts, grapes, figs, thyme, and olive oil. Toss to coat. Spread the mixture evenly on the baking sheet and sprinkle with a generous pinch each of salt and pepper.

3. Roast until evenly caramelized, 20 to 25 minutes, tossing and turning the Brussels sprouts and grapes at least once. The sprouts should look well browned, and the grapes and figs should be slightly shrivelled and bursting with juice. Remove from the oven and drizzle with the balsamic vinegar.

4. Transfer to a platter and garnish with the toasted pecans. Serve warm.

ABBEY'S TIP These Brussels sprouts make a beautiful holiday side dish that can easily be doubled and made ahead of time. Simply roast until caramelized, let cool, and refrigerate for up to 2 days. When ready to eat, pop them back in a preheated 350°F (180°C) oven for 10 minutes until warm, drizzle with the balsamic vinegar, and top with pecans right before serving.

Spicy Honey Lime Blistered Shishitos with Sesame Panko Crunch

Dairy-free • Nut-free • Vegetarian

Serves 4

Shishito peppers are nature's potato chips. I bet you can't eat just one. And what would be the fun in that, anyway? When thrown into a searing-hot skillet, these addictive, hand-held noms get a smoky, delicate flavour and a strangely satisfying wrinkled skin that become purely perfect with a light sprinkle of salt. But be warned: eating shishitos can be like playing a game of Russian roulette. Most are mild and sweet, but one in every ten peppers requires a milk chaser and possibly an antacid. Good luck!

Sesame Panko Crunch
1 teaspoon (5 mL) extra-virgin olive oil
2 tablespoons (30 mL) whole wheat panko breadcrumbs
2 tablespoons (30 mL) sesame seeds

Spicy Honey Lime Blistered Shishitos
1 tablespoon (15 mL) pure liquid honey
2 teaspoons (10 mL) fresh lime juice
1 teaspoon (5 mL) Sriracha
1 tablespoon (15 mL) extra-virgin olive oil
4 cups (1 L) shishito peppers
Maldon salt or fleur de sel

1. **Make the Sesame Panko Crunch** In a large cast-iron skillet, heat the olive oil over medium heat. Add the panko and sesame seeds and toast, stirring frequently, until slightly golden brown, 3 to 5 minutes. Transfer to a small bowl and set aside.

2. **Make the Spicy Honey Lime Blistered Shishitos** In another small bowl, stir together the honey, lime juice, and Sriracha; set aside.

3. Add the olive oil to the skillet and heat over medium-high heat. Add the shishitos and cook, tossing frequently, until tender and blistered, 3 to 4 minutes.

4. Pour the honey-lime mixture over the shishitos in the skillet and cook, tossing, just until they're coated in the sticky goodness. Quickly transfer the peppers to a serving platter.

5. Sprinkle with the Sesame Panko Crunch and a generous pinch of salt and serve.

ABBEY'S TIP Loaded with vitamins C, K, and B6, shishito peppers make getting your vegetables a delicious game. If you're risk averse, or just want to "win" a round, try sticking to the smaller peppers, which some believe are too young to develop heat. If you can't find shishito peppers, Spanish padrón peppers are very similar.

Charred Green Beans with Thai Peanut Sauce and Sriracha

Dairy-free • Gluten-free • Healthy fats • High fibre

Serves 6

Green bean haters, let's get real. If you've only ever had green beans (a) out of a can and doused with fake butter in the hot lunch line at school or (b) smothered in goopy soup at your great aunt's holiday affair, you've been doing it all wrong. Peanut sauce makes everything better. It's the life hack we were using well before life hacks were cool. When we were picky kids, my mom knew that throwing a little of the "awesome sauce" on dinner was always a weeknight win. Update: this hack works equally well on grown-ups. Bright, green, and snappy, my bean babies are charred in a screaming-hot pan, draped in a blanket of sweet and salty peanut sauce, and drizzled with fiery Sriracha. A perfect sidekick to my Veggie Noodle Pad Thai (page 71), this is peanut sauce for the win!

Thai Peanut Sauce

⅓ cup (75 mL) natural peanut butter

½ cup (125 mL) light coconut milk

2 tablespoons (30 mL) fresh lime juice

1 tablespoon (15 mL) coconut sugar

1 teaspoon (5 mL) low-sodium tamari (gluten-free, if required)

1 teaspoon (5 mL) fish sauce (gluten-free, if required)

Charred Green Beans

1 tablespoon (15 mL) virgin coconut oil

1½ pounds (675 g) green beans, trimmed

Sea salt

Sriracha, for drizzling (optional)

¼ cup (60 mL) unsalted natural peanuts, chopped, for garnish

Fresh cilantro leaves, for garnish

1. **Make the Thai Peanut Sauce** In a small saucepan, combine the peanut butter, coconut milk, lime juice, coconut sugar, tamari, and fish sauce. Bring to a simmer over medium-low heat. Simmer and stir until warm and smooth.

2. **Make the Charred Green Beans** Meanwhile, heat a cast-iron skillet over high heat. Add the coconut oil. Add the green beans and cook, turning occasionally, until they're lightly blistered and charred but remain crisp-tender, about 6 minutes. Transfer to a serving platter and season with a pinch of salt.

3. To serve, drizzle the Thai Peanut Sauce over the beans, top with a squirt of Sriracha (if using), and sprinkle with peanuts and cilantro leaves.

ABBEY'S TIP Fish sauce is a staple in Thai dishes, giving that funky, salty, umami-rich flavour that balances the sweet, sour, and spicy sauces. It's almost always gluten-free, but some brands add wheat to their recipe, so double-check the ingredients if gluten is a concern. To make this vegetarian or vegan, replace the fish sauce with an extra ½ teaspoon (2 mL) tamari and ½ teaspoon (2 mL) miso paste. Either way, you can easily double or triple this sauce and store it in the fridge for up to a week. It's delicious on meats, raw veggies, tofu, or you know, by the spoon.

Grilled Peaches with Jalapeño, Walnuts, and Blue Cheese

Gluten-free • Healthy fats • Vegetarian

Serves 4

Drinking and grilling. It's a simple combination that makes summers at the cottage worth the hassle of traffic. As soon as I arrive, I get into my swimsuit, fire up the barbecue, and relax with a batch of Summer Stone Fruit Sparkling Sangria (page 188). Pro tip: Save some of that succulent stone fruit for the grill. Sweet peaches are embellished by a smouldering kiss of the hot grill, before spicy jalapeños, pungent blue cheese, and crunchy walnuts join in the fun. For the best effect, I recommend pairing this with a slight daytime buzz.

4 freestone peaches, pitted, each sliced into 8 wedges
½ lime
Extra-virgin olive oil in an oil atomizer
½ small jalapeño pepper, seeded and sliced into
16 paper-thin rings

¼ cup (60 mL) coarsely chopped toasted natural walnuts
3 tablespoons (45 mL) crumbled blue cheese
4½ teaspoons (22 mL) extra-virgin olive oil
2 teaspoons (10 mL) pure liquid honey
Fleur de sel

1. Prepare a grill for direct cooking over medium-high heat.

2. Lightly spritz the peaches and the cut side of the lime with olive oil in an oil atomizer and place directly over the flames. Grill each side of the peach wedges and the cut side of the lime until they caramelize and get some rich grill marks, 2 to 3 minutes per side.

3. Transfer the peaches to a platter and garnish with jalapeños, walnuts, and blue cheese. Squeeze the grilled lime over the fruit (using an oven mitt if it's still hot), drizzle with the olive oil and honey, and sprinkle with a generous few pinches of fleur de sel.

ABBEY'S TIP There's nothing quite like biting into a fresh summer peach and suckling on its sweet, sticky juices as they try to escape down your chin. But when you're at a summer barbecue, rocking a white linen dress, chatting up a cute friend of a friend, the snacking goes from hot to not pretty quick. All peaches pack cancer-fighting and heart-healthy antioxidants, but I prefer using freestone peaches that separate easily from their pits and slice up nicely without any juicy drama.

Honey Caraway Carrots with Lemon Parsley Sauce

Gluten-free • Nut-free • Vegetarian

Serves 4

I have nothing but love for a vegetable that's sweet like candy and crunchy like chips. When in doubt on the vegetable front, carrots always check out. Upgrading this universal favourite, my carrots get glazed in a sticky-sweet honey butter and scented with nutty caraway reminiscent of a cozy Jewish bakery. Served atop a protein-rich yogurt sauce speckled with citrusy lemon and bright greens, this snacking staple is transformed into an impressive crowd-pleasing side. If you manage not to inhale the entire bunch before they hit the plate, round out the sweet and sticky meal with my Orange Honey Salmon with Pistachio, Olive, and Herb Relish (page 107).

Honey Caraway Carrots

1 pound (450 g) thin multicoloured carrots with
   their greens
1 tablespoon (15 mL) + ½ teaspoon (2 mL)
   extra-virgin olive oil, divided
1 tablespoon (15 mL) unsalted butter, melted
1 teaspoon (5 mL) ground cumin
4 large cloves garlic, peeled and smashed
Sea salt
1 tablespoon (15 mL) pure liquid honey
½ teaspoon (2 mL) caraway seeds
Fleur de sel

Lemon Parsley Sauce

¼ cup (60 mL) plain 2% Greek yogurt
2 tablespoons (30 mL) coarsely chopped fresh
   flat-leaf parsley
4½ teaspoons (22 mL) fresh lemon juice
Sea salt and cracked black pepper

1. Preheat the oven to 425°F (220°C).

2. **Make the Honey Caraway Carrots** Trim the carrot greens, leaving ½ inch (1 cm) intact, and peel the carrots. If the carrots aren't already ½ inch (1 cm) wide, halve or quarter them accordingly.

3. Combine the carrots with 1 tablespoon (15 mL) olive oil, butter, and cumin in a 13- x 9-inch (3 L) baking dish or baking sheet. Toss to ensure the carrots are well coated, and spread them out in a single layer.

4. Place the garlic pieces on a small piece of foil, drizzle with the remaining ½ teaspoon (2 mL) olive oil, and add a small pinch of sea salt. Close up the foil into a little parcel (or scrunch it into a ball) and place in the corner of the baking dish. Roast the carrots and garlic for 20 to 23 minutes, or until a fork inserted into the middle of a carrot meets a little bit of resistance.

5. Drizzle the carrots with honey and sprinkle with the caraway seeds. Return to the oven and roast for an additional 5 to 7 minutes, or until the carrots are tender and lightly caramelized. Sprinkle with fleur de sel and keep warm.

continues

6. **Make the Lemon Parsley Sauce** Unwrap your garlic parcel and squeeze the garlic into a small food processor or blender. Add the yogurt, parsley, lemon juice, and sea salt and pepper to taste. Process until smooth.

7. To serve, smear the Lemon Parsley Sauce on a serving platter and scatter the carrots on top. Finish with a generous pinch of fleur de sel.

ABBEY'S TIP I love crunchy raw carrots as a vehicle for getting hummus (like my Sriracha Peanut Hummus, page 179) into my mouth, but cooking them actually gives them a nutritional edge. Carrots are one of the best sources of beta-carotene, the eye-supporting nutrient that is enhanced more than sixfold when cooked. I like using really pretty colourful heirloom carrots here with a little of their greens intact for show, but you can easily use bagged whole or baby carrots without compromising flavour. These carrots can be roasted and the sauce made and refrigerated up to 2 days ahead. When ready to serve, simply pop the carrots into a 350°F (180°C) oven until warm.

Sunchoke and Pear Soup with Caramelized Shallots and Pepitas

Gluten-free • Healthy fats • High fibre • Nut-free • Vegetarian

Serves 6

I won my first cooking competition with a creamy sunchoke soup when I was seventeen. Sure, it was a tasty soup, but I didn't need to be an Iron Chef to figure out that cream and butter held together by a few vegetables pretty much always tastes good. Although I still love a good cream-based bowl of comfort, these days my palate craves balance. This updated version celebrates the natural sweetness of this nutty tuber with earthy parsnips, sweet pears, and aromatic thyme. Instead of overdosing on the heavy cream and butter, a modest cup of evaporated milk lends a toasty flavour and satisfying body without smothering the delicate vegetable. Whether you're serving this at a fancy dinner party, a casual weeknight meal, or even your own cutthroat competition, this soup is a winner every time.

Sunchoke and Pear Soup

1 tablespoon (15 mL) unsalted butter

1 tablespoon (15 mL) extra-virgin olive oil

1 leek (white and pale green parts only), sliced

1 clove garlic, minced

2 red pears, peeled, cored, and diced

4 cups (1 L) peeled and finely diced sunchokes
   (about 1 pound/450 g; see Tip)

1 cup (250 mL) peeled and finely diced parsnips
   (about 2 large)

2 teaspoons (10 mL) fresh thyme leaves

6 cups (1.5 L) low-sodium vegetable stock
   (gluten-free, if required)

1 cup (250 mL) 2% evaporated milk

2 teaspoons (10 mL) pure maple syrup, or to taste

½ teaspoon (2 mL) cinnamon

¼ teaspoon (1 mL) nutmeg

Sea salt and cracked black pepper

Caramelized Shallots

1 tablespoon (15 mL) unsalted butter

3 shallots, thinly sliced

Sea salt

Garnish

⅓ cup (75 mL) pepitas, toasted

½ red pear, sliced into thin matchsticks

Fresh thyme sprigs

Extra-virgin olive oil, for drizzling

1. **Make the Sunchoke and Pear Soup** Melt the butter with the olive oil in a large saucepan over medium heat. Add the leek and cook until it begins to sweat, about 5 minutes. Then add the garlic and cook, stirring, until fragrant, about another 30 seconds. Stir in the pears, sunchokes, parsnips, and thyme and cook, stirring often, until the vegetables begin to very lightly caramelize, about 7 minutes. Add the vegetable stock, cover with a lid, and simmer for 30 to 35 minutes, or until the vegetables fall apart when pricked with a fork and the liquid has slightly reduced. Stir in the evaporated milk, maple syrup, cinnamon, and nutmeg.

2. Working in batches if necessary, transfer to a high-speed blender and blend until silky smooth. Season with salt and pepper. Keep warm until ready to serve.

continues

3. **Make the Caramelized Shallots** While the soup cooks, in a small nonstick skillet, melt the butter over medium heat. Add the shallots and a pinch of salt, and toss to coat. Cook, stirring occasionally, until the shallots have wilted down a bit, then reduce the heat to medium-low and cook slowly, stirring occasionally, until caramelized, 15 to 20 minutes.

4. To serve, top the soup with a spoonful of Caramelized Shallots, some pepitas, pear, a sprig of thyme, and a drizzle of olive oil.

ABBEY'S TIP Resembling a knobby cross between a potato and ginger root, sunchokes (also known as Jerusalem artichokes) might never win a beauty competition, but they rake up the gold with their sweet, nutty flavour and impressive nutrient dossier. Affectionately nicknamed "fartchokes," these little tubers are one of the best sources of inulin fibre, a prebiotic that helps nourish our healthy gut bacteria. Sunchoke virgins may experience gas if they get a little overzealous their first time, but blending them with other vegetables in this soup minimizes this effect. When peeling your sunchokes, place them in a bowl of water with a touch of acid (like vinegar or lemon juice) to prevent discoloration. And don't worry about removing every bit of peel—if you use a high-speed blender, those bits will melt into the creamy soup.

Smoked Paprika Chicken and Apricot Mason Jar Soup

Dairy-free • Gluten-free • High fibre • High protein • No added sugar • Nut-free

Serves 4

You may remember the crunchy, MSG-laden flavour of dry Mr. Noodles popular in the '90s. While I can't deny that salt on carbs always tastes good, now that my poor-student days are behind me and I've got respectable work lunches to pack, I've come up with a more nutritionally satisfying swap. My simple on-the-go soup is perfect for using your weeknight leftovers and keeps its delicious fresh consistency. Smoky cumin, spicy paprika, and bright cinnamon add a kick of Middle Eastern spice, while the chewy, sweet apricots revitalize pantry-staple chickpeas and tomatoes. A little hot water is all you need for a nourishing and warming soup, but even raw (yes, that means salad), this combo makes for an office-enviable choice. Talk about an adult upgrade from dorm-room dinner!

4 Roma tomatoes, seeded and finely diced

12 dried apricots, finely minced

2 cups (500 mL) shredded carrots

1 can (19 ounces/540 mL) chickpeas, drained and rinsed

8 ounces (225 g) rotisserie or cooked chicken breast, skin and bones removed, meat shredded

6 cups (1.5 L) loosely packed baby spinach

2 teaspoons (10 mL) ground cumin

2 teaspoons (10 mL) sweet smoked paprika

1 teaspoon (5 mL) cinnamon

Cayenne pepper

2 tablespoons (30 mL) fresh lemon juice, more to taste

2 tablespoons (30 mL) vegetable or chicken bouillon paste

Sea salt and cracked black pepper

1. Place 4 clean 1-quart (1 L) mason jars on a work surface.

2. To each jar add a quarter of the tomato, a quarter of the apricots, ½ cup (125 mL) carrots, ½ cup (125 mL) chickpeas, 2 ounces (55 g) chicken breast, 1½ cups (375 mL) spinach, ½ teaspoon (2 mL) cumin, ½ teaspoon (2 mL) paprika, ¼ teaspoon (1 mL) cinnamon, a pinch of cayenne, 1½ teaspoons (7 mL) lemon juice, and 1½ teaspoons (7 mL) bouillon paste. Cover with a lid and refrigerate until ready to eat, up to 2 days in advance.

3. When ready to serve, boil 2 cups (500 mL) water per mason jar and pour over the soup mixture, leaving 1 inch (2.5 cm) headspace. Close the lid tightly, and holding with a towel (just to prevent any hot drips!), shake until well mixed and the spinach has just wilted, about 5 minutes. Season with salt and pepper and eat straight out of the mason jar.

ABBEY'S TIP This recipe was inspired by the $12 I spent at a trendy salad shop where they literally just poured hot chicken stock over my choice of vegetables. It was tasty, but I could have bought a dozen boxes of instant noodles for that kind of dough! Use this recipe as the inspiration for your own cheap-and-cheerful instant soups. This is my personal favourite combination, but feel free to throw in whatever vegetables, proteins, or grains you have on hand.

Chocolate Stout Veggie Chili

Dairy-free • High fibre • High protein • Nut-free • Vegan • Vegetarian

Serves 6 to 8

Rich, meaty, and warming to the bone, chili is feel-good food for cold Canadian days, especially when the hockey game is on. My version skips the meat and builds layers of hearty flavours in its place, but even the burliest men won't mind. Trust me on that. Nutrient-rich, earthy mushrooms get minced to a ground meat–like consistency and mingle with smoky chipotle peppers, bittersweet cocoa, warming cinnamon, and malty beer. And with a trio of satisfying beans, you clock more than half of your daily fibre needs in one bowl! Research suggests that consuming pulses like beans can significantly lower bad LDL cholesterol, reducing the risk of heart attack or stroke by as much as 6 percent.

8 ounces (225 g) cremini mushrooms, stemmed and quartered

1 tablespoon (15 mL) extra-virgin olive oil

½ yellow onion, diced

2 stalks celery, finely diced

2 red, orange, or yellow bell peppers, diced

4 cloves garlic, minced

1 to 2 chipotle peppers in adobo sauce (depending on how spicy you like it), minced

1½ teaspoons (7 mL) unsweetened cocoa powder, sifted

1½ teaspoons (7 mL) ground cumin

1 teaspoon (5 mL) chili powder (more if you like it hot)

1 teaspoon (5 mL) cinnamon

1 can (19 ounces/540 mL) red kidney beans, drained and rinsed

1 can (19 ounces/540 mL) black beans, drained and rinsed

1 can (19 ounces/540 mL) white beans, drained and rinsed

1 can (28 ounces/796 mL) diced tomatoes, drained

1 bottle (12 ounces/341 mL) stout beer

2 tablespoons (30 mL) low-sodium soy sauce

1 tablespoon + 2 teaspoons (25 mL) fresh lime juice

4½ teaspoons (22 mL) pure maple syrup

Sea salt

Garnish

Fresh cilantro leaves

Thinly sliced radish

1 avocado, pitted, peeled, and diced

Lime wedges

1. In a food processor, pulse the mushrooms until they reach the consistency of ground meat.

2. In a large skillet, heat the olive oil over medium heat. Add the onions and celery and cook, stirring from time to time, until they are soft and translucent, about 7 minutes. Add the bell peppers, garlic, and mushrooms and cook for another 2 to 3 minutes.

3. Stir in the chipotle with any adobo sauce, along with the cocoa powder, cumin, chili powder, and cinnamon. Stir until the vegetables are well coated in the spices and super fragrant.

4. Add the kidney beans, black beans, white beans, tomatoes, beer, soy sauce, lime juice, and maple syrup. Reduce the heat to low and simmer, uncovered, for 45 minutes, or until the chili thickens and the flavours marry. Season with salt.

5. Using a hand blender or a regular blender, purée a little less than half of the chili. Stir the puréed half back into the chunky half. Reheat if needed, then ladle into bowls and garnish with cilantro, radishes, avocado, and lime wedges.

ABBEY'S TIP Pulses like beans contain an indigestible carbohydrate that is notorious for causing gas, but eating them more often allows your gut to adapt and quells the effect. To help cut back on the immediate discomfort in the meantime, always make sure to rinse your canned beans thoroughly to help eliminate some of the offending substances.

3 P.M. Fix

Pumpkin Pecan Pie Energy Bites

Dairy-free • Gluten-free • Healthy fats • High fibre • No added sugar • Vegan • Vegetarian

Makes 32 bites

My family aren't bakers, so during the holidays I'm always responsible for the pie. And while it would probably break my mom's heart not to serve traditional pumpkin, I have an affinity for a good gooey, crunchy pecan tart myself. Rather than instigate a sugar-fuelled feud around the holiday table, my solution is to combine the two and enjoy my favourite festive flavours all year round. These tasty little bites may taste like dessert, but they're life savers when you're deciding between stale cookies and stealing a co-worker's snack to fill that 3 p.m. void. Fibre-rich quinoa, flax, and sweet pumpkin will keep the hunger monster at bay, and an energy boost from dates and cranberries will keep you going. You'll even get a hit of heart-healthy fats from crushed pecans. This winning combination makes getting through that last hump of the day a piece of cake (or pie, in this case). And that's something I'm thankful for.

1¼ cups (300 mL) Medjool dates, pitted and coarsely chopped (10 to 12 dates)

1¾ cups (425 mL) coarsely chopped toasted pecans

¼ cup (60 mL) dried cranberries

1¼ cups (300 mL) cooked quinoa (any colour), cooled

6 tablespoons (90 mL) pure pumpkin purée

1 tablespoon (15 mL) ground flaxseed

1 teaspoon (5 mL) pumpkin pie spice

1 teaspoon (5 mL) pure vanilla extract

¼ teaspoon (1 mL) sea salt

½ cup (125 mL) minced toasted pecans, to garnish (optional)

1. In a food processor, process the dates until they turn into a big sticky ball. Break up the ball with your fingers. Add the coarsely chopped pecans and cranberries. Pulse until the cranberries and pecans are incorporated into the dates and the pecans are in very fine shards, but don't over-blend and let them turn into nut butter—you want a little texture.

2. Add the quinoa, pumpkin purée, flaxseed, pumpkin pie spice, vanilla, and salt, then pulse about 5 times, until everything is well combined. Refrigerate the mixture for 10 minutes to make it easier to roll.

3. Using about 2 tablespoons (30 mL) of the mixture at a time, roll between your hands into balls. If the mixture starts to stick, cool your hands with a little water.

4. Sprinkle or roll the energy bites in toasted pecans (if using).

ABBEY'S TIP Unless you're really hungry (or feeding a lot of calorie-torching kids), you're probably not going to eat these all at once. So freeze the energy bites on a baking sheet lined with parchment paper for 1 hour, then transfer them to a large resealable freezer bag for up to 6 months. Pull a few out each morning, give them an hour to thaw out in a baggie, and pop a few in your mouth when you need a hit of energy.

Peaches and Cream Quinoa Bites with Brown Sugar Crackle Glaze

Gluten-free • Vegetarian

Makes 24 bites

Peaches and cream was one of the first treats I learned how to make myself as a kid. By kindergarten, I had nailed the perfect peach to cream ratio (as in, fill mouth with aerosol can cream and pop a peach slice in), and by grade three, I had a massive left bicep from manual whipping labour. I've maybe come a long way in the kitchen, but my affinity for this classic combination endures. Sweet peaches and creamy yogurt mingle with fibre-rich almond flour, oats, and quinoa, finished with an omega-3-loaded sweet, crackly flax glaze. Slightly more impressive than my kindergarten signature dish, but undoubtedly more delicious.

Peaches and Cream Quinoa Bites

1¼ cups (300 mL) quick-cooking rolled oats (gluten-free, if required)

1 cup (250 mL) almond flour

½ cup (125 mL) cooked red or multicoloured quinoa, cooled

3 tablespoons (45 mL) brown rice flour

1 teaspoon (5 mL) cinnamon

½ teaspoon (2 mL) nutmeg

½ teaspoon (2 mL) baking powder (gluten-free, if required)

½ teaspoon (2 mL) baking soda

½ teaspoon (2 mL) salt

1 large egg

¼ cup (60 mL) packed light brown sugar

2 tablespoons (30 mL) unsalted butter, melted

½ cup (125 mL) plain 2% Greek yogurt

1 tablespoon (15 mL) pure vanilla extract

2 teaspoons (10 mL) orange zest

1½ cups (375 mL) very finely diced ripe peaches

Brown Sugar Crackle Glaze

3 tablespoons (45 mL) brown sugar

1 tablespoon (15 mL) ground flaxseed

¼ teaspoon (1 mL) cinnamon

2 tablespoons (30 mL) unsalted butter, melted

1. Preheat the oven to 350°F (180°C). Lightly grease 24 mini muffin cups.

2. **Make the Peaches and Cream Quinoa Bites** In a large bowl, combine the oats, almond flour, quinoa, rice flour, cinnamon, nutmeg, baking powder, baking soda, and salt.

3. In a medium bowl, lightly beat the egg. Stir in the brown sugar, butter, yogurt, vanilla, and orange zest. Add the wet ingredients to the dry and mix until combined. Carefully fold in the peaches.

4. **Make the Brown Sugar Crackle Glaze** In a small bowl, stir together the brown sugar, flaxseed, cinnamon, and butter.

5. Fill 24 mini muffin cups with the batter, and brush generously with the glaze.

6. Bake for 15 to 18 minutes until golden brown on top and around the edges. Let cool slightly in the tin before carefully removing. Serve warm, or cool completely, then pop into a resealable freezer bag and store in the freezer for up to 3 months. Thaw and enjoy at room temperature.

ABBEY'S TIP Once a coveted hipster health-food secret, quinoa is now a readily available whole grain that's considered a "complete" vegetarian protein. In other words, unlike rice, beans, or nuts, it has all the essential amino acids our bodies need in each tiny grain. I always whip up a huge batch at the start of the week by bringing 1 cup (250 mL) rinsed quinoa to a boil with 2 cups (500 mL) water and ½ teaspoon (2 mL) salt. Cover, lower the heat to medium-low, and simmer for 15 minutes, until fluffy and tender. It's delicious in everything from these mini muffins to my Charred Broccoli, Quinoa, and Hazelnut Crunch Salad (page 126).

Edamame Mango Brown Rice Energy Balls

Dairy-free • Gluten-free • Healthy fats • No added sugar • Vegan • Vegetarian

Makes 16 energy balls

I love energy bites, but sometimes I need to switch things up on those days when I have a hankering for something more salty than sweet. I came up with these when I was attempting to make triangular onigiri, but the perfectionist in me was struggling to form precise equilateral triangles. Gah! Making snacks shouldn't require a mathematical degree! And that's why I've decided that balls are always best. These tangy, spicy, savoury, and nutty bites are so delicious right out of the mixing bowl, there's no need to obsess over shape. Packed with energizing carbs from brown rice, protein from edamame, and a dose of healthy fats from nuts and seeds, these balls are all the perfection you need.

¼ cup (60 mL) minced dried mango

¼ cup (60 mL) filtered water, room temperature

1 cup (250 mL) cooked brown sticky rice (sushi rice)

½ cup (125 mL) minced shelled edamame

¼ cup (60 mL) natural cashew butter, room temperature

4 teaspoons (20 mL) white miso paste

2 teaspoons (10 mL) Sriracha, more to taste

1 teaspoon (5 mL) toasted sesame oil

Sea salt and cracked black pepper

3 tablespoons (45 mL) black sesame seeds

3 tablespoons (45 mL) white sesame seeds, toasted

1 sheet nori seaweed, crushed (optional)

1. In a small ramekin, combine the mango and water and let soak for 15 minutes, or until softened. If your mango is already very soft and pliable, you can skip this step, but I find most dried mango very, well, dry. Drain.

2. In a large bowl, combine the softened mango, rice, edamame, cashew butter, miso, Sriracha, and sesame oil. Mix well, then season with salt and pepper, if desired. Refrigerate for 1 hour to make it super easy to roll.

3. Roll the mixture into 16 balls, about 2 tablespoons (30 mL) each. Combine the black and white sesame seeds in a small bowl and give the balls a gentle toss to coat. Garnish with nori, if using.

ABBEY'S TIP These energy balls will last for about 5 days in the fridge, but I prefer to freeze them for up to 6 months. Simply arrange the balls in rows on a baking sheet lined with parchment paper and freeze for 1 hour or until solid, then transfer them to a resealable freezer bag. If you pull them out of the freezer in the morning, by the time you get to work or the gym and need a little nosh, they're thawed and ready to eat.

Lemon Poppy Seed Yogurt Cookie Cups

Healthy fats • Vegetarian

Makes 24 mini cookie cups

When I was a kid, I used to envy American children when I saw commercials for Cookie Crisp cereal that my mom said wasn't sold in Canada. Not that she would have let us have it if it was available here. Thankfully, now that I'm an adult and can make my own life decisions, I can and will eat all the cookies any time of day. My cute cookie cups are packed with natural sweetness from ripe banana and dates, plus an extra hit of fibre from the almond butter, bran buds cereal, oats, and flaxseed. Filled to the brim with yogurt laced with lemon and poppy seeds and crowned with fresh berries, they easily trump any of my childhood whims.

Cookie Cups

¼ cup (60 mL) Medjool dates, pitted and minced
   (2 to 3 dates)
⅓ cup (75 mL) natural almond butter
¼ cup (60 mL) mashed very ripe banana
¼ cup (60 mL) virgin coconut oil, melted
2 tablespoons (30 mL) pure liquid honey
1 teaspoon (5 mL) pure vanilla extract
1¼ cups (300 mL) old-fashioned rolled oats
1 cup (250 mL) high-fibre bran buds cereal
2 tablespoons (30 mL) ground flaxseed
2 teaspoons (10 mL) lemon zest

1 teaspoon (5 mL) poppy seeds
1 teaspoon (5 mL) cinnamon
¼ teaspoon (1 mL) salt

Lemon Poppy Seed Yogurt

2 cups (500 mL) plain 4% Greek yogurt
1 tablespoon (15 mL) pure liquid honey, or to taste
4 teaspoons (20 mL) lemon zest
4 teaspoons (20 mL) fresh lemon juice
2 teaspoons (10 mL) poppy seeds
1½ cups (375 mL) fresh blueberries, for topping

1. Preheat the oven to 350°F (180°C). Lightly grease 24 mini muffin cups.

2. **Make the Cookie Cups** In a large bowl, combine the dates, almond butter, banana, coconut oil, honey, and vanilla. Mix until smooth. Add the oats, bran buds cereal, flaxseed, lemon zest, poppy seeds, cinnamon, and salt. Stir until well combined.

3. Scoop a 2-tablespoon (30 mL) ball of cookie mixture into each muffin cup and press it down to pack it in tightly. Using your thumb, carefully make an indentation in the middle of the puck and spread the mixture up the sides of the muffin cup. Bake for 10 minutes, or until the cookie cups are lightly browned around the edges. Let cool slightly before very carefully removing them from the tin and then let them cool completely on a cooling rack.

4. **Make the Lemon Poppy Seed Yogurt** In a medium bowl, combine the yogurt, honey, lemon zest, lemon juice, and poppy seeds. Stir together well.

5. To serve, add a spoonful of the Lemon Poppy Seed Yogurt to each cookie cup, and top with a few blueberries.

ABBEY'S TIP With about 40 percent of our fibre needs in a modest ⅓ cup (75 mL), crunchy little bran buds are my go-to with yogurt or milk for quickie morning meals. But they're also a nourishing base for these crunchy cups. You can easily make the cookie cups ahead and store them (without the yogurt) in an airtight container for up to 4 days or in the freezer in resealable freezer bags for up to 6 months. The yogurt mixture should keep at least until it's best before date on the container.

Chocolate Hazelnut Granola Bars

Dairy-free • Gluten-free • Healthy fats • High fibre • Vegan • Vegetarian

Makes 16 bars

We all struggle with buying meaningful holiday hostess gifts for the people on our list that we barely know. But when Facebook stalking my Secret Santa for the inspiration for their $10 gift starts to get a little too creepy, I settle on bulk-buying Ferrero Rocher. Let's be honest. That hazelnut-chocolate combination is pretty much as thoughtful as it gets. But when January rolls around—and your own holiday stash runs low—these hearty granola bars help fill the void. Chewy dates and ripe banana provide natural sweetness, while fibre-rich oats, hazelnuts, and hemp hearts give a satisfying chew. Finished with a triple threat of chocolate, they're the treats you'll never re-gift.

Chocolate Hazelnut Granola Bars
⅔ cup (150 mL) pitted and coarsely chopped Medjool dates
½ cup (125 mL) mashed very ripe banana (about 1 large banana)
⅓ cup (75 mL) pure maple syrup
¼ cup (60 mL) natural almond butter
¼ cup (60 mL) hazelnut oil
2 teaspoons (10 mL) pure vanilla extract
2 cups (500 mL) old-fashioned rolled oats (gluten-free, if required)

1 tablespoon (15 mL) unsweetened cocoa powder, sifted
½ teaspoon (2 mL) salt
½ cup (125 mL) finely chopped toasted hazelnuts
¼ cup (60 mL) cacao nibs
2 tablespoons (30 mL) hemp hearts

Chocolate Hazelnut Drizzle
¼ cup (60 mL) finely chopped 70% dark chocolate (vegan or dairy-free, if required)
¼ cup (60 mL) minced toasted hazelnuts

1. Preheat the oven to 350°F (180°C). Line a 9-inch (2.5 L) square baking dish with parchment paper, allowing excess paper to hang over each side.

2. **Make the Chocolate Hazelnut Granola Bars** In a food processor or high-speed blender, combine the dates, banana, maple syrup, almond butter, hazelnut oil, and vanilla. Process until smooth with flecks of dates still visible.

3. In a large bowl, mix together the oats, cocoa powder, and salt.

4. Stir the date mixture into the oat mixture until well combined, then stir in the hazelnuts, cacao nibs, and hemp hearts until evenly combined with crunchy bits strewn throughout. Press the mixture evenly into the baking dish. Bake for 30 to 35 minutes, or until the edges start to lightly brown. Let cool completely before removing from the dish and cutting into 16 bars.

5. **Make the Chocolate Hazelnut Drizzle** Place the chocolate in a heatproof bowl and place it over a small saucepan filled with 1 inch (2.5 cm) of water. Bring the water to a bare simmer and let the chocolate gently melt, stirring often. (*Optional microwave method: Place the chocolate in a microwave-safe dish. Melt in the microwave on 50 percent power in 30-second increments until almost fully melted. Stir once after each 30-second increment.*)

6. Using a fork, drizzle the chocolate over the bars and sprinkle with the minced hazelnuts. Allow the chocolate to set before eating or storing.

ABBEY'S TIP Not only are hazelnuts and chocolate a total dream team, but they're also nutritional superstars all in their own right. Packed with nourishing unsaturated fats, antioxidants, and folate, hazelnuts are as good for the heart as they are for the soul. Make a big batch, transfer to an airtight container, and keep in the fridge for up to 1 week or store in the freezer for up to 3 months.

Chewy Crackle Almond Apple Cookies

Gluten-free • Healthy fats • Vegetarian

Makes 16 cookies

We may all have different beliefs, but I think most people agree on a few societal values and rules. Thou shalt not kill. Thou shalt not steal. And thou shalt not eat bad cookies. I'm just waiting for an official bylaw for that last one. But honestly, I'm rarely interested in a basic store-bought chocolate chip, never mind those detox "cookies" made with vegan mushroom protein powder, organic maca root, and sun-dried kale leaves. It's a cookie, guys—even the word itself should make us smile, not gag. Forget that paleo-blood-type-alkaline-detox bunk and dig into these nourishing, nutty bites. Toasty almond crackle on the outside with chewy caramelized apple bits in the middle, these cookies are packed with the hunger-crushing combo of protein, fibre, and healthy fats. So save those chalky, detox pucks for a pickup game of hockey, these babies pass my rigorous cookie test every time.

⅓ cup (75 mL) pure maple syrup

¼ cup (60 mL) virgin coconut oil, melted

2 tablespoons (30 mL) 2% cottage cheese

2 teaspoons (10 mL) pure vanilla extract

1 cup (250 mL) freeze-dried apple, minced

1 cup (250 mL) almond flour

1 cup (250 mL) sliced unsalted natural almonds, toasted

½ cup (125 mL) old-fashioned rolled oats
  (gluten-free, if required)

2 tablespoons (30 mL) hemp hearts

2 teaspoons (10 mL) cinnamon

1 teaspoon (5 mL) nutmeg

1 teaspoon (5 mL) baking powder
  (gluten-free, if required)

1 teaspoon (5 mL) baking soda

½ teaspoon (2 mL) sea salt

1. Preheat the oven to 350°F (180°C). Line 2 baking sheets with parchment paper or silicone baking mats and position the oven racks in the top ⅓ and lower ⅓ of the oven.

2. In a small food processor, combine the maple syrup, coconut oil, cottage cheese, and vanilla. Process until smooth (little flecks of the cottage cheese are totally cool).

3. In a medium bowl, stir together the freeze-dried apples, almond flour, almonds, rolled oats, hemp hearts, cinnamon, nutmeg, baking powder, baking soda, and salt. Add the cottage cheese mixture and stir thoroughly until it forms a thick mixture.

4. Using lightly greased hands (to prevent a sticky mess), roll 2 tablespoons (30 mL) of the mixture at a time into balls and arrange them on the prepared baking sheets spaced 1 inch (2.5 cm) apart. Flatten the dough balls to about ½ inch (1 cm) thick. Bake for 10 to 12 minutes, or until they are lightly brown on top and around the edges but still feel a bit tender when you touch them on top—don't worry, they'll firm up as they cool. Let cool on the baking sheets for 10 minutes before carefully transferring them with a spatula straight to into your mouth or to a cooling rack to cool completely.

ABBEY'S TIP I'm a snacking queen, so I always keep emergency bags of natural almonds in each of my purses and bags—just ask my husband, who's being crowded out by my collection. With 6 grams of protein and 4 grams of fibre in each cookie, plus antioxidants like vitamin E, from a double whammy of sliced almonds and almond flour, these cookies are a satisfying staple in my day. While I don't imagine you'll have extras, you can store them in an airtight container for up to 5 days or freeze them in a resealable freezer bag for up to 6 months.

Peanut Butter Banana Chocolate Chip Muffins

Dairy-free • Gluten-free • Healthy fats • Vegetarian

Makes 18 to 20 muffins

I originally made these muffins for weekend snacks at the cottage to share with my gluten-free friend. A quick note to self—never travel for an extended period of time with a batch of these on my lap. They didn't stand a chance. My muffins start with the fibre-rich combination of coconut flour, oat flour, and flaxseed for a snack that stays with you all afternoon long. Sweetened with super-ripe bananas, thickened with a dollop of sticky peanut butter, and made kindred spirits with a healthy dose of chocolate, these moist morsels are a great way to make friends (if you don't polish them off first). Yeah, maybe make a double batch.

3 large eggs

2 cups (500 mL) mashed very ripe bananas
    (about 6 medium)

1 cup (250 mL) natural peanut butter, room temperature

¼ cup (60 mL) coconut sugar

¼ cup (60 mL) pure liquid honey

1 tablespoon (15 mL) pure vanilla extract

1 cup (250 mL) oat flour (see page 18 for
    DIY version; gluten-free, if required)

¼ cup (60 mL) coconut flour

2 tablespoons (30 mL) ground flaxseed

1 teaspoon (5 mL) cinnamon

1 teaspoon (5 mL) baking powder
    (gluten-free, if required)

½ teaspoon (2 mL) baking soda

½ teaspoon (2 mL) salt

¼ cup (60 mL) mini dark chocolate chips
    (dairy-free, if required)

2 bananas, thinly sliced, for topping

1. Preheat the oven to 350°F (180°C). Lightly grease 2 muffin tins. Position the baking racks in the top ⅓ and bottom ⅓ of the oven.

2. In a medium bowl, lightly beat the eggs. Add the mashed bananas, peanut butter, coconut sugar, honey, and vanilla. Stir until well combined.

3. In a large bowl, whisk together the oat flour, coconut flour, flaxseed, cinnamon, baking powder, baking soda, and salt.

4. Add the mashed banana mixture to the flour mixture and stir to combine. Stir in the chocolate chips.

5. Fill the muffin cups about three-quarters full. Top each portion with a thin slice of banana. Bake for about 20 minutes, or until lightly golden brown, rotating the muffin tins top to bottom and front to back halfway through. Let cool completely in the muffin tins on a wire rack before removing from the tins.

ABBEY'S TIP Please, do yourself a favour and resist the urge to buy "low fat" peanut butter that replaces fat with added sugar. The monounsaturated fat in regular peanut butter adds luscious mouthfeel, moisture, and richness to these little muffins, plus it packs heart-healthy benefits and that satiety factor. Make a double batch for a month of snack attacks by freezing them in resealable freezer bags for up to 4 months. You can also make these into 55 to 60 mini muffins for those days you just need a little chocolate fix; use a mini muffin tin and reduce the cooking time to about 14 minutes.

Chocolate-Dipped Banana Crunch Roll-Up Pops

Dairy-free • Healthy fats • High fibre • Vegan • Vegetarian

Makes 8 roll-up pops

I have my share of hectic days when I just can't deal with any fork-and-knife foods. Then there are days when even proper finger foods don't entertain my mood. Let's face it: life is more fun when you're eating off a stick—especially when it tastes this good. Whole-grain wraps hug sweet bananas, dark cherries, and crunchy high-fibre cereal with a smear of protein-rich almond butter. Since everything on a stick needs a good dip in something decadent, they're finished in a dark chocolate bath. No fork, no knife, and no civility required.

4 large whole-grain wraps
½ cup (125 mL) natural almond butter,
    room temperature
¼ cup (60 mL) minced dried cherries
½ cup (125 mL) high-fibre bran buds cereal
4 large bananas

Toppings
½ cup (125 mL/about 6 ounces) finely chopped
    70% dark chocolate (vegan or dairy-free, if required)
2 teaspoons (10 mL) virgin coconut oil
¼ cup (60 mL) minced pistachios
¼ cup (60 mL) unsweetened shredded coconut, toasted
3 tablespoons (45 mL) hemp hearts

1. Have ready 8 ice-pop sticks. Line a baking sheet with parchment paper or a silicone baking mat.

2. Lay the wraps on a clean surface and spread almond butter on each wrap. Sprinkle the dried cherries and cereal evenly among the wraps on top of the almond butter. Place a banana at the bottom edge of one wrap, then roll up the banana in the wrap. Repeat with the remaining wraps.

3. Cut each pop in half, then insert an ice-pop stick into the un-cut end of the banana. Place the pops on the baking sheet and freeze for 5 to 10 minutes.

4. **Make the Toppings** Meanwhile, place the chocolate and coconut oil in a heatproof bowl and place it over a small saucepan filled with 1 inch (2.5 cm) of water. Bring the water to a bare simmer and let the chocolate gently melt, stirring often. *(Optional microwave method: Place the chocolate in a microwave-safe dish. Melt in the microwave on 50 percent power in 30-second increments until almost fully melted. Stir once after each 30-second increment.)*

5. Dip the pops cut side down into the chocolate and then, without turning it upright (unless you like streaks), hold it over another bowl and sprinkle the chocolate with pistachios, coconut, and hemp hearts.

ABBEY'S TIP These roll-up pops are a great way to use up any crunchy little odds and ends you find in your pantry. Swap out the nuts, seeds, and dried fruit for whatever you have on hand. These are tastiest when they're enjoyed fresh, but they can also be frozen in resealable freezer bags for up to 1 month. Pull them out in the morning before work, and by the time that energy slump hits you, they'll be thawed and ready to be enjoyed.

Fruity Nut Fro-Yo "Cookies"

Gluten-free • Healthy fats • High protein • No added sugar • Vegetarian

Makes 8 "cookies"

Don't we all love to complain about the weather? We wait all year for sunshine, but then we just don't know how to handle life in clothes when the humidex gets too high. In the hot, sultry dog days of summer, you can usually find me standing over the freezer letting ice cubes melt in my mouth, looking like a dishevelled cat in heat. Attractive image, I know. But since this hot and bothered lady can't live on ice alone, I cool down with these fro-yo "cookies" instead. Creamy-cool, high-protein Greek yogurt gets blitzed with a delicious combination of sweet fruit and crispy, crunchy nuts. Finish it off with a crackly layer of omega-3-rich hemp hearts, and bam! That's how you outsmart the weatherman.

½ cup (125 mL) plain 2% Greek yogurt
½ cup (125 mL) frozen fruit (see below
   for combinations)

⅓ cup (75 mL) crushed nuts (see below
   for combinations)
3 tablespoons (45 mL) hemp hearts

1. In a food processor or high-speed blender, purée the yogurt with the fruit. Stir in the nuts.

2. Spoon 2 to 3 tablespoons (30 to 45 mL) purée into each of 8 regular-size silicone muffin moulds. Sprinkle with the hemp hearts. Freeze until solid.

3. Once frozen, remove from the moulds and transfer to a resealable freezer bag for up to 6 months. Pop one back whenever you need a refreshing nosh.

My favourite combinations
- Cherries + almonds
- Avocado + pistachios
- Blueberries + walnuts
- Mango + cashews
- Banana + 1 tablespoon (15 mL) unsweetened cocoa powder + 1 tablespoon (15 mL) maple syrup + peanuts

ABBEY'S TIP I don't know much about evolution, but I have a theory that complementary flavours must have nutritional benefits, too. Nuts and fruit are a perfect example, and I would happily go back to grad school to write a thesis on this pairing alone. The combination of energizing carbohydrates in the juicy fruit and the satisfying protein from the nuts and hemp hearts makes these refreshing cold cookies a perfect post-workout recovery snack. If you don't have silicone muffin moulds, this recipe can easily be made in an ice cube tray and called "poppers" instead. (Or just eat them before you have to call them anything to anyone.)

Frozen Banana Berry Pie Pops with Berry Crunch Dip

Healthy fats • High fibre • Vegetarian

Makes 6 to 8 pie pops

One of my favourite childhood memories involves the frantic twoonie-snatch from Mom's dresser and chasing that creepy ice-cream-truck jingle down the street. Man, what I would do for some of that fearlessness, energy, and constantly replenished pile of coins today. Since I was cut off long ago from the mommy money tree, and Dickie Dee doesn't visit high-rise condos, today I make my own frozen treats. These ice pops make perfect midday snacks. Layers of berry-studded, banana-sweetened, protein-packed yogurt alternate with a crunchy high-fibre-cereal pie crumble, all topped with a crunchy strawberry crust. So save the sprints for the treadmill, the twoonies for the coffee run, and that jingle for your nightmares—these homemade pops are the nostalgic treats you crave.

Banana Berry Yogurt Layer
1 cup (250 mL) plain 2% Greek yogurt
1 cup (250 mL) mashed very ripe bananas
    (about 3 medium)
⅓ cup (75 mL) fresh or frozen finely chopped strawberries
⅓ cup (75 mL) fresh or frozen wild blueberries
¼ cup (60 mL) fresh or frozen raspberries, halved
Pure liquid honey (optional)

Pie Crust Layer
1 cup (250 mL) high-fibre bran buds cereal
2 tablespoons (30 mL) graham cracker crumbs
¼ cup (60 mL) natural almond butter
1 teaspoon (5 mL) pure liquid honey
Sea salt

Berry Crunch Dip
4½ teaspoons (22 mL) virgin coconut oil, melted
6 tablespoons (90 mL) freeze-dried strawberries crushed
    to a coarse powder

1. **Make the Banana Berry Yogurt Layer** In a food processor or blender, purée the yogurt and bananas. Transfer to a medium bowl and stir in the strawberries, blueberries, raspberries, and honey to taste (if using).

2. **Make the Pie Crust Layer** In a small bowl, mix together the bran buds cereal and graham cracker crumbs. Then stir in the almond butter, honey, and a pinch of salt.

3. Divide half of the Banana Berry Yogurt Layer among 6 to 8 ice-pop moulds. Add 1½ heaping tablespoons (27 mL) of the Pie Crust Layer and pack it down tight. Repeat with the remaining Banana Berry Yogurt Layer and Pie Crust Layer.

4. Insert the ice-pop sticks into the moulds and freeze for at least 4 hours or ideally overnight.

5. **Make the Berry Crunch Dip** Before you're ready to serve, have the coconut oil and strawberry powder in 2 separate small bowls. Run an ice-pop mould briefly under hot water and carefully pull it out. Working quickly, dip the tip of the ice pop into the melted coconut oil and immediately dip it into the strawberry powder. Enjoy immediately.

ABBEY'S TIP Freeze-dried fruits are becoming more popular as an alternative to traditional dehydrated fruit (such as raisins or dried cranberries). Instead of a chewy texture, freeze-dried fruit is light and crunchy, and even a small portion can add loads of colour and flavour. Because freeze-drying removes more moisture than dehydrating, there are usually no additives, preservatives, or added sugars, and the fruits retain their nutrients better. For easy crushing, throw the fruit pieces into a plastic bag and get some aggression out with a pot or pan. Depending on the size of your moulds, you might have a little extra Banana Berry Yogurt and a sprinkle of freeze-dried strawberries left over, so throw them together for a tasty snack while you're assembling the pops.

Two-Ingredient Protein "Ice Cream"

Gluten-free • High fibre • High protein • No added sugar • Nut-free • Vegetarian

Serves 1

I'm a straight-shooting, decisive girl who always knows what she wants. But put me in an ice cream shop and I need to try all thirty-one flavours before I can make a choice. Hey, it's a big commitment. Although I make a point of going out to my favourite ice cream shop weekly to practise my decision-making skills, sometimes I need to find a quick way to satisfy that craving at home. So for that reason, I always keep two ingredients—cottage cheese and frozen fruit—on hand to make this cheater protein-packed treat. When my go-to snack of cottage cheese is whizzed in the food processor with icy frozen fruit, it develops a creamy-cool, ice cream–like consistency. Don't worry, you can still stay faithful and committed to your weekly ice cream date. It's not cheating if it tastes this good.

⅔ cup (150 mL) low-sodium 2% cottage cheese
1 cup (250 mL) frozen fruit (see below for combinations)
Pure liquid honey (optional)
Fruit, nuts, seeds, dark chocolate, or fresh herbs (see below for combinations; optional)

1. In a food processor or high-speed blender, combine the cottage cheese with your choice of frozen fruit. Process until very smooth. Sweeten with honey to taste, if desired. Enjoy as is, stir in the suggested flavour add-ins, or stir in any other fruit, nuts, seeds, chocolate, or fresh herbs you desire.

My favourite combinations

- 1 cup (250 mL) frozen chopped banana + 1 tablespoon (15 mL) peanut butter. Stir in 1 tablespoon (15 mL) cacao nibs.

- 1 cup (250 mL) frozen mixed berries. Stir in 2 tablespoons (30 mL) finely chopped fresh mint.

- 1 cup (250 mL) frozen chopped banana + 2 teaspoons (10 mL) unsweetened cocoa powder. Stir in 1 tablespoon (15 mL) mini marshmallows + 1 tablespoon (15 mL) mini dark chocolate chips.

- ½ cup (125 mL) frozen mango + ½ cup (125 mL) frozen chopped banana. Stir in 1 tablespoon (15 mL) toasted coconut.

- 1 cup (250 mL) frozen cherries. Stir in 1 tablespoon (15 mL) shaved dark chocolate.

- ½ cup (125 mL) frozen blueberries + ½ cup (125 mL) frozen peaches. Stir in 1 tablespoon (15 mL) finely chopped fresh basil.

ABBEY'S TIP This snack is super quick and simple to pull off, but it must be enjoyed right after you make it so it doesn't lose its wonderful texture of chilly soft-serve ice cream. Can't find low-sodium cottage cheese? All good. The regular kind tastes just the same, but if you want to cut back on the salt, you can just give your cottage cheese a gentle rinse in a colander before processing.

Carrot "Cake" Protein Parfait

Gluten-free • Healthy fats • High protein • Vegetarian

Serves 4

There are two types of people in this world: those who hate cream cheese frosting, and those who literally throw out their cupcake after licking it off the top. I'm only friends with the latter. Tangy, sweet, and lusciously smooth, cream cheese frosting has the power to make a vegetable-based cake an irresistible, must-have treat. While I usually give the frosting on my carrot cake more love than the actual cake, in this recipe, the sum is far greater than its parts. Layers of whipped cottage cheese scented with the sprightly kick of lemon make it taste like a lighter, dreamier cake topper with all the usual dessert fixings strewn throughout. It's my favourite cake without the cake, and for once, I'm cool with that.

Cream Cheese Protein Pudding
2 cups (500 mL) low-sodium 2% cottage cheese
1 teaspoon (5 mL) lemon zest
1 tablespoon (15 mL) fresh lemon juice
1 teaspoon (5 mL) pure vanilla extract
¼ teaspoon (1 mL) cinnamon, or to taste
Pure liquid honey

Carrot "Cake" Mixture
1 cup (250 mL) minced fresh pineapple
¾ cup (175 mL) coarsely chopped toasted natural walnuts
½ cup (125 mL) finely grated carrots, squeezed to remove excess water
¼ cup (60 mL) unsweetened shredded coconut, toasted
3 tablespoons (45 mL) golden raisins
2 tablespoons (30 mL) minced crystallized ginger

1. **Make the Cream Cheese Protein Pudding** In a food processor or high-speed blender, purée the cottage cheese. Add the lemon zest, lemon juice, vanilla, cinnamon, and honey. Blitz quickly to combine.

2. **Make the Carrot "Cake" Mixture** In a medium bowl, mix together the pineapple, walnuts, carrots, coconut, raisins, and ginger.

3. To serve, divide half of the Cream Cheese Protein Pudding among four 1-cup (250 mL) glasses or mason jars, then top with half of the Carrot "Cake" Mixture. Repeat with the rest of the pudding and carrot mixture. Enjoy right away or refrigerate for 1 hour before serving.

ABBEY'S TIP Want to whip up a big batch for the week? I like to use an entire container of cottage cheese in my Cream Cheese Protein Pudding and store it in the fridge until the best-before date. On the day you're ready to eat, just layer the pudding with the rest of the yummy accoutrements into 1-cup (250 mL) mason jars and refrigerate until snack time.

Savoury Beet and Avocado Yogurt Bowl

Gluten-free • Healthy fats • High protein • No added sugar • Nut-free • Vegetarian

Serves 4

Yogurt parfaits—the token "healthy choice" on brunch menus and at fast-food restaurants everywhere. You know exactly what I'm talking about. It's a crappy plastic cup filled with cloyingly sweet, runny yogurt, a few handfuls of stale granola, and some sweaty chunks of melon that nobody eats. I say skip this faux dieter's delight, order those pancakes you really want, and then go home and reimagine a parfait with a satisfying savoury edge. Mine starts with a luscious high-protein Icelandic yogurt topped with crisp cucumbers, sweet beets, and buttery avocado. Finished with a sprinkle of lemony sumac and aromatic sesame, it's the healthy choice you'll actually want to choose.

2 cups (500 mL) plain 0% or 2% skyr

1 cup (250 mL) sliced mini cucumber

½ cup (125 mL) peeled and finely shredded
  raw red beet

1 avocado, pitted, peeled, and diced

2 teaspoons (10 mL) fresh lemon juice

½ teaspoon (2 mL) sumac

1 teaspoon (5 mL) white sesame seeds, toasted

Sea salt and cracked black pepper

Drizzle of extra-virgin olive oil (optional)

1. Divide the yogurt among 4 bowls. Top with the cucumber, beet, avocado, lemon juice, sumac, and sesame seeds. Season with a pinch each of salt and pepper and drizzle with some olive oil (if using).

ABBEY'S TIP Tired of classic Greek? Switch things up in this recipe with skyr! While Greek yogurt is crazy popular for damn good reason, skyr (pronounced skeer) is admittedly more qualified for the job. Skyr is an Icelandic cheese made from skim milk that has the same probiotic and bone-supporting benefits of yogurt, but with a thicker stick-to-your-spoon texture, a softer tart flavour, and more power-promoting protein. Try it side by side with your favourite Greek yogurt, and then go with your favourite!

Sriracha Peanut Hummus

Gluten-free • Healthy fats • High protein • Vegetarian

Makes 2¼ cups (550 mL)

Hummus has come a long way from being the uncool obligatory vegetarian snack at the Super Bowl buffet or the hippie-dip no one wanted to trade their Dunkaroos for at school. The offerings in the hummus aisle today are undeniably convenient and tasty, but there's no skirting around the simplicity (and frugality) of a humble homemade version. My go-to hummus smooths out the beany flavour with rich, savoury peanuts, spicy Sriracha, and tangy lime juice. And with a hit of satiating protein and satiny finish from Greek yogurt, it's the snack you'll never trade.

1 can (14 ounces/398 mL) chickpeas, drained and rinsed
½ cup (125 mL) plain 2% Greek yogurt
⅓ cup (75 mL) natural peanut butter
3 tablespoons (45 mL) fresh lime juice
1 tablespoon (15 mL) coconut sugar
1 tablespoon (15 mL) Sriracha, or to taste
1 tablespoon (15 mL) low-sodium tamari
   (gluten-free, if required)
½ teaspoon (2 mL) sesame oil
2 cloves garlic, finely minced
Kosher salt and cracked black pepper

Garnish
¼ cup (60 mL) minced unsalted natural peanuts
1 green onion, thinly sliced on a diagonal
2 tablespoons (30 mL) fresh cilantro leaves
Extra Sriracha (optional)

1. In a food processor, combine the chickpeas, yogurt, peanut butter, lime juice, coconut sugar, Sriracha, tamari, sesame oil, and garlic. Process until very smooth. Season with salt and pepper.

2. Transfer the hummus to a serving bowl. Garnish with peanuts, green onion, cilantro, and a drizzle of Sriracha (if using). Enjoy with fresh veggies or whole-grain pita.

ABBEY'S TIP Next time you think about your bowels, I want you to think about beans (and not just because of their booty-belching quirks). Beans are loaded with the antioxidant kaempferol, which research suggests may play a role in preventing colorectal cancer. Beans also deliver almost a quarter of your daily fibre needs in a modest ½ cup (125 mL), another key to optimal health (and to keep things moving smoothly, if you know what I mean). Make a batch of hummus for the work week, divvy it up into individual containers, and keep refrigerated for up to 5 days.

Chinese Five-Spice Edamame and Cashews

Dairy-free • Gluten-free • Healthy fats • No added sugar • Vegan • Vegetarian

Makes about 1 ¼ cups (300 mL)

I once fell in love with a Szechuan peppercorn–dusted chicken wing at a charity food event. It was a "one per person" deal, and while I used my charm to nail seconds, I had to round up a friend for reinforcements to get my third. I wasn't hungry; I was hooked. If you're unacquainted, these distinctive peppercorns start as a gentle little tingle, then burst into an exhilarating cascade of electricity on the tongue. Their intensity can be a little hard core for spice newbies, so let me introduce you to their gateway drug: Chinese five-spice. Four balancing aromatic spices complement these super-charged peppers, dusting up a duo of protein-rich edamame and toasty cashews. I'm all for charity, but this is a no-limits kind of snack.

¾ cup (175 mL) frozen shelled edamame, thawed and
   patted very dry
2 teaspoons (10 mL) extra-virgin olive oil, divided
2 teaspoons (10 mL) Chinese five-spice
1 teaspoon (5 mL) coconut sugar (optional)
1 teaspoon (5 mL) lime zest

½ teaspoon (2 mL) toasted sesame oil
¼ teaspoon (1 mL) sea salt, more to taste
¾ cup (175 mL) unsalted natural cashews
1 teaspoon (5 mL) black or white sesame seeds,
   for garnish (optional)

1. Preheat the oven to 375°F (190°C).

2. On a baking sheet, toss the well-dried edamame with 1 teaspoon (5 mL) of the olive oil. Bake, stirring halfway through, for 18 to 20 minutes, or until golden brown and fairly crispy.

3. Meanwhile, in a small ramekin, stir together the remaining 1 teaspoon (5 mL) olive oil, the Chinese five-spice, coconut sugar (if using), lime zest, sesame oil, and salt.

4. Add the cashews to the edamame, sprinkle with the spice mix, and toss until well coated. Bake, stirring halfway through, for another 8 to 10 minutes, or until the cashews are a light golden brown and the edamame are browned and super crispy.

5. Season with additional salt, if desired, and sprinkle with sesame seeds (if using). Let cool completely on the baking sheet before transferring to an airtight container. Store at room temperature for up to 1 week.

ABBEY'S TIP This crispy mix is equally addictive straight up savoury or with a hint of sweet—add the optional coconut sugar, if you like! If you can't find Chinese five-spice, you can easily mix up your own with equal parts ground cinnamon, cloves, fennel seeds, star anise, and those addictive Szechuan peppercorns. Store in an airtight container out of sunlight for several months, and put it on everything you eat.

Turmeric Chickpea Apricot Trail Mix

Dairy-free • Gluten-free • Healthy fats • High fibre • High protein • No added sugar • Vegan • Vegetarian

Makes about 3¼ cups (800 mL)

"Trail mix" used to be a derogatory term for the tasteless fuel stuffed into boho bags for the summer hikes of hippie offspring. It's amazing how things have changed. These days, the health-food store probably has a whole aisle devoted to $12 bags of gourmet trail mix, so you know it's trendy stuff. Whereas gas station blends are packed with candies and chocolate chips, mine adds natural sweetness with chewy apricots and warm spice. I also boost fibre and protein while stretching out those pricier nuts and seeds with a can of humble chickpeas. Crispy, crunchy, sweet, and spicy! Save the $12 for your double foam, extra whip, super-hot morning latte, and let this trail mix get you through the afternoon.

1 can (19 ounces/540 mL) chickpeas, drained and rinsed

1 tablespoon (15 mL) + 1 teaspoon (5 mL) extra-virgin olive oil, divided

½ teaspoon (2 mL) cinnamon

½ teaspoon (2 mL) turmeric

¼ teaspoon (1 mL) ground ginger

¼ teaspoon (1 mL) ground cumin

¼ teaspoon (1 mL) sweet smoked paprika

¼ teaspoon (1 mL) chili powder, more to taste

½ teaspoon (2 mL) fleur de sel, divided

½ cup (125 mL) shelled unsalted natural pistachios

½ cup (125 mL) unsalted natural pepitas

¾ cup (175 mL) dried apricots, minced

1. Preheat the oven to 425°F (220°C). Line a baking sheet with parchment paper.

2. Spread the chickpeas on a clean kitchen towel, top with another towel, and gently rub the chickpeas until they start to pop out of their thin, translucent skins. Getting rid of the skins and thoroughly drying the chickpeas helps ensure the beans get and stay extra crisp. It's not necessary to remove *all* the skins, but be sure to pick out any that easily slip off from the rubdown.

3. Transfer the dried chickpeas to the baking sheet. Toss the chickpeas with 1 tablespoon (15 mL) of the olive oil. Bake for 20 to 22 minutes, or until golden brown and crispy, stirring and tossing them at least once. Remove from the oven and turn the oven off.

4. In a small bowl, stir together the cinnamon, turmeric, ginger, cumin, paprika, chili powder, and ¼ teaspoon (1 mL) of the fleur de sel. Add the pistachios, pepitas, the remaining 1 teaspoon (5 mL) olive oil, and the remaining ¼ teaspoon (1 mL) fleur de sel; stir well. Add the mixture to the chickpeas and toss to coat. Return the baking sheet to the oven (with the temperature off) and leave the chickpeas in the oven (with the oven door closed) until the pan is cool to the touch, at least 1 hour.

5. Stir in the apricots and season with additional fleur de sel and chili powder to taste. Store in an airtight container or resealable plastic bag at room temperature for up to 10 days.

ABBEY'S TIP With its vibrant golden hue, turmeric possesses anti-inflammatory properties thanks to its active ingredient, curcumin. But if you're careless like me while tossing these crispy chickpeas, everything you touch will turn to gold (and not the bling-bling kind). Sprinkle a little cornstarch onto any stained linens and scrub fresh lemon onto yellowed nails so you don't go out looking like a chain smoker.

Happy Hour

Kombucha Dark and Stormy

Dairy-free • Gluten-free • Nut-free • Vegan • Vegetarian

Serves 1 (option for 12)

You can tell a lot about a person by what drink they order at the bar. Long Island Iced Tea? You're out on parole and not afraid of a shared jail cell. Screwdriver? You're a sleep-deprived mom. Gin rickey? You probably just watched *The Great Gatsby* and think Leo is super hot. My take? It's booze—don't worry about what others think. You just do you, and then focus on what matters—*your liquor-fuelled dance moves*. For me, it's all about the spicy, tangy combination of ginger and rum in a Dark and Stormy. My version swaps out the ginger beer for a fresher, yet equally fizzy, probiotic-rich ginger kombucha. I guess I like the contrast of a strong, tempestuous, hair-on-your-chest bevvy with good-for-your-belly bacteria. So, what does that say about me?

Ginger Simple Syrup (for 12 cocktails)
¼ cup (60 mL) filtered water
2 tablespoons (30 mL) pure maple syrup
4 teaspoons (20 mL) minced peeled fresh ginger

Kombucha Dark and Stormy (for 1 cocktail)
2 tablespoons (30 mL) dark rum
2 tablespoons (30 mL) fresh lime juice
1 teaspoon (5 mL) Ginger Simple Syrup
½ cup (125 mL) ginger kombucha
1 lime wedge
1 slice crystalized ginger

1. **Make the Ginger Simple Syrup** In a small saucepan, heat the filtered water and maple syrup on medium-high heat until the syrup dissolves, then add the ginger. Remove from the heat, cover, and let steep for 20 minutes. Transfer the syrup (with the ginger) to a small jar and keep refrigerated.

2. **Make the Kombucha Dark and Stormy** When ready to serve each cocktail, add a heaping scoop of ice cubes to a cocktail shaker, then add the rum, lime juice, Ginger Simple Syrup, and ginger kombucha. Shake until cold.

3. Serve in a tall glass over crushed ice, and garnish with a lime wedge and a piece of crystallized ginger on a metal pick.

ABBEY'S TIP Kombucha is a fermented-tea drink that's naturally low in sugar but fizzy and tangy like soda pop. It's packed with probiotics (good bacteria) for healthy digestion and gut health, as well as a range of antioxidants from the tea. This drink is best made à la minute (it also makes you look fancy), but you can totally whip up a full batch in a pitcher or punch bowl and add the kombucha right before serving to keep the fizz. To make a full batch of cocktails to serve 12 people, you'll need 1½ cups (12 ounces/375 mL) dark rum, 1 cup (250 mL) fresh lime juice, 6 cups (1.5 L) ginger kombucha, 12 lime wedges, and 12 slices of crystallized ginger. You can store the Ginger Simple Syrup for up to 1 month in the fridge—it's great for adding a little zing to any drink or dessert.

Summer Stone Fruit Sparkling Sangria

Dairy-free • Gluten-free • Nut-free • Vegetarian

Serves 8 to 10

In first-year university, we used to hang out at a local dive bar where the servers were dreamy and the sangria was cheap. I was too young and desperate to appreciate the quality of the cocktail (or lack thereof), but as a starving student, I appreciated the boozy fruit salad in the bottom of every pitcher. Who doesn't like getting a free dessert with their drink? Well, after a few too many glasses, I could usually be caught fishing out the canned cherries with my bare hands in some savage attempt to soak up the cheap booze. My grown-up version skips the cloying juice and stretches a high-quality bottle of sparkling white with aromatic peach tea. Sweet and sparkly, this sangria is made for long summer days, while all that seasonal fruit is well worth the dive. Hey, I don't judge!

1 cup (250 mL) boiling filtered water

2 herbal peach tea bags

1 cup (250 mL) ice-cold filtered water

½ cup (125 mL) peach schnapps

1 orange, thinly sliced

1 peach, pitted and thinly sliced

1 purple plum, pitted and thinly sliced

1 nectarine, pitted and thinly sliced

1 cup (250 mL) sweet cherries, pitted and halved

1 tablespoon (15 mL) pure liquid honey (optional)

1 bottle (26 ounces/750 mL) good-quality sparkling white wine, well chilled

1. Place the boiling water and tea bags in a teapot or other container with a spout and let steep for 8 minutes. Add the ice-cold water to quickly cool it down, remove the tea bags, and pour the prepared tea into a large pitcher.

2. Add the peach schnapps, orange, peach, plum, nectarine, cherries, and honey (if using). Chill in the fridge for at least 30 minutes or until ready to serve.

3. When ready to party, pour the sparkling wine into the pitcher, add ice, and give it a good stir to let the flavours muddle. Serve immediately in chilled glasses.

ABBEY'S TIP I don't think you need any excuse to pop a good bottle of Champagne, but I save the swanky Dom Pérignon and Moët for sipping au naturel. If I'm going to mix my sparkling into a sangria or another bubbly cocktail, a more affordable but still stellar option is a dry and zesty sparkler like Spanish cava or a light, fruity, and floral Brut (extra-dry) Italian Prosecco. They both boast a beautiful effervescence and flavour. A bonus reason to toast: like red wine, they're chock full of heart-healthy antioxidants. I can cheers to that!

Pineapple Coconut Margaritas

Dairy-free • Gluten-free • Nut-free • Vegan • Vegetarian

Serves 1 (option for 4)

If your twenties played out any way like mine, you likely still associate tequila with a wide range of bad life decisions. I get it. Leaving your ex a voicemail at 2 a.m. of you singing to Whitney Houston probably didn't leave a great taste in your mouth, but that, my friend, is all about to change. Skip the salt-chased shots and graduate to my pineapple coconut margaritas. Mixed with sprightly lime, bittersweet orange, sweet pineapple, and aromatic coconut water, your rekindled BFF is smooth, satisfying, and still ready to party, but without the messy drama. Finally, a glass of tequila is the best decision of the night.

Coconut Rim (for 4 cocktails)

½ cup (125 mL) unsweetened finely shredded coconut, toasted

¼ cup (60 mL) kosher salt

1 lime, quartered

Pineapple Coconut Margarita (for 1 cocktail)

2 tablespoons (30 mL) fresh pineapple juice

1 tablespoon (15 mL) fresh lime juice

1 tablespoon (15 mL) silver tequila

1½ teaspoons (7 mL) orange liqueur (such as Triple Sec or Cointreau)

½ to 1 teaspoon (2 to 5 mL) agave nectar

2 to 3 tablespoons (30 to 45 mL) unsweetened coconut water

1. **Make the Coconut Rim** In a saucer, stir together the coconut and salt. Moisten the rims of 4 margarita glasses with the lime wedges. Dip the rims of the glasses into the coconut mixture.

2. **Make the Pineapple Coconut Margarita** To make one cocktail, add a handful of ice, pineapple juice, lime juice, tequila, orange liqueur, and agave nectar to a cocktail shaker. Shake until chilled. Pour into a glass and top up with the coconut water. Repeat to make the remaining 3 drinks, and cheers!

ABBEY'S TIP I don't expect you'll be refuelling from a marathon with this boozy bevvy, but if you did, you'd actually be pretty smart. Coconut water is nature's Gatorade, packed with the essential electrolytes we need to replenish after a hard sweat session at the gym. When choosing a coconut water, look for one without added sugars or flavours so that you can control the sweetness of your drink. To make a full recipe for 4 cocktails, you will need ½ cup (125 mL) fresh pineapple juice, ¼ cup (60 mL) fresh lime juice, ¼ cup (60 mL) silver tequila, 2 tablespoons (30 mL) orange liqueur (such as Triple Sec or Cointreau), 2 to 4 teaspoons (10 to 20 mL) agave nectar, and ½ to ¾ cup (125 to 175 mL) coconut water.

Riesling-Soaked Frozen Grapes

Dairy-free • Gluten-free • Nut-free • Vegetarian

Serves 12 to 16

Remember when we used to get our buzz from booze-soaked candy because the adult juice was too strong? Ah, yes, the innocent days. Now, I can't imagine throwing back a handful of slippery gummy bears for any reason, let alone to disguise good wine. But I have no qualms about finding more boozy ways to enjoy fruit. If you, like me, sometimes order sangria just for the inebriated fruit (see page 188 for my favourite version), I say just cut to the chase with these grapes. Bright, crisp, floral Riesling is infused with aromatic lemon, honey, and thyme, creating a perfect soak for antioxidant-rich grapes. Melt them slowly in your mouth, or bite down for a tipsy explosion. A few handfuls in, and you won't even notice the brain freeze.

6 cups (1.5 L) grapes (red, green, or a combination), stemmed
1 bottle (26 ounces/750 mL) semi-dry Riesling wine
3 tablespoons (45 mL) pure liquid honey
Small bunch of fresh thyme (about 15 sprigs)
Rind of 1 lemon, peeled with a vegetable peeler in large strips

1. Using a toothpick or skewer, poke holes all over the grapes.

2. In a large bowl, stir together the wine and honey until the honey dissolves. Add the thyme, lemon rind, and grapes. Cover and refrigerate for 12 to 24 hours—the longer the grapes marinate, the more boozy they will taste!

3. Line a baking sheet with parchment paper, wax paper, or a silicone baking mat. Strain the grapes, reserving the marinade (see the Tip). Discard the thyme and lemon peel. Transfer the grapes to the baking sheet and freeze until solid, 2 to 3 hours. Transfer to a large resealable freezer bag and store in the freezer for up to 3 months. Pull a few out and when ready to indulge serve in a chilled bowl.

ABBEY'S TIP Please, please, please, on behalf of my desperately thirsty former-student self, do not throw out the wine marinade! It makes a delicious summer spritzer mixed halfsies with club soda or sparkling water, with a few wine-soaked grapes doing double duty as ice cubes that won't water down your drink.

ABBEY'S TIP Sometimes called husk tomatoes or tomate verde, tomatillos are packed with fibre, potassium, and a range of powerful antioxidants. In fact, new research on wild tomatillos has discovered new compounds that may have a protective effect against colon cancer. When choosing these summer staples, look for firm, dry, hard fruits that are tightly covered by their husks. Store them in an unsealed paper bag for up to 3 weeks in the fridge and resist peeking under their husks until you're ready to eat them to keep them fresh. This gazpacho can be made 1 day ahead and stored in the fridge, but the speedy salsa is best made the day of serving.

Honeydew Tomatillo Gazpacho Shooters with Strawberry Salsa

Dairy-free • Gluten-free • Healthy fats • High fibre • Nut-free • Vegan • Vegetarian

Makes 16 shooters

When I was growing up, my father was always so proud of his backyard tomato garden. Like tiny pets, each and every misshapen fruit got its own name and destiny, but most were headed into a batch of classic gazpacho. I'm always down for a bowl of Mindy, Frank, and their juicy cousins, but my tomatillo version is a welcome and refreshing twist. If you've never had a tomatillo, consider them the love child of a tomato and a lime. They're sprightly tart darlings in their raw state, but when sizzled on a hot grill and paired with sweet melon and buttery avocado, they make for a perfect summer starter. Yes, you can totally serve this with a spoon and bowl at a table as a first course, but if your parties are like my parties, hand-held items always do best. Plus, a spoon is one more thing to wash, and lord knows, this girl grills, but she doesn't clean.

Honeydew Tomatillo Gazpacho

1 pound (450 g) tomatillos, husks removed

½ English cucumber, peeled

2 ripe avocados, pitted and peeled

1 jalapeño pepper, chopped (ribs and seeds optional, depending how spicy you like it)

2 cups (500 mL) diced honeydew melon

1 cup (250 mL) low-sodium vegetable stock (gluten-free, if required)

3 tablespoons (45 mL) fresh lime juice, more if needed

2 teaspoons (10 mL) coconut sugar

Sea salt and cracked black pepper

Strawberry Salsa

1 cup (250 mL) minced fresh strawberries

1 tablespoon (15 mL) thinly sliced fresh mint

Sea salt and cracked black pepper

1. **Make the Honeydew Tomatillo Gazpacho** Prepare a grill for direct cooking over medium-high heat. Grill the tomatillos, with the lid open, turning every few minutes, until they're well charred all over, 5 to 6 minutes.

2. In a high-speed blender or food processor, combine the grilled tomatillos, cucumber, avocados, jalapeño, melon, vegetable stock, lime juice, and coconut sugar. Blend until smooth. Season with salt and pepper, and add additional lime juice as needed, depending on the acidity of your tomatillos. Transfer to a pitcher and refrigerate until cold, at least 1 hour.

3. **Make the Strawberry Salsa** In a medium bowl, stir together the strawberries, mint, and salt and pepper to taste.

4. To serve, pour about ¼ cup (60 mL) Honeydew Tomatillo Gazpacho into each shooter glass. Top with a spoonful of Strawberry Salsa.

Chili and Chocolate Nut Mix

Dairy-free • Gluten-free • Healthy fats • Vegetarian

Makes about 3 cups (750 mL)

Nut mixes are a gift you give to get. I know you feel me on this one. Like a box of chocolates, you give hosts or family members nut mixes because you hope they'll put them out and you can eat some too. Win, win! I developed this recipe as a holiday gift for my nut-loving dad, and it has since become a go-to party snack.

Chili Cashews
1 tablespoon (15 mL) egg white
1 tablespoon (15 mL) coconut sugar
½ teaspoon (2 mL) finely grated lime zest
¼ teaspoon (1 mL) chili powder
¼ teaspoon (1 mL) ground cumin
1½ cups (375 mL) raw cashews
¾ teaspoon (4 mL) fleur de sel

Chocolate Hemp Almonds
3½ ounces (100 g) 70% to 80% dark chocolate
   (dairy-free, if required), finely chopped
1½ cups (375 mL) unsalted natural almonds
1 teaspoon (5 mL) hemp hearts
¼ teaspoon (1 mL) fleur de sel

1. Preheat the oven to 350°F (180°C). Line 2 baking sheets with parchment paper or silicone baking mats.

2. **Make the Chili Cashews** In a medium bowl, whisk the egg white until very frothy. Add the coconut sugar, lime zest, chili powder, and cumin. Whisk until well combined. Add the cashews and toss until well coated in the spice mixture.

3. Spread the cashews on one of the prepared baking sheets, sprinkle with fleur de sel and bake, stirring halfway through, for 15 to 20 minutes, or until golden brown and dry to the touch. Let cool completely on the baking sheet before handling.

4. **Make the Chocolate Hemp Almonds** Meanwhile, place the chocolate in a heatproof bowl and place it over a small saucepan filled with 1 inch (2.5 cm) of water. Bring the water to a bare simmer and let the chocolate gently melt, stirring often. *(Optional microwave method: Place the chocolate in a microwave-safe dish. Melt in the microwave on 50 percent power in 30-second increments until almost fully melted. Stir once after each 30-second increment.)*

5. Add the almonds to the melted chocolate and stir them until fully coated. Spread the nuts out on the second baking sheet and sprinkle with hemp hearts and fleur de sel. Set aside until the chocolate has set completely, or transfer to the fridge to quicken the process.

6. Once cooled, break up any stuck-together pieces, and mix the chocolate almonds with the chili cashews. Store in an airtight container for up to 2 weeks.

ABBEY'S TIP Nuts are must-have drinking food in my home. They're packed with protein, fat, and fibre to help slow alcohol absorption so randos don't get passed-out drunk on boxed wine. On party day, just serve these in candy dishes, on cheese platters, or packaged as thank-you gifts for guests or hosts.

Beet Tartare with Cashew Caper Cream and Crispy Kasha

Dairy-free • Gluten-free • Healthy fats • High fibre • No added sugar • Vegan • Vegetarian

Makes 16 beet tartare spoons; Serves 8

Planning a party menu for a family with every single imaginable food intolerance is like trying to get from one end of the city to the other in rush-hour traffic. Of course, every route on Google is closed for construction, and you're getting desperate, frustrated, and hangry. Patience has never been my forte, so when challenged with too many menu restrictions, I used to throw a generic tub of hummus and baby carrots on the spread in sheer defeat. Not anymore. This is one of my favourite elegant recipes that satisfies my vegan, dairy-free, and gluten-free friends. Sweet, earthy beets get pulsed to the consistency of beef tartare, dressed in a pungent mustard sauce, and served in an endive spoon. A little caper-laced cashew purée on top adds a briny bite to the luscious cream, with a crackly finishing crunch from pan-fried kasha grains. It's my secret route to party success!

Beet Tartare

½ pound (225 g) red beets, scrubbed
½ pound (225 g) golden beets, scrubbed
¼ cup (60 mL) whole-grain Dijon mustard
4 teaspoons (20 mL) extra virgin olive oil
2 teaspoons (10 mL) sherry vinegar
1 teaspoon (5 mL) low-sodium tamari
   (gluten free, if required)
1 teaspoon (5 mL) fresh lemon juice
2 tablespoons (30 mL) minced shallot
1 tablespoon (15 mL) minced fresh parsley
1 teaspoon (5 mL) fresh lemon zest
Kosher salt and cracked black pepper

Cashew Caper Cream

1 cup (250 mL) unsalted natural cashews, soaked
   in water in the fridge overnight and drained
¼ cup + 2 tablespoons (90 mL) cashew milk
4 teaspoons (20 mL) drained capers
4 teaspoons (20 mL) fresh lemon juice
Kosher salt and cracked black pepper

To Serve

1 tablespoon (15 mL) extra-virgin olive oil
⅓ cup (75 mL) kasha
2 Belgian endives, leaves separated

1. Preheat the oven to 450°F (230°C).

2. **Make the Beet Tartare** Wrap the red beets in a foil package and the golden beets in a separate foil package, and place both packages on a baking sheet. Roast for 1 to 1½ hours, or until very tender when pricked with a fork. (For a speedier version, simply place the red beets in a microwave-safe dish, cover in plastic wrap, and microwave on high for 10 minutes, or until tender. Repeat with the golden beets.) When the beets are cool enough to handle, peel and roughly chop.

3. Transfer the red beets to a food processor and pulse until finely chopped but not puréed—you're looking for a tartare-like consistency. Transfer to a medium bowl. Repeat with the golden beets and add to the bowl with the red beets.

continues

4. In a large bowl, combine the mustard, olive oil, sherry vinegar, tamari, lemon juice, shallots, parsley, and lemon zest. Stir until well combined. Add the beets, toss until coated in the dressing, and season with salt and pepper. The golden beets will get stained, but I like the sunset-like hue they take on. Set aside.

5. **Make the Cashew Caper Cream** In a high-speed blender, combine the cashews, cashew milk, capers, and lemon juice. Blend until smooth. Season with salt and pepper and set aside.

6. To serve, in a small nonstick skillet, heat the olive oil over medium-high heat. Add the kasha and toast, stirring, for 30 to 60 seconds, or until it smells toasty and nutty. Quickly transfer to a plate or bowl lined with paper towel to drain.

7. Top each endive leaf with a generous spoonful of the Beet Tartare. Finish with a dollop of Cashew Caper Cream and a sprinkle of kasha. Serve at room temperature.

ABBEY'S TIP Kasha is the toasted version of buckwheat groats, a naturally gluten-free whole grain that's packed with fibre and heart-healthy antioxidants. I love its subtle, nutty flavour and irresistible crispy crunch, but if you want to skip this step, a light sprinkle of finely chopped pistachios or walnuts makes a beautiful substitute.

Layered Everything Bagel Dip and Baked Pita Chips

Dairy-free • Healthy fats • High fibre • High protein • No added sugar • Vegan • Vegetarian

Serves 12

The Everything Bagel may be the grand-Bubbie in the bagel hierarchy, but I have a big confession to make. While I love the salty, garlicky, nutty flavour of "everything" spice, I don't love bagels. I've been known to lick the densely packed spice right off the top of the bagel and scrape the cream cheese right into my mouth. I know, the chutzpah! So when I'm hosting the nosh, I skip the dense bread and get straight to the goods. This layered plant-based dip combines a creamy cashew-dill cream cheese, protein-rich hummus spiked with everything bagel spice mix, and candy-like onions. Serve with some crispy baked "everything" chips, and help grand-Bubbie get her groove back.

Caramelized Onions

1 tablespoon (15 mL) extra-virgin olive oil
1 yellow onion, finely diced
Kosher salt and cracked black pepper

Everything Bagel Spice Mix

2 teaspoons (10 mL) white sesame seeds
2 teaspoons (10 mL) poppy seeds
1 teaspoon (5 mL) onion flakes
1 teaspoon (5 mL) garlic flakes
¾ teaspoon (4 mL) kosher salt

Dill "Cream Cheese"

1¼ cups (300 mL) unsalted natural cashews, soaked
   in water overnight in the fridge and drained
¼ cup (60 mL) cashew milk (more, if mixture is
   too thick)
2 teaspoons (10 mL) lemon zest
5 teaspoons (25 mL) fresh lemon juice
5 teaspoons (25 mL) finely chopped fresh dill
Kosher salt and cracked black pepper

White Bean Hummus

1 can (19 ounces/540 mL) cannellini beans,
   drained and rinsed
2 teaspoons (10 mL) lemon zest
3 tablespoons (45 mL) fresh lemon juice
1 tablespoon (15 mL) tahini
1 tablespoon (15 mL) extra-virgin olive oil
½ teaspoon (2 mL) ground cumin
Kosher salt and cracked black pepper

Baked Pita Chips

6 small pita breads, cut into small triangular pieces
2 tablespoons (30 mL) extra-virgin olive oil

To Serve

4 cups (1 L) cut-up fresh vegetables (carrots, celery,
   fennel, cucumber, bell peppers)
Chopped fresh dill (optional)

1. **Make the Caramelized Onions** Heat the olive oil in a medium nonstick skillet over medium-low heat. Add the onions and stir to coat them in the oil. Stirring every 5 minutes, cook the onions until they reach a caramelized, amber colour, 45 to 60 minutes. Season with salt and pepper and set aside.

2. **Make the Everything Bagel Spice Mix** In a small bowl, stir together the sesame seeds, poppy seeds, onion flakes, garlic flakes, and salt. Set aside.

continues

3. **Make the Dill "Cream Cheese"** In a food processor or high-speed blender, process the cashews until they break down into a paste. Add the cashew milk, lemon zest, and lemon juice and process until very smooth—it can take a few minutes, so be patient. Add the dill and pulse until little flecks of herb are strewn throughout the dip. Season with salt and pepper, transfer to a bowl, and clean out the food processor or blender.

4. **Make the White Bean Hummus** In the food processor or blender, combine the beans, lemon zest, lemon juice, tahini, olive oil, cumin, 1 teaspoon (5 mL) of the Everything Bagel Spice Mix, and ¼ cup (60 mL) of the Caramelized Onions. Process until very smooth, then season with salt and pepper. Set aside.

5. Preheat the oven to 375°F (190°C). Position the oven racks to the top ⅓ and bottom ⅓ of the oven.

6. **Make the Baked Pita Chips** Arrange the pita triangles on 2 baking sheets (making sure they're not touching), and brush with olive oil. Sprinkle with 1 tablespoon (15 mL) of the Everything Bagel Spice Mix. Bake for about 10 minutes, rotating the pans once, until the chips are crisp and golden brown.

7. To serve, spread the White Bean Hummus in a 5-inch (12 cm) serving dish. Top with the remaining Caramelized Onions, making an even layer, and then top with a layer of the Dill "Cream Cheese." Sprinkle generously with the Everything Bagel Spice Mix and fresh dill (if using). Serve with the Baked Pita Chips and cut-up vegetables.

ABBEY'S TIP The dill-scented cashew cream cheese layer is loose enough for dipping, but if you want to make extra to smear on actual bagels, wrap it in cheesecloth and squeeze out some of the excess moisture. You can also make a big batch of the spice mix and keep it in a sealed container for up to a year—it's delicious on freshly baked breads, chicken breasts, baked potatoes, and pasta. Meanwhile, both of the dip layers can be made up to 4 days ahead and stored in a covered container in the fridge. The pita chips are best enjoyed fresh.

Almond Coconut Zucchini Chips with Ginger Plum Dipping Sauce

Dairy-free • Gluten-free • Healthy fats • High fibre • Vegan • Vegetarian

Serves 6 to 8

I'm a city gal, so I get that living space is often such a hot commodity that there's no room to entertain with a formal sit-down meal. But just because it's standing room only—and the food is fork-optional—crudités don't have to be the only vegetable on the spread. The tastiest way to party green is with these crispy zucchini chips. No, they're neither wafer thin nor made of potatoes, but hey, after a few cocktails, people love foods called chips, and these never disappoint. Coated with fibre-rich flax, fragrant, crispy coconut, savoury sesame, and satiating almond flour, my crispy minis are so much more than your token party green-thing. I serve mine with a zesty ginger plum sauce that's addictively fresh and fiery. Finally, a reason to purge those expired Chinese take-out packets of sauce you've been hoarding. Hello, #adulting!

Almond Coconut Zucchini Chips

4 large zucchini, cut into ¼-inch (5 mm) rounds
½ teaspoon (2 mL) kosher salt (optional)
¼ cup (60 mL) ground flaxseed
⅔ cup (150 mL) filtered water
1½ cups (375 mL) almond flour
½ cup (125 mL) unsweetened finely shredded coconut
2 teaspoons (10 mL) black sesame seeds
2 teaspoons (10 mL) white sesame seeds
½ teaspoon (2 mL) ground ginger
½ teaspoon (2 mL) sea salt
½ teaspoon (2 mL) black pepper
2 tablespoons (30 mL) Dijon mustard
Extra-virgin olive oil in an oil atomizer

Ginger Plum Dipping Sauce

2 cups (500 mL) pitted and diced red plums
1 clove garlic, finely minced
1 tablespoon (15 mL) finely grated fresh ginger
1 tablespoon (15 mL) coconut sugar
1 tablespoon (15 mL) seasoned rice vinegar
1½ teaspoons (7 mL) low-sodium tamari
   (gluten-free, if required)
½ cup (125 mL) filtered water

1. Place a baking sheet in the oven and preheat the oven to 425°F (220°C).

2. **Make the Almond Coconut Zucchini Chips** Line a baking sheet with a few layers of paper towel or kitchen towel. Spread the zucchini rounds over the paper towel, overlapping as little as possible, and sprinkle with kosher salt (if using). Cover with a few more layers of paper towel, another baking sheet, and some heavy items. Let sit for 10 minutes.

3. Lightly rinse the zucchini in a colander. Replace the paper towel on the baking sheet. Again spread the rinsed zucchini over the paper towel, top with another few layers of paper towel, and another baking sheet, then press down with heavy items and let dry for 10 minutes. (Yes, you can skip this step, but I highly recommend following it to fully dry the zucchini so they get super crispy.)

continues

4. To make a flaxseed egg, stir together the flaxseed and water in a small bowl until well combined. Refrigerate for 15 minutes, until thickened and slightly goopy.

5. In a medium bowl, stir together the almond flour, coconut, black and white sesame seeds, ginger, salt, and pepper. Set aside.

6. Place the mustard in another medium bowl. Toss the zucchini rounds in the mustard until well coated. Add the flaxseed egg and toss until well coated.

7. Working with a few at a time, dredge the zucchini rounds in the almond flour mixture, gently turning them until they're fully coated.

8. Remove the hot baking sheet from the oven and spritz it with olive oil in an oil atomizer. Place the coated zucchini rounds in a single layer on the baking sheet and spritz again with olive oil. Bake for 15 minutes. Turn the zucchini rounds, give them another spritz, and bake for an additional 15 minutes, or until they're golden brown and crispy.

9. **Make the Ginger Plum Dipping Sauce** Meanwhile, in a small saucepan, combine the plums, garlic, ginger, coconut sugar, rice vinegar, tamari, and water. Bring to a boil over medium-high heat, then cover, reduce the heat to medium-low, and simmer for 7 minutes. Uncover and cook until thick, about 3 minutes. Transfer to a high-speed blender or food processor and purée.

10. Serve the Almond Coconut Zucchini Chips with the Ginger Plum Dipping Sauce on the side.

ABBEY'S TIP What this recipe lacks in gluten and dairy, it more than makes up for in good-for-you fats. Coconut brings a hit of medium-chain fatty acids, flax offers omega-3s, and almonds pack healthy monounsaturated fats and protein. Not only does this trio offer a ton of satiating nutrition, but it also provides a wickedly crispy crust. To enhance the crunch factor, take the time to salt and "sweat" your zucchini to remove some of the excess moisture, turning those humdrum veggies into amazing chips.

Five-Spice Sesame Panko Tofu Poppers with Sweet-and-Sour Orange Dip

Dairy-free • Nut-free • Vegan • Vegetarian

Makes 40 poppers; Serves 20

There are three notorious party fouls I've learned never to commit: (1) underestimating the drinking capacity of your guests, (2) playing Nickelback, and (3) serving bland tofu without a crispy golden crust and a wicked dip. I trust you can figure out how to avoid #1 and #2 by yourself, but here's a little life hack for getting through #3: make these poppers. Crispy golden panko, crackly sesame seeds, and aromatic Chinese five-spice turn basic tofu into something totally party ready. Served with a sassy, tangy sweet-and-sour orange dip, these poppers can turn any liquorless party with painfully horrible tunes into a delicious success.

Five-Spice Panko Tofu Poppers

1 package (12 ounces/350 g) extra-firm tofu,
    cut into ¾-inch (2 cm) cubes
Extra-virgin olive oil in an oil atomizer
1 cup (250 mL) whole wheat panko breadcrumbs
2 tablespoons (30 mL) white sesame seeds
4 teaspoons (20 mL) black sesame seeds
2 teaspoons (10 mL) Chinese five-spice
1 teaspoon (5 mL) sea salt
1 teaspoon (5 mL) black pepper
½ cup (125 mL) Dijon mustard

Sweet-and-Sour Orange Dip

2 teaspoons (10 mL) virgin coconut oil
2 cloves garlic, finely minced
2 teaspoons (10 mL) finely grated fresh ginger
½ cup (125 mL) frozen orange juice concentrate
2 tablespoons (30 mL) seasoned rice vinegar
2 tablespoons (30 mL) low-sodium soy sauce
1 tablespoon (15 mL) coconut sugar, more to taste
1 teaspoon (5 mL) Sriracha, or to taste
2 teaspoons (10 mL) cornstarch, tapioca starch,
    or brown rice flour
1 cup (250 mL) filtered water
Salt and pepper

1. Preheat the oven to 425°F (220°C).

2. **Make the Five-Spice Panko Tofu Poppers** Line a baking sheet with a few layers of paper towel or kitchen towel. Arrange the tofu cubes on the paper towel. Top with another layer of paper towel, then cover with a second baking sheet and weigh it down with some heavy objects such as cast-iron skillets topped with canned goods. Let sit for 1 hour so the tofu releases some of its moisture.

3. When ready to bake, transfer the tofu cubes to a cutting board or large plate. Discard the paper towel and lightly grease the baking sheet with olive oil in an oil atomizer. Place the baking sheet in the preheated oven.

4. In a small bowl, stir together the panko, white and black sesame seeds, Chinese five-spice, salt, and pepper.

5. Brush the tofu all over with the mustard. Working with a few pieces at a time, toss the tofu in the panko mixture, coating it well.

continues

6. Remove the baking sheet from the oven and arrange the tofu cubes on it, being careful that the pieces don't touch. Season with a pinch each of sea salt and pepper and spritz lightly with olive oil in an oil atomizer. Bake for 25 to 35 minutes, or until golden brown and crispy on all sides, turning at least once.

7. **Make the Sweet-and-Sour Orange Dip** Meanwhile, heat the coconut oil in a small skillet over medium heat. Add the garlic and ginger and cook until fragrant, about 30 seconds. Add the orange juice concentrate, rice vinegar, soy sauce, coconut sugar, and Sriracha. Stir until it starts to simmer gently.

8. In a small bowl, stir together the cornstarch and water until smooth, then stir into the sauce. Simmer until the sauce reaches a thick dip-like consistency, 7 to 10 minutes. Season with salt and pepper and add more coconut sugar, if desired.

9. To serve, arrange the tofu on a serving platter with toothpicks, and serve the Sweet-and-Sour Orange Dip in a bowl for dipping.

ABBEY'S TIP I don't care if you have to schlep out your university textbooks to get some good heavy weight in there (you'll never resell them anyway), but don't skip the pressing step with your tofu. While it's a heavy lifter in the protein department, tofu is also water-rich, which gets in the way of us nailing that crispy crust if we don't wring them out a little with some weight. These poppers are best made and served right away, but they can also be made 1 day ahead, stored in single layers between parchment paper in the fridge, and warmed in a 400°F (200°C) oven for 5 minutes or until crispy and hot.

Cheese-Explosion Cauliflower Tots

High protein • No added sugar • Nut-free • Vegetarian

Makes 24 tots; Serves 6

Everything is just better with a side of tots. My mom knows this. Your babysitter knows this. Hipster restaurants know this. A lesser-known fact is that the "other white vegetable," cauliflower, is just as tasty as traditional taters, but it comes with a whole new world of powerful antioxidants. These poppable tots start with tender cauliflower rice bound together with crispy panko and fresh herbs before being finished with a melted ooey-gooey cheese surprise. See, moms are always right.

Cheese-Explosion Cauliflower Tots

4 cups (1 L) cauliflower florets

2 teaspoons (10 mL) extra-virgin olive oil

½ cup (125 mL) finely minced yellow onion

1 clove garlic, minced

½ cup (125 mL) whole wheat panko breadcrumbs

½ cup (125 mL) finely grated Parmigiano-Reggiano cheese

¼ cup (60 mL) whole wheat flour

¼ cup (60 mL) finely minced fresh flat-leaf parsley

¼ teaspoon (1 mL) sea salt

¼ teaspoon (1 mL) cracked black pepper

1 large egg white, lightly beaten

6 mini bocconcini balls, quartered

Breading

2 large eggs

½ cup (125 mL) whole wheat panko crumbs

2 tablespoons (30 mL) finely grated Parmigiano-Reggiano cheese

1 tablespoon (15 mL) finely minced fresh flat-leaf parsley

⅛ teaspoon (0.5 mL) sea salt

⅛ teaspoon (0.5 mL) cracked black pepper

Olive oil in an oil atomizer

To Serve

Marinara sauce, warmed, for dipping

1. **Make the Cheese-Explosion Cauliflower Tots** Place the cauliflower in a food processor and pulse until it reaches a rice-like consistency. Set aside.

2. Heat the olive oil in a large nonstick skillet over medium heat. Add the onions and cook, stirring often, until translucent, about 2 minutes. Add the garlic and cook for another 30 seconds, until fragrant.

3. Add the cauliflower rice along with 2 tablespoons (30 mL) water, cover the pan, and steam for 2 minutes. Remove the lid and allow the moisture to evaporate for an additional 2 minutes. Remove from the heat and let cool to room temperature.

4. Preheat the oven to 425°F (220°C). Line a baking sheet with parchment paper and lightly grease the paper.

5. Transfer the cauliflower to a piece of cheesecloth and squeeze the liquid out. Put some muscle into it—you really want to get every last drop out so you don't have soggy tots.

6. Add the cauliflower rice into a large bowl and add the panko, Parmesan, flour, parsley, salt, pepper, and egg white. Mix until well combined.

continues

7. **Make the Breading** In a small bowl, beat the eggs. In another small bowl, stir together the panko, Parmesan, parsley, salt, and pepper.

8. **Assemble and Cook** Carefully press 2 tablespoons (30 mL) of the cauliflower mixture around one piece of bocconcini cheese, making a log-like shape. Repeat with the remaining bocconcini and cauliflower mixture. Working with a few at a time, carefully toss the cauliflower tots in the beaten eggs, then in the breading, gently tossing until they're fully coated in the breading. Transfer to the prepared baking sheet, making sure the tots aren't touching each other.

9. Spritz the tots with a little olive oil in an oil atomizer. Bake for 10 minutes. Turn the tots over, spritz them again with oil, and bake for an additional 12 to 14 minutes, or until golden brown and crispy. Serve warm (ideally fresh out of the oven so the cheese is extra melty) with warm marinara sauce.

ABBEY'S TIP Once strictly reserved as a vehicle for cheese sauce, cauliflower has been winning the PR game as of late. With cauliflower rice, pizza, mash, and flour swaps blowing up your Instagram and Pinterest feeds, this humble vegetable is white hot. But cauliflower is so much more than a low-carb swap. It is rich in a sulphur-containing compound, glucosinolate, which some research has linked to a reduced risk of lung, stomach, breast, colon, and prostate cancers. Cutting your cauliflower into small pieces like we do in these cheesy tots provides the best access to those cancer-fighting compounds.

Grilled Wild Blueberry and Corn Flatbread

Nut-free • **Vegetarian**

Serves 16

When we head to the cottage every summer, the only stop we make before turning down the dirt road is at the wild blueberry farm. It's only another five minutes to the cottage, but I've usually inhaled half a bushel by the time we get there. They say what grows together, goes together, so juicy blueberries meet their sweet vegetable match in this stunningly delicious blueberry and corn flatbread. Spicy arugula and chili oil balance out the sweet, supple duo, with a tangy bite from the luscious and light goat cheese. Simple, seasonal, and unapologetically satisfying, it's a crowd-pleasing nibble to kick off any summer night.

Extra-virgin olive oil in an oil atomizer
½ lemon
1 corn cob, shucked
4 teaspoons (20 mL) extra-virgin olive oil
½ teaspoon (2 mL) pure liquid honey
Pinch of red chili flakes
Sea salt and cracked black pepper
4 whole-grain naan or pocketless pita breads (6 to 7 inches/15 to 18 cm each)
½ cup (125 mL) soft goat cheese
½ cup (125 mL) wild blueberries
½ cup (125 mL) mini bocconcini balls, cut in half
1 cup (250 mL) arugula
3 tablespoons (45 mL) fresh basil thinly sliced on a diagonal
Fleur de sel and cracked black pepper, for garnish

1. Prepare a grill for direct cooking over medium-high heat on one side of the grill. Lightly grease the grate.

2. Spritz the cut side of the lemon half and the corn with a bit of olive oil in an oil atomizer, place them both on the grill over the direct heat (place the lemon cut side down), and close the lid. Grill the lemon until you see some nice grill marks, about 4 minutes. Grill the corn, turning frequently, until evenly charred, about 10 minutes total. Remove from the grill and, once cool enough to handle, cut the corn kernels from the cob and transfer to a small bowl.

3. In another small bowl, juice the grilled lemon. Add the olive oil, honey, chili flakes, and a pinch each of salt and pepper. Stir well and set aside.

4. Spritz both sides of the naan with the olive oil in the oil atomizer. Smear each naan with 2 tablespoons (30 mL) of the goat cheese, then evenly top each naan with the corn kernels, blueberries, and bocconcini.

continues

5. Grill, with the lid closed, over direct heat until lightly charred on the bottom, 3 to 4 minutes. Transfer to the side without direct flames (indirect heat), close the lid, and cook for another 2 to 4 minutes, or until the bottom is golden brown and the bocconcini just starts to melt.

6. Transfer the naan to a cutting board and let rest for 2 minutes before cutting into pieces. Top with arugula, basil, the reserved lemon chili oil, and a generous sprinkle of fleur de sel and cracked black pepper.

ABBEY'S TIP Wild blueberries may be tiny, but each itty-bitty orb packs a hefty load of heart-healthy antioxidants—twice as much as ordinary blueberries and more than twenty times that of the other top fruits and veggies. Research has linked consuming wild blueberries with helping to reduce the "bad" LDL cholesterol, reduce the risk of heart disease, improve insulin sensitivity, and slow cognitive decline associated with age. I suggest keeping the rest of the bushel nearby for nibbling while manning the grill—you know, to keep your barbecue skills sharp.

Pickled Honeydew and Radish Toast with Whipped Feta Yogurt

Nut-free • Vegetarian

Serves 12

Watermelon radish is the speakeasy of the plant world. Humble and unassuming on the outside, and one hell of a hot party inside. Not only is it pungent and spicy all on its own, it also makes a wicked wingman to my new obsession, pickled melon. Confession time: I would pickle everything if I could (and trust me, I've tried). Pickling honeydew melon in a spicy jalapeño brine brings its natural sweetness to the forefront and turns everyone's least favourite fruit-platter melon into a must-have bite. Expert tip: double the whipped feta yogurt for a savoury protein-packed spread to continue the party until the early morning on your breakfast toast.

Pickled Honeydew Melon

1 cup (250 mL) boiling water

½ cup (125 mL) seasoned rice vinegar

¼ cup (60 mL) pure liquid honey

8 ounces (225 g) honeydew melon, thinly sliced
   into ribbons (about 2 cups/500 mL)

¼ jalapeño pepper, seeded

Whipped Feta Yogurt

2 cups (500 mL) plain 2% Greek yogurt

½ cup (125 mL) crumbled feta cheese

Radish Toast

6 slices crusty whole-grain bread,
   each 1 inch (2.5 cm) thick and cut in half

Extra-virgin olive oil in an oil atomizer

Salt and pepper

3 watermelon radishes, sliced paper thin

Sugar

Garnish

Crumbled feta cheese

Toasted sunflower seeds

Fresh micro basil

1. **Make the Pickled Honeydew Melon** In a medium bowl, combine the boiling water, rice vinegar, and honey Stir until the honey has dissolved. Add the melon and jalapeño, cover, and refrigerate for 1 hour. Drain the melon mixture in a colander.

2. **Make the Whipped Feta Yogurt** In a food processor, process the yogurt and feta until smooth. Set aside.

3. Preheat the oven to 375°F (190°C). Line a baking sheet with parchment paper or a silicone baking mat.

4. **Make the Radish Toast** Spritz the bread slices on both sides with olive oil in an oil atomizer, and sprinkle with a pinch each of salt and pepper. Bake for 9 to 12 minutes, turning halfway through, until golden brown. If you like your toast extra crispy and a little charred like I do, pop it under the broiler for 1 to 2 minutes. Just keep an eye on it to make sure it doesn't burn.

5. Place the radish slices in a colander and sprinkle with a pinch each of salt and sugar. Massage for 30 seconds, then rinse under cold water. Pat very dry with paper towels to remove any excess water.

6. To assemble, smear the Whipped Feta Yogurt on the toasted bread. Top each slice with some pretty ribbons of Honeydew Pickled Melon and a few radish slices. Garnish each serving with a little extra feta, sunflower seeds, and micro basil.

Loaded with hydrating water, heart-healthy potassium, and antioxidants, honeydew melon is the fruit you should have never forgotten. The best way to get those pretty melon ribbons is to cut the melon in half, remove the "guts," and then slice it into 1½-inch (4 cm) wedges. Run a vegetable peeler across the curve to remove thin slices of fruit in long, windy strands.

Caponata and Ricotta Sweet Potato Bites

Gluten-free • Healthy fats • High fibre • No added sugar • Vegetarian

Makes about 36 round bites; Serves 12

In my university days, I used to think "party snacks" was the universal code for fully loaded jalapeño poppers. Hey, sometimes a girl just needs something deep-fried, wrapped in bacon, and stuffed with oozing cheese. But, when I remember I don't have the digestive stamina of my twenty-year-old self, I realize a little balance just tastes better. Whether you're living out the glory days of your former under-aged self or looking for a classier grown-up snack, these darling little appies do the trick. A warm Sicilian-inspired salad of caramelized eggplant, sweet tomatoes, and briny olives is piled high onto a bed of pillowy protein-rich ricotta cheese with a roasted sweet potato "toast." Consider this a fork-free introduction to the sexy adult world of antipasto.

Sweet Potato Bites

5 large sweet potatoes, each peeled and sliced into
   about eight ¼-inch (5 mm) rounds
Extra-virgin olive oil in an oil atomizer
Sea salt and cracked black pepper

Caponata

4 teaspoons (20 mL) extra-virgin olive oil
3 cups (750 mL) finely diced eggplant
⅓ cup (75 mL) minced sweet onion
2 cloves garlic, finely minced
Sea salt and cracked black pepper
1 teaspoon (5 mL) tomato paste

¼ teaspoon (1 mL) cinnamon
1½ cups (375 mL) canned diced tomatoes (with some juice)
¼ cup (60 mL) golden raisins
2 tablespoons (30 mL) finely chopped roasted red pepper
2 teaspoons (10 mL) fresh lemon juice
⅓ cup (75 mL) finely chopped pimento-stuffed green olives
2 tablespoons (30 mL) thinly sliced fresh basil

Toppings

2 cups (500 mL) ricotta cheese
½ cup (125 mL) pine nuts, toasted
Fresh basil leaves, gently torn, for garnish

1. Preheat the oven to 450°F (230°F). Line a baking sheet with parchment paper.

2. **Make the Sweet Potato Bites** Arrange the sweet potato rounds on the prepared baking sheet. Spritz both sides with olive oil in an oil atomizer and season with a pinch each of salt and pepper. Roast for 10 minutes, or until golden brown. Turn and roast for another 10 minutes, or until tender and golden on the other side. Let cool to room temperature on the baking sheet.

3. **Make the Caponata** Meanwhile, heat the olive oil in a large nonstick skillet over medium heat. Add the eggplant, onion, garlic, and a pinch each of salt and pepper. Cook, stirring often, until the eggplant is soft and lightly caramelized, about 10 minutes. Add the tomato paste and cinnamon and stir until fragrant. Then add the tomatoes, raisins, red pepper, and lemon juice. Cover and cook for about 5 minutes, until the vegetables are tender. Remove the lid and allow the excess moisture to evaporate, another 4 to 5 minutes.

continues

4. Remove from the heat and stir in the olives and basil. Season with salt and pepper. Let the caponata cool to room temperature before serving.

5. When ready to serve, dollop a little fresh ricotta onto each of the sweet potato rounds, and top with a pinch each of salt and pepper. Finish with about 1 tablespoon (15 mL) of the Caponata, a few toasted pine nuts, and fresh basil. Enjoy at room temperature.

ABBEY'S TIP I know I'm a total Type A, but I've lost sleep from the stress of making appetizers. I've spent way too many holidays coated in gravy and flour, filling tiny little pastry shells with two hands and sometimes even my mouth, just trying to get everything to the table hot. It's a party, guys. Make it fun. This recipe is perfect for feeding a crowd without having a meltdown because everything can be made in advance and served at room temperature. You know you're getting old when the words "serve at room temperature" make you smile.

Crispy Avocado Fries with Mango Chili Coconut Dip

Dairy-free • Gluten-free • Healthy fats • High fibre • No added sugar • Nut-free • Vegan • Vegetarian

Serves 8

Being a good party host today is less about how well you can keep the conversation going while effortlessly stirring gravy and more about how you can accommodate your guests' varied and completely different dietary restrictions. I don't know about your circles, but in mine, just trying to find a menu item that everyone can enjoy consumes more time than the meal prep itself. The good news for you is that I put the time in here so that you don't have to. Legit, this dish is one of the tastiest things I've ever made, yet it's totally dairy-free, vegan, gluten-free, and nut-free. Buttery avocados get coated in a light and crispy chip crust and served with a refreshing yet fiery mango dip. You may be accommodating, but you definitely won't be compromising when serving this beauty of an appetizer.

Crispy Avocado Fries

¼ cup (60 mL) ground flaxseed

⅔ cup (150 mL) filtered water

⅓ cup (75 mL) oat flour (see page 18 for
   DIY version; gluten-free, if required)

½ teaspoon (2 mL) ground cumin

½ teaspoon (2 mL) salt

¼ teaspoon (1 mL) chili powder

¼ teaspoon (1 mL) cracked black pepper

4 cups (1 L) baked potato or vegetable chips
   (ideally low-sodium), crushed

2 slightly firm but not hard avocados, each pitted, peeled,
   and cut into 8 slices

Chili powder (if you want a little extra heat)

Fleur de sel (depending on your chips)

Mango Chili Coconut Dip

2 cups (500 mL) diced ripe mango (about 2 mangos)

2 tablespoons (30 mL) fresh cilantro leaves (optional)

1 tablespoon (15 mL) fresh lime juice, or to taste

½ teaspoon (2 mL) chili powder, or to taste

2 tablespoons (30 mL) coconut cream (or the thick white
   cream from the top of the can)

Pure maple syrup (optional)

Sea salt

1. Preheat the oven to 450°F (230°C). Line a baking sheet with parchment paper or a silicone baking mat.

2. **Make the Crispy Avocado Fries** In a shallow bowl, make a flaxseed egg by stirring together the flaxseed and water until well combined. Refrigerate for 20 to 25 minutes. It should look goopy and thick like an egg white.

3. In small bowl, stir together the oat flour, cumin, salt, chili powder, and pepper. Place the crushed chips in a large bowl.

4. Working with one slice at a time, dip the avocado into the oat mixture, then into the flaxseed egg, then into the chip crumbs, coating well. Arrange on the baking sheet, making sure they don't touch, and bake for 20 to 25 minutes, or until lightly golden brown, turning once halfway through. Sprinkle with chili powder, if desired, and if you used unsalted chips, sprinkle with a pinch of fleur de sel.

continues

5. **Make the Mango Chili Coconut Dip** Meanwhile, in a blender or food processor, combine the mango, cilantro (if using), lime juice, and chili powder. Blend until smooth. Add the coconut cream and blend just for a few seconds, until creamy and incorporated. Taste, and season with maple syrup (if using) and salt.

6. Serve the Crispy Avocado Fries with the Mango Chili Coconut Dip.

ABBEY'S TIP Stop the fat shaming and embrace the fatty goodness of avocados. One large study found that avocado eaters tended to have more nutritious diets overall, had better weight management strategies, and had lower risk of metabolic disorders. That's not surprising, considering that avocados are packed with heart-healthy monounsaturated fats and fibre that together keep you satisfied far longer than any of your typical deep-fried party snacks. These crispy avocado darlings are best hot out of the oven, but if you must make them ahead, simply refrigerate in an airtight container for up to 1 day before you're ready to serve, then recrisp them on a baking sheet in a 450°F (230°C) oven for 5 minutes.

Golden Pork Wontons with Hoisin Applesauce

Dairy-free • High protein • Nut-free

Makes 40 wontons; Serves 12 to 14

I grew up in a proper British home where deep-fried chicken balls and egg rolls were as far outside our meat-and-potatoes comfort zone as we would get. Today, I swoon over a good basket of steamed dim sum delights, but when I'm entertaining, I find most people crave a subtle, pan-fried crunch. These babies deliver it all. Supple, chewy wonton meets caramelized crispy edges with a sweet and tangy lean pork filling. I like stretching my meat budget with antioxidant-rich mushrooms minced to a meaty grind, adding that umami flavour but without any of that MSG crap. This is one of those hors d'oeuvres that is fun to make as a team, so grab the #squad and make a night of it!

Hoisin Applesauce

1 cup (250 mL) unsweetened applesauce

¼ cup (60 mL) hoisin sauce

¼ cup (60 mL) seasoned rice vinegar

2 tablespoons (30 mL) apple butter

1 tablespoon (15 mL) low-sodium soy sauce

1 teaspoon (5 mL) toasted sesame oil

Golden Pork Wontons

4 ounces (115 g) cremini mushrooms, stemmed

½ pound (225 g) extra-lean ground pork

¼ cup (60 mL) minced water chestnuts

3 tablespoons (45 mL) minced fresh cilantro leaves

2 tablespoons (30 mL) minced green onions
   (white and light green parts)

2 tablespoons (30 mL) hoisin sauce

2 teaspoons (10 mL) low-sodium soy sauce

1 teaspoon (5 mL) tapioca starch or cornstarch

1 teaspoon (5 mL) toasted sesame oil

½ teaspoon (2 mL) sea salt

½ teaspoon (2 mL) ground black pepper

40 wonton wrappers (from a 12-ounce/340 g package)

2 tablespoons (30 mL) extra-virgin olive oil, divided

1 cup (250 mL) filtered water

To Serve

1 cup (250 mL) fresh cilantro leaves

3 green onions (white and light green parts),
   thinly sliced on a diagonal

1 Thai red chili, thinly sliced

1. Preheat the oven to 150°F (65°C). Line a baking sheet with parchment paper or a silicone baking mat.

2. **Make the Hoisin Applesauce** In a small saucepan, combine the applesauce, hoisin sauce, rice vinegar, apple butter, soy sauce, and sesame oil. Stir over medium heat until warm, and keep warm until you're ready to serve.

3. **Make the Golden Pork Wontons** In a small food processor, pulse the mushrooms until they have the consistency of ground meat. Transfer to a large bowl and add the pork, water chestnuts, cilantro, green onions, hoisin sauce, soy sauce, tapioca starch, sesame oil, salt, and pepper. Mix well.

4. Lay a wonton wrapper on a clean surface. (Keep the remaining wrappers in plastic wrap so they don't dry out.) Using your finger, brush a bit of water all around the edges. Mound about 1½ teaspoons (7 mL) filling in the centre, and fold the wrapper over into a triangle shape. Press the dampened edges together with your thumb and index finger to seal. Repeat with the remaining wonton wrappers and filling.

continues

5. Heat a large nonstick skillet over medium-high heat, and keep the filtered water close by. Heat 2 teaspoons (10 mL) of the olive oil in the skillet until hot. Working with about a dozen wontons at a time, add the wontons and cook until golden brown on one side, about 1 minute. Flip them over and cook until they start to brown on the other side, another 1 minute. Working quickly, add about ¼ cup (60 mL) of the water and cover the pan with the lid. Let the wontons steam for 3 minutes. Remove the lid and continue to cook just until the water has evaporated and the wontons begin to crisp back up. Transfer to the prepared baking sheet and keep warm in the oven while you cook the remaining wontons.

6. To serve, arrange the Golden Pork Wontons on a platter, sprinkle with cilantro, green onions, and chili, and serve with the Hoisin Applesauce for dipping.

ABBEY'S TIP Take the stress out of entertaining by stuffing and freezing your wontons ahead. Arrange the uncooked wontons in a single layer on a baking sheet lined with parchment paper or a silicone baking mat, cover with plastic wrap, and freeze for 3 to 4 hours. Transfer them to a large resealable freezer bag and store in the freezer for up to 4 months. On party day, simply cook them from frozen, adding an extra minute or two to the steaming time.

Buffalo Chicken Egg Rolls with Blue Cheese Dip

High protein • **Nut-free**

Makes 12 rolls

Long before I could order myself a pint, the Brit in me loved going to the pub with my family for buffalo wing night. With each fiery bite of saucy chicken, my dad's face would turn as red as a British phone booth, and he'd say, "These make my head sweat, but hey, I think I like it." It might seem like questionable logic, but Dad was actually making a lot of sense. Whether heat activates a series of endorphins to counteract the spicy pain, or we just get a thrill from daring experiences like tipping the Scoville scale—eating spicy food definitely spanks those senses. My take on buffalo chicken wings loses the skin and bones but keeps the satisfying heat and packs that lean meat into a crispy baked egg roll shell. I serve mine with a creamy protein-packed cheese dip to quell that iconic fire, but as my dad might say, "If you still can't stand the heat, just take off your sweater vest and keep eating."

Buffalo Chicken Egg Rolls

1 rotisserie chicken (2 pounds/900 g)

¾ cup (175 mL) minced celery

¾ cup (175 mL) peeled and minced carrots

Sea salt

1 teaspoon (5 mL) cornstarch, tapioca starch, or brown rice flour

1 cup (250 mL) hot sauce (such as Frank's Original), divided

3 tablespoons (45 mL) unsalted butter

2 tablespoons (30 mL) pure liquid honey

2 teaspoons (10 mL) fresh lemon juice

12 egg roll wrappers

Extra-virgin olive oil in an oil atomizer

Blue Cheese Dip

1 cup (250 mL) plain 4% or 5% Greek yogurt

½ cup (125 mL) crumbled blue cheese

1 large clove garlic, minced

3 tablespoons (45 mL) fresh lemon juice

3 tablespoons (45 mL) olive oil mayonnaise

Sea salt and cracked black pepper

1. Preheat the oven to 400°F (200°C) and position the racks in the top ⅓ and bottom ⅓ of the oven. Line 2 baking sheets with parchment paper.

2. **Make the Buffalo Chicken Egg Rolls** Remove and discard the skin and bones from the chicken and finely shred the meat. You should have about 3 cups (750 mL) meat. In a medium bowl, combine the chicken, celery, carrots, and salt to taste. (You likely won't need pepper, unless you're a glutton for punishment.) Mix well and set aside.

3. In a small ramekin, stir together the cornstarch and ¼ cup (60 mL) of the hot sauce.

4. In a small saucepan, combine the remaining ¾ cup (175 mL) hot sauce, the butter, honey, and lemon juice. Bring to a boil over medium-high heat, then reduce the heat and simmer for 5 minutes. Give the cornstarch mixture a stir, stir it into the sauce, and cook for an additional 1 to 2 minutes, until the sauce thickens slightly. Let cool for 10 minutes. Add the sauce to the chicken mixture in a large bowl and stir to coat.

continues

5. Lay an egg roll wrapper in a diamond on a clean surface. (Keep the remaining wrappers in plastic wrap so they don't dry out.) Using your finger, brush a bit of water all around the edges. Spread about ¼ cup (60 mL) of the filling horizontally across the lower third of the wrapper to form a log. Fold the bottom corner over the filling, then brush a little water onto the newly exposed edges of the wrapper. Fold the side corners tightly in towards the middle, then roll the egg roll to close tightly. Make sure to seal any openings or gaps, using a bit of water as your super glue. Place the egg roll on the baking sheet, seam side down. Repeat with the remaining wrappers and filling. If any juices seem to have leaked out, just pat the egg rolls dry using a paper towel.

6. Spritz the egg rolls with a little olive oil in an oil atomizer. Bake for 10 minutes. Turn the egg rolls and sprinkle with a touch of salt. Bake for an additional 10 to 12 minutes, or until super crispy and browned. Transfer to a plate lined with paper towel.

7. **Make the Blue Cheese Dip** Meanwhile, in a food processor, combine the yogurt, cheese, garlic, lemon juice, mayonnaise, and salt and pepper to taste. Process until smooth.

8. Slice the Buffalo Chicken Egg Rolls in half with a strong knife and serve with the Blue Cheese Dip.

ABBEY'S TIP Entertaining often means making things ahead of time so that you can save your sanity on the day of. Bake these babies as instructed, then cool the egg rolls completely on a rack. Place the egg rolls on a parchment-lined baking sheet and freeze for at least 3 hours before transferring them to a resealable freezer bag for up to 3 months. As the party gets started, pop them into a 350°F (180°C) oven for about 10 minutes, or until heated through.

Pistachio-Crusted Lamb Lollies with Harissa Yogurt Dip

Gluten-free • Healthy fats • High protein • No added sugar

Makes 16 lollies; Serves 8

Back in my restaurant-reviewing days, I mastered the art of juggling a cocktail, three plated food samples, and the necessary cutlery in my hands, all while still getting a wicked Instagram shot. But after enduring a tragic saucy-pork-belly-meets-blouse incident—hey, what food blogger hasn't?!—I came to a realization so many before me had already had: food on sticks are your party BFFs. These lovely lamb lollies crust bite-size morsels of juicy lean meat with toasty, fragrant pistachios. And after a quick (and carefully calculated) dunk in a spicy, smoky protein-packed dip, you've got a party-perfect one-hand wonder. So elegant to serve, so easy to eat, and best of all, you avoid any post-party dry cleaning drama.

Pistachio-Crusted Lamb Lollies

⅓ cup (75 mL) finely minced unsalted natural pistachios

1 pound (450 g) lean ground lamb

2 small cloves garlic, finely minced

2 tablespoons (30 mL) thinly sliced fresh mint

2 teaspoons (10 mL) lemon zest

2 teaspoons (10 mL) ground coriander

1½ teaspoons (7 mL) ground cumin

1 teaspoon (5 mL) harissa

½ teaspoon (2 mL) sea salt

¼ teaspoon (1 mL) cracked black pepper

Harissa Yogurt Dip

4 teaspoons (20 mL) extra-virgin olive oil

2 teaspoons (10 mL) harissa

1½ cups (375 mL) plain 4% Greek yogurt

¼ cup (60 mL) fresh mint, thinly sliced

¼ cup (60 mL) fresh cilantro, finely chopped

2 teaspoons (10 mL) lemon zest

2 tablespoons (30 mL) fresh lemon juice

½ teaspoon (2 mL) ground cumin

Sea salt and cracked black pepper

1. Place a baking sheet in the oven and preheat the oven to 375°F (190°C). Have ready 16 cocktail skewers or ice-pop sticks.

2. **Make the Pistachio-Crusted Lamb Lollies** Place the pistachios in a shallow dish and set aside.

3. In a large bowl, combine the lamb, garlic, mint, lemon zest, coriander, cumin, harissa, salt, and pepper. Mix thoroughly with your hands, but be careful not to overwork the meat. Roll 2 tablespoons (30 mL) at a time into balls, then roll the balls in the pistachios.

4. Place on the hot baking sheet and bake for 12 to 15 minutes, or until the internal temperature is 160°F (70°C). Remove from the oven and immediately insert a cocktail skewer or ice-pop stick into each ball and transfer to a serving dish.

5. **Make the Harissa Yogurt Dip** Meanwhile, in a small bowl, whisk together the olive oil and harissa until well combined.

6. In a medium bowl, combine the yogurt, mint, cilantro, lemon zest, lemon juice, cumin, and a pinch each of salt and pepper. Stir well. Transfer to a serving bowl and swirl the harissa oil on top of the yogurt in a pretty pattern.

7. Serve the Pistachio-Crusted Lamb Lollies warm from the oven with the Harissa Yogurt Dip.

ABBEY'S TIP Often called "land salmon" (as strange as that visual is), lamb often has an omega-6 to omega-3 ratio closer to fatty fish than any other domestic meat. With 40 percent of its fats coming from heart-healthy monounsaturated fat and a boatload of high-value protein on board, it's a shame we don't eat more lamb. To get the most nutrient bang (especially for those healthy fats) for your buck, I suggest using 100 percent grass-fed lamb. If you're averse to its mild gamy flavour, you can easily substitute lean beef. These lollies can be made ahead and refrigerated for up to 4 days ahead, or frozen for up to 6 months. Thaw if necessary and reheat in a 375°F (190°C) oven for 5 to 8 minutes until hot.

Something
Sweet

Mayan Salted Avocado Hot Chocolate Brookies

Dairy-free • Nut-free • Vegetarian

Makes 24 cookies

I first enjoyed Mayan hot chocolate at a winter festival in Toronto. The unexpected kick of chili and the soothing aroma of cinnamon added an extra hit of warmth to an otherwise drizzly day. Named affectionately for their cookie appearance and dense brownie texture, these brookies deliver that same unexpected jolt of heat. With a gentle tickle of chili spice peeping through the salty, crackly crust, these fudgy chocolate treats melt on the tongue. And don't be rattled by the avocado. With its creamy, buttery texture and mild flavour, this luscious fruit is a nutrient-packed substitute for butter and oil that's brimming with heart-healthy fats. Sweet, spicy, salty, and bitter, these beauties fire all the pleasure buttons on your tongue. Drizzly day? You got this.

¾ cup (175 mL) mashed very ripe avocado
 (about 1½ small avocados)
½ cup (125 mL) coconut sugar
¼ cup (60 mL) virgin coconut oil, melted
2 tablespoons (30 mL) pure liquid honey
1 large egg
1 teaspoon (5 mL) pure vanilla extract
½ cup (125 mL) whole wheat flour
2 tablespoons (30 mL) unsweetened cocoa powder, sifted

1 teaspoon (5 mL) chili powder, more for sprinkling
 if desired
½ teaspoon (2 mL) cinnamon
½ teaspoon (2 mL) baking powder
⅛ teaspoon (0.5 mL) salt
⅛ teaspoon (0.5 mL) cayenne pepper
½ cup (125 mL/about 3 ounces) finely chopped
 70% dark chocolate (dairy-free, if required)
Fleur de sel, for sprinkling

1. Preheat the oven to 350°F (180°C). Line a baking sheet with parchment paper or a silicone baking mat.

2. In a large bowl, beat together the avocado, coconut sugar, coconut oil, and honey until well incorporated. Gently stir in the egg and vanilla until just combined.

3. In a medium bowl, combine the whole wheat flour, cocoa powder, chili powder, cinnamon, baking powder, salt, and cayenne. Gently stir the dry ingredients into the wet ingredients until just combined. Stir in the finely chopped chocolate.

4. Transfer the dough to a piping bag fitted with a 1-inch (2.5 cm) pipe tip, and pipe into 1½-inch (4 cm) circles spaced ¾ inch (2 cm) apart. Flatten any mounds with a damp finger. Sprinkle cookies with fleur de sel. The heat in the cookies is fairly subtle, so if you want an extra little kick, sprinkle with a little pinch of chili powder.

5. Bake for 15 minutes, or until the cookies feel dry and are set on the bottom. Transfer to a rack and let cool completely.

ABBEY'S TIP Don't have a piping bag? All good. Fill a large plastic bag with the dough, and with the bag open squeeze it down into one corner, then seal the bag and snip out a ¼-inch (5 mm) hole in that corner. Pipe away! These cookies are best kept in an airtight container for up to 3 days, but you can also store them in the freezer for up to 6 months. Be sure to freeze until solid on a baking sheet before transferring to a resealable freezer bag to prevent them from sticking together.

Samoas Doughnuts

Dairy-free • Gluten-free • High fibre • Nut-free • Vegetarian

Makes 6 doughnuts

I was never a Girl Guide. I'm pretty sure my mom thought the whole thing was a bit hokey and that the uniform was lame, but mainly I think she didn't want to get stuck selling $5 boxes of cookies. So while I never learned how to tie a fisherman's knot, I did develop my own affinity for the chocolate, caramel, and coconutty goodness that is Samoas cookies. These moist, spongy cake doughnuts are topped with a thick, sticky caramel made from fresh Medjool dates, fibre-rich coconut, and luscious dark chocolate. Skip the annual cookie haul and get your Chef's Badge with these babies instead.

Doughnuts

Olive oil in an oil atomizer

2 large eggs

½ cup (125 mL) light brown sugar, lightly packed

¼ cup (60 mL) virgin coconut oil

¼ cup (60 mL) unsweetened vanilla soy milk or almond milk

1 tablespoon (15 mL) unpasteurized apple cider vinegar

1 teaspoon (5 mL) pure vanilla extract

½ cup (125 mL) brown rice flour

¼ cup (60 mL) coconut flour

1 tablespoon (15 mL) unsweetened cocoa powder, sifted

1 teaspoon (5 mL) cinnamon

¼ teaspoon (1 mL) nutmeg

¼ teaspoon (1 mL) salt

Samoas Topping

½ cup (125 mL) Medjool dates, pitted and finely chopped (5 to 6 dates)

¼ cup (60 mL) unsweetened vanilla soy milk or almond milk

¼ cup (60 mL) pure maple syrup

Pinch of sea salt

¾ cup (175 mL) unsweetened shredded coconut, toasted

2 ounces (55 g) 70% dark chocolate (dairy-free, if required), finely chopped

1. Preheat the oven to 350°F (180°C). Lightly grease a 6-cavity doughnut pan with olive oil in an oil atomizer.

2. **Make the Doughnuts** In a stand mixer or using a hand mixer, beat the eggs until light and pale yellow, about 4 minutes. Add the sugar and coconut oil and slowly beat until combined. Add the milk, apple cider vinegar, and vanilla and stir just until mixed.

3. In a small bowl, stir together the rice flour, coconut flour, cocoa powder, cinnamon, nutmeg, and salt. Stir the dry ingredients into the wet ingredients just until mixed. Transfer the batter to a piping bag.

4. Pipe the batter into the doughnut pan, filling each mould about three-quarters full. Bake for 15 minutes, or until a toothpick inserted in the centre of a doughnut comes out clean. Let cool in the pan to room temperature.

5. **Make the Samoas Topping** In a small saucepan, combine the dates and soy milk. Cover with a lid and bring to a gentle simmer over medium heat, about 4 minutes. Transfer the mixture to a food processor and process until the dates are well broken down. Add the maple syrup and salt and process until smooth.

continues

6. Pour the mixture back into the saucepan and bring to a boil. Reduce the heat and simmer until it thickens slightly, about 5 minutes. Remove from the heat, stir in the coconut, and let cool to room temperature.

7. Place the chocolate in a heatproof bowl and place it over a small saucepan filled with 1 inch (2.5 cm) of water. Bring the water to a bare simmer and let the chocolate gently melt, stirring often. *(Optional microwave method: Place the chocolate in a microwave-safe dish. Melt in the microwave on 50 percent power in 30-second increments until almost fully melted. Stir once after each 30-second increment.)*

8. To assemble, remove the doughnuts from the pan and arrange them flat side up (the side that was facing upwards in the oven). Smear a generous amount of the Samoas Topping onto each doughnut, then use a fork to drizzle the tops with melted chocolate. Allow the chocolate to set for 5 minutes.

ABBEY'S TIP Don't leave out either of the two flours and think you can just increase the other one. Trust me, I didn't just use two types to seem fancy. I love hearty coconut flour because it has far more satiating protein and fibre than even the gold-standard whole wheat. But without the lighter brown rice flour in there, you would lose that ethereal doughnut texture. I'm all for experimenting in the kitchen, but doughnuts are sacred territory, and trust me, this combination works. Store your doughnuts in an airtight container at room temperature for up to 3 days, or transfer to resealable freezer bags and freeze for up to 3 months.

Ultimate Sticky Toffee Puddings

Gluten-free • Dairy-free • Nut-free • Vegetarian

Makes 8 large puddings or 24 mini puddings

I'm a British girl, so naturally, sticky toffee pudding isn't just a dessert to me, it's a lifestyle. I've proudly eaten my way through Toronto studying official STP science, and once planned an entire U.K. trip around finding the best pud. Honestly, it's a miracle this book ever made it past this one recipe after taste-testing it for months, but I was determined to do my pudding palate proud. Long, sticky story short—I nailed it. My version starts with dense, spicy little sponge cakes so good you'll almost forget about the sauce. But that would be sacrilege, so please just don't. I suggest tucking into a generous pool of my sweet and salty date toffee that's so addictive you'll want an extra shot to drink. So save those air miles and call off the local pudding tour. These puds bring the best of the U.K. home.

Sticky Toffee Pudding
½ cup (125 mL) Medjool dates, pitted and diced
¼ cup (60 mL) boiling water
¼ teaspoon (1 mL) baking soda
¼ cup (60 mL) virgin coconut oil, melted
¼ cup (60 mL) fancy molasses
¼ cup (60 mL) mashed very ripe banana
1 tablespoon (15 mL) grated fresh ginger
2 large eggs
1 cup (250 mL) oat flour (see page 18 for DIY version; gluten-free, if required)
2 tablespoons (30 mL) tapioca starch
1 teaspoon (5 mL) salt
½ teaspoon (2 mL) cinnamon

Toffee Sauce
¾ cup (175 mL) Medjool dates, pitted and diced
¾ cup (175 mL) unsweetened vanilla soy milk or almond milk
¼ cup + 2 tablespoons (90 mL) pure maple syrup
A few pinches of sea salt

To Serve (optional)
Coconut yogurt

1. Preheat the oven to 350°F (180°C). Lightly grease 8 large muffin cups or 24 mini muffin cups.

2. **Make the Sticky Toffee Pudding** In a small bowl, combine the dates, boiling water, and baking soda, and let sit for 5 minutes.

3. Transfer the dates and their soaking water to a food processor and add the coconut oil, molasses, banana, and ginger. Process until very smooth. Add the eggs and process just until incorporated. Be careful not to overwhip the eggs.

4. In a large bowl, stir together the oat flour, tapioca starch, salt, and cinnamon. Stir in the date mixture until combined.

5. Pour about 3 tablespoons (45 mL) batter into each large muffin cup or 1 heaping tablespoon (18 mL) per mini muffin cup. Bake for about 20 minutes for the large puddings or 10 minutes for the minis. Let cool for a few moments before carefully popping them out onto dessert plates.

continues

6. **Make the Toffee Sauce** While the puddings are cooking, in a small saucepan, combine the dates and soy milk. Cover with a lid and bring to a simmer, about 4 minutes. Transfer to a food processor or high-speed blender and purée. Add the maple syrup and salt and whirl until super smooth.

7. Return the mixture to the saucepan and bring to a boil. Reduce the heat and simmer until it bubbles and thickens into a luscious caramel-like consistency, about 1 minute. If it gets too thick, just add a few more tablespoons of soy milk.

8. To serve, while the puddings are still warm, poke a few holes into each with a toothpick and smother them with a spoonful of Toffee Sauce. Garnish with a dollop of coconut yogurt, if desired.

ABBEY'S TIP These puddings are best eaten within 2 days, stored at room temperature, but you can freeze them (without the sauce topping) on a baking sheet for 1 hour before transferring to a resealable freezer bag for up to 3 months. When you're ready to eat, remove them from the freezer bag, place on a plate, cover with plastic wrap, and thaw on the counter until they reach room temperature. Add an extra splash of soy or almond milk before rewarming the sauce in the microwave or a saucepan, and tuck in.

Tiramisu Paletas

Healthy fats • Nut-free • Vegetarian

Makes 6 frozen pops

A few years back, I read some health magazine where they listed the unexpected foods women should avoid when pregnant. At the top? Tiramisu. Really. What the article should have been called is "Reasons Women Hate Pregnancy." Let's get real. Tiramisu is a beautiful thing. Even the name rolls off the tongue like romantic free-verse poetry. Moist, booze-soaked cookies, coffee-spiked cream, and luscious dark chocolate—seems to me that's exactly what expectant mothers need. My version boosts the protein with satiny-smooth Greek yogurt and packs the whole thing into a no-spoon-required fro-yo pop. The hardest part is waiting for the paletas to freeze, but I say patience is a virtue. Deprivation is not.

Tiramisu Paletas

4 ladyfingers

¼ cup (60 mL) Marsala wine (or non-alcoholic substitute; see Tip)

¼ cup (60 mL) finely grated 70% dark chocolate (about 1½ ounces)

1½ cups (375 mL) plain 4% Greek yogurt

¾ cup (175 mL) mascarpone cheese

3 tablespoons (45 mL) pure liquid honey

1 tablespoon (15 mL) instant espresso powder

Chocolate Dip

½ cup (125 mL) chopped 70% dark chocolate (about 3 ounces)

1 tablespoon (15 mL) virgin coconut oil

1. **Make the Tiramisu Paletas** Cut each ladyfinger into 3 equal pieces. Pour the wine into a small bowl and place the grated dark chocolate in another small bowl. Dip the ladyfinger pieces into the wine, then roll them in the chocolate. Transfer to a plate and set aside. Reserve any remaining dark chocolate.

2. In a medium bowl, beat together the yogurt, mascarpone, honey, and espresso powder. Transfer to a piping bag fitted with a ½-inch (1 cm) plain tip or a plastic bag with the corner cut off.

3. Pipe about 1 inch (2.5 cm) of the yogurt filling into each of 6 ice-pop moulds. Drop in one piece of ladyfinger and press it into the yogurt filling. Pipe the yogurt filling around the ladyfinger, making sure the filling completely surrounds the ladyfinger to help hold it in place—this is *key* to making sure your pops stay together. Fill each mould with another inch of yogurt filling, and then press in another piece of ladyfinger. Finish with the remaining yogurt filling, again being sure the filling completely surrounds the ladyfinger. Sprinkle any remaining grated dark chocolate on top. Carefully insert the ice-pop sticks and freeze until solid, at least 4 hours.

4. **Make the Chocolate Dip** Before serving, place the chocolate and coconut oil in a heatproof bowl and place it over a small saucepan filled with 1 inch (2.5 cm) of water. Bring the water to a bare simmer and let the chocolate gently melt, stirring often. Remove the bowl from the pot. (*Optional microwave method: Place the chocolate in a microwave-safe dish. Melt in the microwave on 50 percent power in 30-second increments until almost fully melted. Stir once after each 30-second increment.*)

continues

5. When ready to serve, run the ice-pop mould under hot water until the pop easily releases, then carefully pull it out. Dip about ¾ inch (2 cm) of the tip into the chocolate. Let any excess chocolate drip off as it freezes into a shell. Repeat with the remaining ice-pops and enjoy immediately.

ABBEY'S TIP Although the amount of alcohol per pop is likely fairly negligible (unless you let those ladyfingers linger extra long like I "accidentally" do sometimes), if you want to cut it out completely, simply soak your cookies in brewed coffee instead. Because of the shape of the ladyfingers, it's best to use a classic large rectangle ice-pop mould rather than a round, short, or rocket-shaped mould.

Piña Colada Napoleons

Gluten-free • Nut-free • Vegetarian

Serves 4

I'm not much for nature, but I wait all year to light up the grill and get outdoors. Okay, so I could—and honestly sometimes do—barbecue during a minus-ten blizzard, but it's far more enjoyable without the insulated gloves and parka. Regardless of the weather forecast, this dessert will transport you away on a tropical vacation. A lick of fire caramelizes sweet rings of pineapple to a crackling, succulent state, contrasting with a creamy coconut filling laced with marshmallowy bites. Even in a hailstorm of epic proportion, this recipe nails that vacation vibe.

Lime-Honey Pineapple
1 lime, halved
2 tablespoons (30 mL) pure liquid honey
12 rings fresh pineapple (about ⅛ inch/3 mm thick)

Napoleon Filling
1 can (14 ounces/400 mL) full-fat coconut milk, refrigerated overnight
1 cup (250 mL) plain 2% Greek yogurt

2 teaspoons (10 mL) pure liquid honey, more to taste
2 teaspoons (10 mL) light rum
1 teaspoon (5 mL) pure vanilla extract
3 teaspoons (15 mL) lime zest, divided
1 medium banana, cut into bite-size cubes
1½ cups (375 mL) coarsely crushed meringue cookies or pavlova pieces
¼ cup (60 mL) + 3 tablespoons (45 mL) unsweetened flaked coconut, toasted, divided

1. Prepare a grill for direct cooking over medium heat. Lightly grease the grate.

2. **Grill the Lime-Honey Pineapple** Grill the lime halves cut side down until charred and juicy, about 3 minutes. Transfer to a plate and let cool enough that you can pick them up. In a small bowl, juice the grilled limes (I suggest using a citrus reamer to save your fingers!) into a small bowl. Stir in the honey. Lightly brush both sides of the pineapple rings with the lime-honey mixture, reserving any extra for garnish.

3. Grill the pineapple rings with the lid open until both sides are charred, 4 to 5 minutes per side. Set the pineapple aside to cool to at least room temperature.

4. **Make the Napoleon Filling** Open the can of coconut milk and scoop the solid white coconut cream on the top into a large bowl. Discard (or drink!) the remaining coconut water. Using a hand mixer, whip the coconut cream until very smooth and fluffy. Add the yogurt, honey, rum, vanilla, and 2 teaspoons (10 mL) of the lime zest. Beat until the filling is fluffy, lusciously smooth, and thick.

5. Fold in the banana, crushed meringue cookies, and ¼ cup (60 mL) toasted coconut. Set aside.

6. To serve, place 4 pineapple rings on a platter. Top each with a spoonful of the coconut cream, using about half the cream. Top with another 4 pineapple rings, the remaining coconut cream, and then the remaining 4 pineapple rings. Garnish with the remaining 3 tablespoons (45 mL) toasted coconut, the remaining 1 teaspoon (5 mL) lime zest, and a drizzle of any remaining lime-honey mixture.

continues

ABBEY'S TIP Pineapple is one of my all-time favourite fruits, and it is packed with a protein-digesting enzyme called bromelain. The research is still young, but bromelain may help reduce the duration of sinus infections, improve immunity, and reduce inflammation. Grill up extra slices and serve them on yogurt or cottage cheese for a quick snack. The pineapple and filling (without the banana and meringue cookies) can be made 1 day ahead and refrigerated until you're ready to serve. Add the bananas and meringue cookie to the coconut cream just before assembling.

Meyer Lemon Raspberry Cheesecakes

Healthy fats • Vegetarian

Makes 8 mini cheesecakes

Once I had a dream that I was invited to be the official cheesecake tester at the Cheesecake Factory, and I took my role very seriously. Sometimes I wouldn't be sure" about a cheesecake until I had eaten the whole slice and then compared that slice to a slice of every other cake in the display case. I'm convinced this was actually a premonition of just how many versions of this recipe I tried in my quest for tangy-sweet cheesecake perfection. That, or I just kept making them so I could eat more. My hand-held version upgrades the classic graham cracker crust with protein-rich almonds and fibre-loaded cereal. Since no dream-state cheesecake expert would ever condone fat-free cream cheese, I boost the protein and lighten up the texture with tangy Greek yogurt. Scented with the oh-so-floral notes of Meyer lemons, it's finished with a sprightly, tangy swirl of raspberries. Maybe dreams do come true (at least when you're in my kitchen).

Cheesecake Crust

¼ cup (60 mL) high-fibre bran shreds cereal
   (such as All-Bran Original)
¼ cup (60 mL) graham cracker crumbs
¼ cup (60 mL) almond flour
1 tablespoon (15 mL) pure liquid honey
1 tablespoon (15 mL) unsalted butter, melted
½ teaspoon (2 mL) Meyer lemon zest

Meyer Lemon Cheesecake Filling

4 ounces (115 g) cream cheese, softened and diced
1 cup (250 mL) plain 2% Greek yogurt
¼ cup (60 mL) pure liquid honey
1 tablespoon (15 mL) Meyer lemon zest
1 tablespoon (15 mL) fresh Meyer lemon juice
1 teaspoon (5 mL) pure vanilla extract
1 large egg, beaten

Raspberry Swirl

¼ cup (60 mL) frozen or fresh raspberries
1 teaspoon (5 mL) pure liquid honey

1. Preheat the oven to 350°F (180°C). Line a mini muffin tin with 8 paper liners.

2. **Make the Cheesecake Crust** In a food processor, pulse the cereal, graham cracker crumbs, and almond flour until the cereal crushes down to crumbs. Add the honey, melted butter, and lemon zest and pulse until combined. Spoon just under 1 tablespoon (15 mL) of the mixture into each liner and press down firmly with your fingers. Bake until lightly browned around the edges, about 5 minutes. Set aside.

3. **Make the Meyer Lemon Cheesecake Filling** Wipe out the food processor, then purée the cream cheese. Add the yogurt, honey, lemon zest, lemon juice, and vanilla. Purée again. Add the egg and whiz for 2 seconds. Transfer filling to a glass measuring cup with a spout. Rinse and dry the food processor bowl.

4. **Make the Raspberry Swirl** Place the raspberries in a microwave-safe bowl and cover with plastic wrap. Microwave for 30 seconds, or until softened and juicy. In the food processor, combine the softened raspberries and the honey and give it a quick whiz to combine. If your food processor is being difficult about puréeing such a small volume, give it a few good pulses to get it going or simply mash any remaining raspberry pieces with the back of a spoon until smooth.

continues

5. Evenly divide the Meyer Lemon Cheesecake Filling among the crusts and give the pan a gentle tap on the counter to level the filling. Using a small spoon, make tiny circle droplets of the raspberry sauce in rows on each of the cheesecakes. Then, drag a toothpick through the raspberry sauce to create a swirled effect. (Don't worry if they aren't perfect swirls. It will taste so good, no one will mind.)

6. Bake for 20 to 22 minutes, or until the centres look set with nothing more than a tiny little jiggle. Let cool in the muffin pan on a rack until room temperature, Carefully lift the cheesecakes out of the pan. Chill for at least 1 hour before eating.

ABBEY'S TIP Greek yogurt is a luscious creamy strained yogurt that tastes like tangy whipped cream while packing a whopping 15 grams of protein per serving. It's lower in lactose (and therefore sugar) than traditional yogurt and is a natural source of probiotics (a.k.a. healthy gut bacteria). Translation? It's perfect for promoting good digestion after your main meal (or as in the case of my dream, after thirty-three different cakes). When choosing a Greek yogurt, look for one without stabilizers, thickeners, or fillers. Ideally the ingredients should be just dairy and a healthy bacteria such as *L. acidophilus, L. casei,* or *B. bifidum.*

These cheesecakes will keep in an airtight container in the fridge for up to 5 days. They can also be wrapped individually in plastic wrap and gently stored in a resealable freezer bag for up to 3 months.

Flourless Chocolate Almond Cake with Cherry Amaretto Sauce

Dairy-free • Gluten-free • Healthy fats • Vegetarian

Makes one 9-inch (23 cm) round cake; Serves 12

I like to think that Moses parted the Red Sea for flourless chocolate cake, and I'd totally be right behind him through the pass. In fact, I first enjoyed flourless cake at a Passover dinner, but spent the entire Seder choking down dry matzah while eyeing the thing from across the room. Getting through the Haggadah can be challenging on a good day, but delaying cake gratification makes that struggle so much more real. Thankfully, it was worth the wait. My version is simultaneously rich and light, with a crackly crust and a molten fudge centre. Made with natural almond butter, almond flour, and almond liqueur, it delivers a delicate nutty aroma to balance the decadent dark chocolate, with a sweet, boozy finish of cherry sauce. I promise you, it's worth crossing any desert for.

Flourless Chocolate Almond Cake

Extra-virgin olive oil in an oil atomizer

Unsweetened cocoa powder, for dusting

5¼ ounces (150 g) 70% dark chocolate
  (dairy-free, if required), coarsely chopped

⅓ cup (75 mL) virgin coconut oil

½ cup (125 mL) natural almond butter

4 large egg yolks

½ cup (125 mL) mashed very ripe banana
  (about 1 large banana)

⅓ cup (75 mL) almond flour

2 tablespoons (30 mL) unsweetened cocoa powder, sifted

2 tablespoons (30 mL) Amaretto liqueur

1 tablespoon (15 mL) pure vanilla extract

¼ teaspoon (1 mL) salt

6 large egg whites

½ teaspoon (2 mL) cream of tartar

⅓ cup (75 mL) pure maple syrup

Cherry Amaretto Sauce

5 cups (1.25 L) fresh or thawed frozen pitted dark cherries

½ cup (125 mL) Amaretto liqueur

2 tablespoons (30 mL) pure maple syrup

1 teaspoon (5 mL) fresh lemon juice

4 teaspoons (20 mL) cornstarch, tapioca starch,
  or brown rice flour

4 teaspoons (20 mL) filtered water

Sea salt

To Serve (optional)

Icing sugar, for dusting

Crushed unsalted natural almonds

1. Preheat the oven to 325°F (160°C). Line the bottom of a 9-inch (2.5 L) springform pan with parchment paper. Using your oil atomizer, lightly grease the pan's sides and the parchment paper with olive oil, and then dust the insides with cocoa powder, knocking out the excess.

2. **Make the Flourless Chocolate Almond Cake** Place the chocolate and coconut oil in a heatproof bowl and place it over a small saucepan filled with 1 inch (2.5 cm) of water. Bring the water to a bare simmer and let the chocolate gently melt, stirring often. Stir in the almond butter and heat, stirring, for another 30 seconds, until well incorporated. *(Optional microwave method: Place the chocolate and coconut oil in a microwave-safe dish. Melt in the microwave on 50 percent power in 30-second increments until almost fully melted. Stir once after each 30-second increment. Once melted, stir in the almond butter and microwave for an additional 15 seconds.)*

continues

3. Let the chocolate cool to room temperature. Stir in the egg yolks, banana, almond flour, cocoa powder, Amaretto, vanilla, and salt.

4. In a very clean bowl, beat the egg whites on medium speed until they are very foamy. Add the cream of tartar and continue to beat until you get voluptuous peaks and poofs. Continue to beat on medium speed while slowly adding the maple syrup until you get stiff peaks when you lift the beaters. This usually takes just a few minutes, but it really depends on your egg whites and your beaters.

5. Using a whisk (or the big whisk attachment of the stand mixer), gingerly whisk a quarter of the egg whites into the chocolate mixture to loosen and lighten the texture. Once fairly incorporated (you may still see some streaks), switch to a spatula and gently fold in the rest of the egg whites until barely incorporated and cohesive.

6. Pour the batter into the prepared springform pan. and gently tap the pan on the counter to level the batter. Bake for 30 minutes, or until the cake has puffed up, the top feels smooth and dry, and the centre doesn't jiggle. Let the cake cool completely on a wire rack for at least 1 hour before removing the sides of the pan.

7. **Make the Cherry Amaretto Sauce** In a medium saucepan, combine the cherries, Amaretto, maple syrup, and lemon juice. Bring to a simmer over medium heat, stirring. In a small bowl, stir together the cornstarch and the filtered water until thick and smooth, then stir it into the bubbling sauce. Simmer until the sauce reaches a thick, syrup-like consistency. Remove from the heat and stir in a pinch of salt.

8. To serve, dust the cake with icing sugar and top with crushed almonds, if desired. Using a sharp knife, cut into thin slices (running the knife under hot water between slices), and serve with the Cherry Amaretto Sauce.

ABBEY'S TIP Almond flour is a naturally gluten-free flour alternative that's made by finely grinding whole blanched almonds. Almonds are packed with protein, healthy monounsaturated fats, and fibre, so you can have your cake and eat it too (without the unpleasant sugar coma). Almond meal (what I use in my Almond-Crusted French Toast on page 40) is nutritionally comparable but is generally a coarser grind and usually includes the almond skins. I've tried this cake with both, and while I prefer the light texture of the finer almond flour, you can substitute almond meal in a pinch.

This cake can be covered in plastic wrap or stored in an airtight container in the fridge for up to 3 days and brought to room temperature before serving. You can also wrap it tightly in plastic wrap, place in a resealable freezer bag, and store in the freezer for up to 3 months. Thaw in the fridge overnight before serving.

Sweet Summer Watermelon Cake

Dairy-free • Gluten-free • Healthy fats • High fibre • No added sugar • Vegan • Vegetarian

Serves 12 to 16

In the words of the great Julia Child, a party without cake is just a meeting. But in the heat of summer, cakes are known to get gloopy and sad (if it wasn't already that way when you chose it from the budget grocery store display). So, to keep the party outdoors, where it belongs, I've created a "cake" that is as fun to make as it is to eat, using a flavour ninja: fresh watermelon. While this sweet and juicy fruit makes for a hydrating summer treat au naturel, a fibre-rich almond and yogurt "frosting" and fruity decals give it a festive cake-over. I think Julia would agree: we clearly know how to throw a proper party.

1 large seedless watermelon (see Tip)

1 cup + 2 tablespoons (280 mL) almond meal or almond flour

¾ cup (175 mL) unsweetened coconut yogurt

1½ teaspoons (7 mL) pure maple syrup (optional)

Suggested Decorations

½ cup (125 mL) unsweetened finely shredded coconut

¼ cup (60 mL) thinly sliced unsalted natural almonds

1 ripe banana, thinly sliced

12 strawberries, halved

1 cup (250 mL) red raspberries

¼ cup (60 mL) pomegranate arils

1. Cut off the ends of the watermelon and stand it up straight. Cut the rind off the watermelon, then trim any rough edges so the outside is smooth.

2. Pat the watermelon a bit dry with paper towel or a kitchen towel that you don't mind getting a bit sticky and pink. Spread newspaper under a serving platter and stand the watermelon upright on the platter. (You may make a little mess while decorating.)

3. To make the "icing," in a small bowl, stir together the almond meal, yogurt, and maple syrup (if using). Using an offset spatula, coat the watermelon in a very thin layer of icing. You may have leftover icing depending on the size of your watermelon, but don't be too generous with it—the thinner the layer, the easier it is to decorate.

4. To decorate, have fun with this cake. There really aren't any rules, and it's a great activity to involve the kids. I sometimes like to gently "slap" the sides with coconut and add some sliced almonds for crunch, then make a ring of sliced banana around the edges, and finish the top with a mountain of berries and pomegranate arils. You do you.

5. Refrigerate until ready to serve, then slice into tall cake wedges.

ABBEY'S TIP Watermelon is the richest source of lycopene, a powerful antioxidant that may play an important role in protecting against prostate cancer. When choosing a watermelon to "cake up," look for one with an oval or rectangular shape rather than a perfect sphere, which will give you more room to get clean, smooth sides. I love serving this cake for Canada Day (hence why I go all out on the white-and-red colour scheme), but my friends south of the border can add their own patriotic flair with a few blueberries for fourth of July celebrations!

ABBEY'S TIP I use natural peanut butter made without added sugar, because the chocolate and ripe banana have got the sweet thing down. Just need a tiny PB-chocolate fix? This recipe can also be made in mini candy moulds, using about ½ teaspoon (2 mL) of filling per mould to yield 50 mini cups. If you can't eat them all at once (hey, I don't judge), these keep in the freezer for up to 6 months, ready to be quickly thawed and devoured in the throes of your next chocolate emergency.

Chocolate Banana Peanut Butter Cups

Dairy-free • Gluten-free • Healthy fats • Vegan • Vegetarian

Makes 10 peanut butter cups

Dietitian confession: I may load up on Reese's Peanut Butter Cups when I see the family-size boxes go on sale the day after Halloween. Follow-up confession: the "family" I'm serving consists of just me. Yes, I am a dietitian, but as far as I'm concerned, peanut butter + chocolate is one of the key pillars to a healthy, happy relationship with yourself. And as much as I adore the iconic orange-wrapped candies, I'll take one of my homemade little morsels of happiness any day of the year. Rich, dark chocolate envelopes a luscious nutty core sweetened naturally with ripe banana, all finished with a flaky, salty crust. No tricks here, just irresistible peanut buttery treats.

Banana Peanut Butter Filling
1 very ripe banana, diced
½ cup (125 mL) natural peanut butter
2 teaspoons (10 mL) virgin coconut oil, melted
   (omit if your peanut butter is smooth and oily)
¼ teaspoon (1 mL) pure vanilla extract

Chocolate Shell
10½ ounces (300 g) 70% dark chocolate
   (vegan or dairy-free, if required), finely chopped
4 teaspoons (20 mL) virgin coconut oil, melted

Garnish
Fleur de sel

1. **Make the Banana Peanut Butter Filling** In a small food processor, combine the banana, peanut butter, coconut oil (if needed), and vanilla. Process until smooth and creamy. Set aside.

2. **Make the Chocolate Shell** Place the chocolate and coconut oil in a heatproof bowl and place it over a small saucepan filled with 1 inch (2.5 cm) of water. Bring the water to a bare simmer and let the chocolate gently melt, stirring often. *(Optional microwave method: Place the chocolate and coconut oil in a microwave-safe dish. Melt in the microwave on 50 percent power in 30-second increments until almost fully melted. Stir once after each 30-second increment.)*

3. To assemble, using a small spoon, carefully spoon a thin layer of the dark chocolate into the bottoms of 10 regular-size silicone muffin moulds. Place the moulds on a baking sheet and transfer to the freezer until hardened, at least 5 minutes.

4. Once set, roll 1 tablespoon (15 mL) of the Banana Peanut Butter Filling into a ball narrower than the diameter of the muffin mould and gently press it onto the chocolate base. Using your finger, gently press on the top to make as flat a surface as possible, but be careful that the filling does not touch the sides of the mould.

5. If your melted chocolate has cooled, reheat it over barely simmering water. Using a small spoon, gingerly pour the chocolate down the sides of each muffin cup to envelop and fully cover the filling. Transfer to the freezer until fully set, at least 20 minutes.

6. Just before serving, sprinkle the cups with a pinch of fleur de sel.

Key Lime Mousse Parfait with Coconut Cashew Crumble

Gluten-free • Healthy fats

Makes 8 parfaits

Florida may not be considered the culinary capital of North America, but what they lack in innovative cuisine, they make up for in pie (and portion sizes, too!). Since childhood, I've always loved pie filling, but I've felt indifferent about the crust, so this recipe forgoes the fussy recipe elements and punches up the flavour of fresh, sprightly limes where it counts. Ethereal mountains of whipped meringue get folded into thick and creamy lime yogurt with crunchy, tropical coconut and cashew crumble strewn throughout. It's my family Florida holiday without the drama (or crust).

Coconut Cashew Crumble

1 cup (250 mL) unsweetened flaked coconut, toasted
1 cup (250 mL) coarsely crushed unsalted natural cashews, toasted
4 teaspoons (20 mL) key lime zest
Generous pinch of sea salt

Key Lime Mousse

¼ cup (60 mL) cold filtered water
4 teaspoons (20 mL) unflavoured gelatin
3 pasteurized egg whites, room temperature
¾ cup (175 mL) pure liquid honey
⅛ teaspoon (0.5 mL) salt
¼ teaspoon (1 mL) cream of tartar
2 cups (500 mL) plain 4% Greek yogurt
2 teaspoons (10 mL) Key lime zest
3 tablespoons (45 mL) fresh Key lime juice
1 teaspoon (5 mL) pure vanilla extract

1. **Make the Coconut Cashew Crumble** In a small bowl, stir together the toasted coconut, cashews, lime zest, and salt. Set aside.

2. **Make the Key Lime Mousse** Pour the filtered water into a small bowl and sprinkle the gelatin on top. Stir until combined. Set aside.

3. In the bowl of a stand mixer or a large heatproof bowl, whisk together the egg whites, honey, and salt. Set the bowl over a saucepan filled with 1 inch (2.5 cm) of water. Bring the water to a simmer over medium heat and cook, whisking constantly, until the honey has dissolved into the egg whites and the mixture is very warm when you stick your finger in it, about 5 minutes. Add the gelatin mixture and whisk until dissolved. Remove the bowl from the saucepan.

4. Add the cream of tartar and beat on high speed until the egg whites have tripled in volume, are gorgeously shiny, and the outside of the bowl is completely cool to the touch, 8 to 9 minutes if using a stand mixer.

5. In another large bowl, stir together the yogurt, lime zest, lime juice, and vanilla. Stir a large spoonful of the egg whites into the yogurt to loosen and lighten the texture, then gently fold the egg whites into the yogurt until just combined.

6. To assemble, divide two-thirds of the Coconut Cashew Crumble among 8 small mason jars or small glasses. Top with the Key Lime Mousse, and garnish with the remaining Coconut Cashew Crumble. Cover the mason jars with lids or plastic wrap and refrigerate until set, 2 to 3 hours.

ABBEY'S TIP Key limes may be smaller, but they pack a far better punch of acidity and a complex floral aroma that pales when compared with their Persian lime counterparts. Yes, their petite size may mean a little more squeezing to get enough juice, so if you're short on time (or your fist has had enough work for the day), skip the plastic shelf-stabled bottled stuff and substitute 2 tablespoons (30 mL) fresh Persian lime juice and 1 tablespoon (15 mL) fresh lemon juice. This mousse can be made up to 1 day ahead and kept refrigerated until ready to eat.

Creamsicle Granita Parfait with Candied Kumquats

Gluten-free • Nut-free • Vegetarian

Makes 6 parfaits

When I was a kid, nothing was better than taking a walk with my mom and my sister down to the "treat store" for a little afternoon delight. Okay, so the treat store was actually just a corner drugstore, but when you're a kid, you only see what you want to see—and I always had my head in the ice cream cooler. My go-to? The classic Creamsicle with its iconic orange crust and creamy vanilla centre, a frozen staple that always ends with a sticky smile. Now I'm all for nostalgic treats, but serving a store-bought ice pop at a dinner party doesn't always fly, so we can easily adult this up. Crispy, crackly, and refreshing orange granita meets layers of vanilla bean–studded yogurt, topped with tangy, bittersweet bits of chewy kumquat candies. It's the flavours of your childhood without the gooey face.

Creamsicle Granita Parfait

½ cup (125 mL) filtered water

½ cup (125 mL) pure liquid honey, divided

2 teaspoons (10 mL) orange zest

2 cups (500 mL) freshly squeezed orange juice

2½ cups (625 mL) plain 4% Greek yogurt

1 vanilla bean, split lengthwise, seeds scraped out
and reserved

Candied Kumquats

¼ cup (60 mL) thinly sliced kumquats (each cut crosswise
into 4 to 6 rings), seeds removed

¼ cup (60 mL) filtered water

2 tablespoons (30 mL) pure liquid honey

6 small fresh mint leaves, for garnish

1. **Make the Creamsicle Granita Parfait** Combine the filtered water and ¼ cup (60 mL) of the honey in a small saucepan over medium heat and simmer until the honey has dissolved. Stir in the orange zest and juice. Pour the mixture into a 9-inch (2.5 L) square metal baking pan and let cool to room temperature. Transfer the mixture to the freezer and freeze for 2 to 3 hours, scraping it with a fork every 30 minutes to yield a crispy icy texture.

2. Meanwhile, in a medium bowl, stir together the yogurt, vanilla seeds, and the remaining ¼ cup (60 mL) honey. Refrigerate until ready to serve.

3. **Make the Candied Kumquats** In a small saucepan, bring 1 inch (2.5 cm) of water to a boil. Add the kumquats and blanch for 30 to 60 seconds, then drain. Refill the pot with 1 inch of water. Bring to a boil, return the kumquats, and blanch for another 30 to 60 seconds. Drain again.

4. Return the saucepan to medium-high heat and bring the filtered water and honey to a boil, stirring until the honey dissolves. Add the kumquats, cover, and reduce the heat to medium-low heat. Simmer for 10 minutes, or until the kumquats are tender and sticky-sweet. Using a slotted spoon, transfer the kumquats to a plate lined with parchment paper to dry.

continues

5. To assemble, divide a third of the yogurt mixture among 6 small glasses or small mason jars. Top with half of the granita, then another third of the yogurt mixture, the remaining granita, and the remaining yogurt mixture. Garnish with a few small slices of Candied Kumquats and a fresh mint leaf.

ABBEY'S TIP In kindergarten, I once ate an orange with its peel, and my face fell asleep (true, yet sad, story). Had it been a kumquat, I could have gotten away with it. Kumquats skin is not only packed with fibre, fragrant essential oils, and flavonoid antioxidants, but also it's deliciously sweet. Blanching the kumquat rings helps to tone down some of their bitterness and soften them enough to absorb the honey syrup nicely. If you're making this dessert for a group, all the components can be made ahead—the granita can last covered well for a few weeks, the yogurt can be mixed up until it's best-before date, and the kumquats can hang out in the fridge for up to a week.

Dark Chocolate—Dipped Figs with Rosemary Goat Cheese Mousse

Gluten-free • Vegetarian

Serves 4

Biting into a perfect fig—jammy, sweet, and blushingly vibrant—is like getting triple 7s on the slot machine. It's culinary gold, my friends. When I was travelling in California, I discovered the motherlode of hidden treasure when I ran into a voluptuous fig tree in my hotel's courtyard. As far as I was concerned, it wasn't theft because those figs were just aching for a stealthy grab. Every day before my morning run, I'd give a quick look over my shoulder before snatching a few beauties and hoping the staff wouldn't notice my bulging cheeks. Although figs are delicious in their unadulterated state, I take them to the next level by filling them with a goat cheese mousse scented with orange zest and rosemary and dunking their plump little bottoms into decadent dark chocolate. Tangy, sweet, rich, and bright, they hit the flavour jackpot every time.

3 tablespoons (45 mL) soft goat cheese
2 tablespoons (30 mL) plain 2% Greek yogurt
¼ teaspoon (1 mL) orange zest, more for garnish
¼ teaspoon (1 mL) finely minced fresh rosemary, more for garnish
Fleur de sel and cracked black pepper
4 large figs (such as Black Mission or Brown Turkey)
1¾ ounces (50 g) 70% to 80% dark chocolate, finely chopped
¼ cup (60 mL) finely crushed unsalted natural pistachios
Pure liquid honey, for drizzling

1. Line a baking sheet with wax paper or a silicone baking mat.

2. In a small food processor, combine the goat cheese, yogurt, orange zest, and rosemary. Process until smooth and light. Season with a pinch each of fleur de sel and pepper. Transfer the goat cheese mousse to a piping bag with a small star tip or a plastic resealable bag with a small hole cut in one corner. Set aside.

3. Cut the stems off the figs and cut an X into the top of each one, slicing almost all the way down to the base. Be careful not to cut all the way through the figs. Set aside.

4. Place the chocolate in a heatproof bowl and place it over a small saucepan filled with 1 inch (2.5 cm) of water. Bring the water to a bare simmer and let the chocolate gently melt, stirring often. Once melted, remove the bowl from the pan. (Optional microwave method: Place the chocolate in a microwave-safe dish. Melt in the microwave on 50 percent power in 30-second increments until almost fully melted. Stir once after each 30-second increment.)

5. Dip the bottom third of each fig into the melted chocolate, swirling to coat the figs. Place on the prepared baking sheet.

continues

6. While the chocolate is still wet, carefully pry the figs open and pipe the goat cheese mousse into the figs, making sure the mousse gets all of the way down to the base. Once filled, gently press the corners together a bit to seal in the filling.

7. Transfer to the fridge until the chocolate is fully set and looks dry, at least 15 minutes. When you're ready to eat, top the figs with crushed pistachios, a drizzle of honey, and additional orange zest and rosemary. Enjoy immediately.

ABBEY'S TIP Often regarded as the original forbidden fruit, fibre-rich figs are a surprising source of calcium, working alongside the creamy Greek yogurt and goat cheese to help promote strong bones. Ripe figs are usually available May through November, and you can spot a good one by looking for fruit that is plump with a slight weariness to the skin, a deep, unblemished purple hue, and a sweet, jammy perfume. Nothing is more disappointing than a mediocre fig, so if you can't get any good ones, feel free to hull and fill jumbo strawberries in their place.

Macerated Balsamic Pepper Strawberries with Rosé Sabayon

Dairy-free • Gluten-free • Nut-free • Vegetarian

Serves 4

On my first big vacation with my hubby, we ate (and drank) our way through Italy's deep, delicious wine-soaked history. Yet amidst the beautiful bolognese, pizza, gelato, and gallons of vino, the only dish I remember in vivid detail is a simple bowl of berries. Macerated with spicy black pepper and tangy balsamic vinegar, local strawberries got a table side toss before being served in a silver goblet. I can still taste that vivacious flavour tickling my tongue. The effortless combination is perfection all on its own, but adding a pillowy blanket of sparkling sabayon brûléed into a caramelized crust gives it that company-worthy finish. The Italians know—and now you do too—that sometimes, simplicity tastes best.

Macerated Balsamic Pepper Strawberries
4 cups (1 L) thickly sliced fresh strawberries
3 tablespoons (45 mL) aged balsamic vinegar
1½ teaspoons (7 mL) pure liquid honey
½ teaspoon (2 mL) cracked black pepper

Rosé Sabayon
¼ cup (60 mL) sparkling rosé wine
2 tablespoons (30 mL) pure liquid honey
2 large egg yolks
4 teaspoons (20 mL) brown sugar (optional)

1. **Make the Macerated Balsamic Pepper Strawberries** In a bowl, stir together the strawberries, balsamic vinegar, honey, and pepper. Allow to macerate in the fridge for 30 to 60 minutes.

2. **Make the Rosé Sabayon** In a medium saucepan, bring 1 inch (2.5 cm) of water to a simmer over medium heat.

3. In a heatproof bowl, combine the sparkling wine and honey. Place the bowl over the saucepan. Whisk together the wine and honey, then whisk in the egg yolks. Continue to whisk the sauce until it turns a pale yellow, doubles in volume, and when you lift your whisk and swirl it, it leaves behind a trail that is visible for a second or two before merging back into the bowl. This usually requires 6 to 7 minutes of heavy whisking. Remove the bowl from the saucepan.

4. To serve, divide the strawberries among 4 bowls and drape each serving with a layer of sabayon. If desired, sprinkle each serving with 1 teaspoon (5 mL) of brown sugar and brûlée using a kitchen torch until caramelized and bubbly.

ABBEY'S TIP Call it art imitating science, but these little heart-shaped berries are packed with potassium that's been shown to help reduce the risk of heart attack and stroke. Eating strawberries more than twice a week has also been shown to delay cognitive aging by up to two and a half years. I say make a double batch of the macerated strawberries to serve on ice cream, yogurt, or pancakes. They will keep in the fridge for up to 2 days, though the longer they sit, the more liquid will separate, so before adding the sabayon, you may want to drain (and drink!) some of the juice. You can also reduce the juice in a small saucepan over medium heat with 1 tablespoon (15 mL) of honey until sticky and thick for drizzling on top.

Riesling-Roasted Pears with Blue Cheese Mousse and Sweet Walnut Pesto

Gluten-free • Healthy fats • High fibre • Vegetarian

Serves 8

Sometimes restaurants are so judgy when it comes to the socially acceptable order of a meal. I spend most of my dinner just waiting to see the dessert menu, and then I get anxious trying to decide between sweets or cheese. Life is too short for these sorts of pressures, so I say have both with my roasted pears and blue cheese mousse. Wine-soaked sweet pears get dressed with a buttery blue cheese mousse lightened up with protein-rich Greek yogurt. Topped with a refreshing herb-and-honey-laced walnut pesto and a pinch of fiery cracked pepper, these pears are the Switzerland of your meal. You'll never need to choose sweet or savoury sides again.

Riesling-Roasted Pears

Extra-virgin olive oil in an oil atomizer

4 firm red pears, cored and quartered

2 teaspoons (10 mL) fresh lemon juice

½ cup (125 mL) dry Riesling wine

1 tablespoon (15 mL) pure liquid honey

4 cinnamon sticks

Sweet Walnut Pesto

2 tablespoons (30 mL) dried cranberries

1 cup (250 mL) natural walnuts, coarsely chopped

½ cup (125 mL) fresh basil leaves

½ cup (125 mL) fresh mint leaves

2 tablespoons (30 mL) pure liquid honey

4 teaspoons (20 mL) fresh lemon juice

Blue Cheese Mousse

½ cup (125 mL) crumbled blue cheese, room temperature

½ cup (125 mL) plain 4% Greek yogurt

Garnish (optional)

Cracked black pepper

Dried cranberries, finely chopped

Pure liquid honey

Fresh mint or basil leaves

1. Preheat the oven to 375°F (190°C). Lightly grease a 9-inch (2.5 L) square baking dish with extra-virgin olive oil in an oil atomizer.

2. **Make the Riesling-Roasted Pears** Place the pears, cut side up, in the baking dish. Pour the lemon juice and wine evenly over the pears. Drizzle with honey, and nestle the cinnamon sticks in the bottom of the baking dish. Bake for about 30 minutes, basting with the wine mixture every 10 minutes, until the edges look slightly shrivelled and golden and the pears are fork-tender.

3. **Make the Sweet Walnut Pesto** Meanwhile, in a small food processor, pulse the cranberries until they are in small pieces. Add the walnuts, basil, and mint, and pulse until the mixture is a thick pesto-like consistency. Add the honey and lemon juice and pulse just to combine. Set aside.

4. **Make the Blue Cheese Mousse** In a medium bowl, whisk together the blue cheese and yogurt until smooth. (If the cheese is a bit hard, you can use a food processor to mix.)

5. To assemble, spoon a dollop of the Blue Cheese Mousse into the cavity of each pear. Top with a spoonful of the Sweet Walnut Pesto, and garnish, if desired, with a pinch of cracked black pepper, a few extra pieces of dried cranberries, a drizzle of honey, and mint or basil leaves.

ABBEY'S TIP Even though I've been known to clean off a cheese platter all by myself, you don't need much of a good blue to get a major flavour impact. If you are new to blue cheese, avoid the super-fragrant bold blues like Roquefort and Stilton, and ask your cheesemonger for a milder, creamier option such as Saint Agur or Bleu d'Auvergne. The mousse and pesto can be made up to 2 days in advance, while the pears are prettiest made the day you want to serve.

Saffron Rice Pudding with Rose Water Caramelized Apricots

Dairy-free • Gluten-free • Vegetarian

Serves 6

My mom was more of a boxed cake mix kind of baker, but she did make an impossibly delicious rice pudding. She used to call rice pudding the ultimate poor man's dessert, since it was an easy way for mom to use up our leftover rice. Now, it's not that I don't like to save a dollar, but sometimes dessert deserves a little more luxury, and my saffron-laced version fits the bill. Spicy cardamom and cinnamon scent a creamy coconut custard dotted with fibre-rich brown rice. Served with plump, caramelized apricots in an aromatic rose honey, it's the Cinderella story of sweets.

Saffron Rice Pudding

2 cups (500 mL) cooked whole-grain brown rice

1 can (14 ounces/400 mL) light coconut milk, shaken

1 vanilla bean, split lengthwise, seeds scraped out and reserved

3 tablespoons (45 mL) pure liquid honey, more to taste

½ teaspoon (2 mL) cinnamon

¼ teaspoon (1 mL) ground cardamom

Pinch of saffron threads

Sea salt

¼ cup (60 mL) minced dried apricots

2 large eggs, beaten

⅓ cup (75 mL) finely chopped unsalted natural pistachios, for garnish

Rose Water Caramelized Apricots

12 large dried apricots

¼ cup (60 mL) filtered water

2 teaspoons (10 mL) pure liquid honey

½ teaspoon (2 mL) rose water

1. **Make the Saffron Rice Pudding** In a medium saucepan, combine the rice, coconut milk, vanilla bean and seeds, honey, cinnamon, cardamom, saffron, and a pinch of salt. Bring to a boil, then reduce the heat to medium-low, cover with a lid, and simmer for 15 minutes, stirring every 2 to 4 minutes. The pudding should look creamy and thick.

2. Remove the vanilla bean and reduce the heat to low. Stir in the minced apricots and beaten eggs and cook, stirring constantly to prevent the egg from scrambling, for 2 to 3 more minutes. Remove from the heat and keep warm.

3. **Make the Rose Water Caramelized Apricots** Meanwhile, combine the dried apricots, water, honey, and rose water in a small saucepan and bring to a boil. Once boiling, cover with a lid, reduce the heat to medium-low, and simmer the apricots for about 7 minutes. Remove the lid, increase the heat to medium, and cook until the moisture has evaporated and the honey starts to bubble. Watch the apricots closely, and turn them as they start to caramelize and the liquid has reduced to a thick rose water honey syrup, 1 to 2 minutes. As soon as they're golden brown, remove them from the heat before the honey burns.

4. To serve, divide the pudding among 6 glasses. Top with a couple of the caramelized apricots and a sprinkle of pistachios.

ABBEY'S TIP Prized for its stunning colour, flavour, and antioxidants, saffron holds the title as the most expensive spice on earth, priced at up to $10,000 a pound. If you're going for it, you might as well go for gold. Skip the stale grocery-store varieties or suspiciously cheap options (which are sometimes laced with bark and chemical additives) and visit a specialty food market instead. Iranian or Spanish saffron is usually your best bet, but be sure to give it a whiff to make sure you get a strong, sweet perfume. Having said that, if you want to dial this back a notch on the luxe scale, you can use a very small pinch of turmeric in the saffron's place.

Brûléed Grapefruit with Mascarpone Thyme Cream

Gluten-free • Vegetarian

Serves 4

I was fifteen when my friend and I decided to do the grapefruit diet. It was my first, real taste of slavish diet culture—something I would spend most of my adult life wrestling myself out of. It was also an obvious way to ruin a perfectly good fruit. I had to free this blushing pink citrus from its unsatisfying marriage, and a sprinkle of sweet sugar becomes its perfect new mate. "Sugar" doesn't have to be a bad word. It's simply just one of the many tools in a chef's toolbox for making nourishing foods even more pleasurable—and a crackly, brûléed crust is always convincing. Paired with a luscious, herbaceous cream of mascarpone, Greek yogurt, and thyme, this grapefruit's both gorgeous and delicious. Ditch the diet, and dig into this.

Mascarpone Thyme Cream
¼ cup (60 mL) mascarpone cheese
¼ cup (60 mL) plain 2% Greek yogurt
½ teaspoon (2 mL) fresh thyme leaves, more for garnish
½ teaspoon (2 mL) pure liquid honey

Brûléed Grapefruit
2 red grapefruits, halved and sectioned (see Tip)
2 tablespoons (30 mL) light brown sugar

1. **Make the Mascarpone Thyme Cream** In a medium bowl, whip together the mascarpone, yogurt, thyme, and honey. Set aside.

2. **Make the Brûléed Grapefruit** Working with one grapefruit half at a time (to prevent the grapefruit from getting soggy), pat the cut side super dry with paper towel or a kitchen towel and sprinkle with brown sugar. Using a kitchen torch, immediately heat the sugar on the top of the grapefruit until melted and beginning to turn dark amber. (If you don't have a kitchen torch you can place the grapefruit under the broiler for about 8 minutes, but be sure to watch it closely because that sugar can easily burn.) Repeat with the remaining grapefruit halves.

3. Serve each grapefruit with a dollop of Mascarpone Thyme Cream and a sprinkle of thyme leaves.

ABBEY'S TIP Grapefruit was always a breakfast staple in my home (yes, even with a sprinkle of sugar on top). With 2 grams of fibre and a boatload of vitamin C, vitamin A, and cancer-fighting antioxidants like lycopene, grapefruit has been shown to help reduce the risk of heart disease by improving triglycerides. To dive into that goodness, start by cutting your grapefruit in half and taking a little sliver off the bottom so the halves sit up straight. Then run your serrated knife on a slight angle pointing inwards around the perimeter of the fruit where the pulp and the rind meet. Then release the juicy segments by carefully cutting on each side of the thin membrane using a slow sawing movement. There you go—a new essential skill for your résumé.

Thank You

Thank you, world, we made it out alive! Birthing this book baby was one of the hardest yet most rewarding experiences of my life (not to mention an exceptionally long and gruelling "pregnancy"). But unlike with a human child, it took far more than two people to help this little babe grow and thrive. I have a lot of people to thank for *The Mindful Glow Cookbook.*

First and foremost, a big thank you to my adoring husband, Justin. Thank you for letting me mess up the kitchen again, and again, and again. I know by the end of the recipe-testing phase you probably didn't want to come home at the end of the workday, but thank you for just closing your eyes and letting me do my thing. (Hey, you did get fed well!) Not only have you been patient and supportive while I create this book baby, but you're a big part of the reason I was ever able to take the scary leap to pursue my dreams. Without you, there would be no *Abbey's Kitchen*, so thank you for being my number-one fan.

To my family, Mom (Deborah), Dad (Blake), and my rad sister, Skye. You three were the OG taste testers, so thank you for being my daily experiment. I maybe can't say I got all my culinary prowess from any of you, but I can say I got your unfailing sense of determination and ambition. You taught me how to dream big, fight for everything I want in life, and create happiness for myself, and because of those lessons, I've managed to build a career and life for myself that I truly love. While I'm sure most parents would look disapprovingly on a daughter who dropped out of prestigious grad school to blog, thank you for knowing it was the right choice.

To my dream team who helped me bring this baby to life. Kyla, you're so much more than just my badass photographer. You've supported my vision from the early beginnings of *Abbey's Kitchen* and you walked with me every step of this crazy journey. You're a true gem, and I'm so lucky to be your business partner and friend. Dara and Houston, thank you for making this book look so crazy good, and thank you, Sofia, for literally running *Abbey's Kitchen* (and my life) for me every day. You are all damn good not only at your jobs but also at helping this neurotic girl stay sane. Go ahead, you can add "therapist" to your CV now.

To my wicked recipe testers, thank you for your incredible in-depth feedback, tasting notes, and enthusiasm. These recipes wouldn't be as perfect as they are without you.

To my editor, Andrea Magyar, and the Penguin team, thank you for believing in me and in *The Mindful Glow Cookbook.* I'm so grateful that you understood the importance of this empowering message.

And most important, to the *Abbey's Kitchen* community. Every day I have to legit pinch myself just thinking about the fact that my job involves making pancakes in my kitchen, shooting hilarious videos in a gold onesie, and seeing you all love it. My mind is pretty much blown. Thank you for your continual support, comments, shares, likes, views, visits, and love. You are the reason I am continually inspired to turn on the stove, and I'm so excited to see what you think of *The Mindful Glow Cookbook.*

Deliciously yours,
Abbey xoxo

Index